POST
MID-CENTURY KID

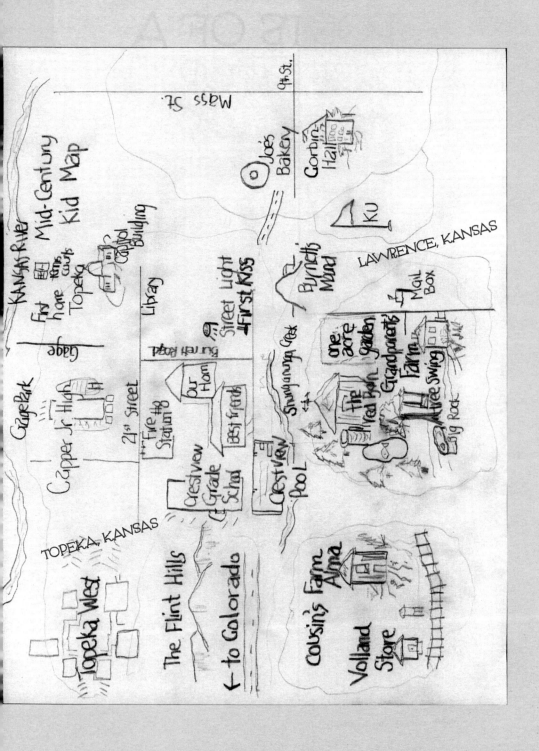

My little brother, Mike, and me,
ready for life's adventures together

POSTS OF A MID-CENTURY KID

Doing my best.
Having fun.

Ann Vigola Anderson

Anamcara Press LLC

Published in 2021 by Anamcara Press LLC
Author © 2021 Ann Anderson
Cover & Book design by Maureen Carroll
Arial, Timeburner, Minion Pro, Timeburner, Escoffier Capitaux, and Ink Free

Printed in the United States of America.

Book Description: Anderson takes us on a journey to 1950s and 60s Kansas and treats the reader to hometown cooking in her tasty memoir Posts of a Mid-Century Kid. With humor and richly crafted details, she chronicles her mid-century childhood, offering a sampling of another era. This delightful and mischievous memoir advocates coloring vividly outside of the lines!

ANAMCARA PRESS LLC
P.O. Box 442072, Lawrence, KS 66044

https://anamcara-press.com/

Ordering Information:
Quantity sales. Special discounts are available on quantity purchases by corporations, associations, and others. For details, contact the publisher at the address above.
Orders by U.S. trade bookstores and wholesalers. Please contact Ingram Distribution.

Posts of a Mid-Century Kid / Ann Anderson

BIO026000, BIOGRAPHY & AUTOBIOGRAPHY / Personal Memoirs
BIO029000, BIOGRAPHY & AUTOBIOGRAPHY / Culinary
OCC000000, BODY, MIND & SPIRIT / General

ISBN-13: 978-1-941237-73-1 (Paperback)
ISBN-13: 978-1-941237-75-5 (Hardcover)
ISBN-13: 978-1-941237-74-8 (EBook)

Library of Congress Control Number: 2021940681

DEDICATION

To my childhood hero, my mom;
To my grown-up hero, Vann;
To my kitties Jazzy, Queenie, and Muffy;
And to my red-tailed hawk who keeps Nature in me.

Contents

To make a prairie,
it takes a clover and one bee.
One clover, and a bee.
And revery.
The revery alone will do,
If bees are few.

—Emily Dickinson

Momma may have,
Papa may have
But God bless the child that's got his own,
That's got his own.

—Billie Holiday

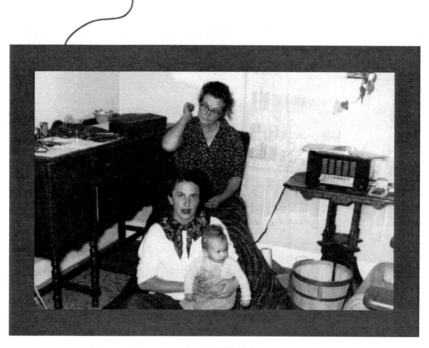

Listening to the WIBW farm report
while Grandma made the rocking chair rug

PROLOGUE

She came at life sideways, maybe from not having the anchor of a dad, so there was always a drift to her journey. A lighthouse for a mom with a bright light to lead back to a happy shore.

Bad choices, good choices, and all the in-between, but a path that always veered a little to the sideways, maybe from being left-handed, too.

Wearing clothes that were homemade, some from cousins, some new, and always that feeling that it wasn't quite right, and sometimes getting it right for a day.

Wanting to wear somebody's ID bracelet, but nobody offered. Finally, easier to buy one of her own. Very pretty and shiny.

A girl makes her way in this world, sideways and sometimes, if she's lucky, she goes right to where she was intended to be and all the better for coming at it sideways.

MAY · 67

The coolest mom

Chapter One

BLOWING KISSES GOODBYE

A small scent of cherry blossoms...

I am twenty-six. My mom is fifty-two. We are sitting in a room so small and airless that I trace it back to the beginning of being claustrophobic. I feel my childhood slipping away from me.

My hands are clinched into fists, and I open one. For a moment, I think of the handfuls of kisses Mom and I have blown to each other over the years. Mom seems to read my thoughts and turns to smile at me. I see my childhood in her eyes.

I am mad that my stepdad is in the waiting room. He should be sitting here with us, but then, I am also glad it's just my mom and me as it usually has been throughout my life.

Just like a jury that has convicted a defendant, the doctor walks in, no eye contact, no handshakes. I take this as the first sign of the bad news to come.

He sits. I look at the clock marking 3:38 p.m. I think that it will begin clicking back our time when he speaks. He settles uneasily and opens a folder.

My mom must sense that I am about to faint as she reaches for my hand and holds it. Just like when I was small, my fingers wrap into it. It is soft despite years of painting, gardening, raising two kids, and all the things a mom's hands must do. They are soft from Jergens lotion, and a small scent of cherry blossoms floats up to me and keeps me from fainting.

The doctor looks at my mom finally and says, "Irene, you have breast cancer."

My heart stops, my breath does not come, and I fight the hot tears that edge my eyes. My mom looks at him and in her ever-positive voice says, "So what's next?"

All that would come for the next four years would not be enough. Our time was marked by some very good days, and then toward the end, there were days that felt like the Devil had come to visit our house.

At my mom's service, I sat with the words I had written clutched in my hands. I wore the navy-blue suit with the white lace blouse that my mom always pronounced made me look like Coco Chanel. When I gave her eulogy, it was about her many accomplishments – President of the PTA, Chairman of the committee to build sidewalks on 21st Street, and all those things that made her life.

I could not give the eulogy in my heart. I could not describe how she smelled like Chanel No. 5, or how everybody who came to our house for a short visit never wanted to leave, how she could make a beautiful meal in minutes when somebody stopped by, how every holiday seemed like a Macy's Day parade because she made it that way, how she solved every problem I had, wiped away every tear, encouraged me in everything I took on, and always with a gentle word and smile. I thought we would grow old together.

This fall day, I sit here in our Kansas home and think of those times as we prepare to retire to South Carolina. I am filled with feelings of not wanting to leave all that is familiar in my prairie state and an anticipation of what life might hold in a new place.

I wrap each item carefully in tissue and think of my memories of a child who grew up in the '50s, in a small town and the years spent visiting my grandparents' farm. I hold each object like a talisman of my journey from a child to an adult.

This is the story of how we lived our mid-century lives. Most of the memories are as sweet as the lilacs that grew in my grandma's backyard and others as dark as the thunderclouds over the vast Kansas prairie. All the memories are stitched into me with the colors and softness of the pieces of fabric scraps my grandma used to sew her quilts so many years ago.

Grandma and me with the rug

1958

A Toni perm and ready for first grade at Crestview

Chapter Two

MOTHER NATURE

So, stop, be still in your place and watch what
Mother Nature shows us this time.

That beautiful, strange feeling that I might be the only one awake. Sitting with the cats at dawn, I am wrapped in a hoodie for the first time this fall, drinking hot tea with honey. Three deer raise their heads and seem to nod good morning to me. I have no pond, but feel like Thoreau surrounded by the dark morning beauty of Kansas.

Ocean waves, thunderstorms, and Kansas winds are Nature's sleeping pill. I heard the wind all night, like a drowsy sleeping tonic, the smell of the Gulf barely in the air, manatees swimming on the wind and lulling me back to sleep. The people of the south wind.

Homecoming, Friday night lights, our first frost advisory. Making sure my pantry is stocked with hot cocoa and marshmallows and digging out the pink, fuzzy slippers. The cats' noses are tucked in their paws. Outside, a leaf turns red.

Ann Anderson

Sunday morning takes me back fifty years to Mom fixing sausage and eggs, my church outfit carefully laid out the night before with gloves, a hat, and my beloved patent leather shoes saved only for this day. My brother had a tiny, clip-on tie that was always missing at the last moment and found and reattached. An hour of worship surrounded by people dressed just so and then off to the church basement for donuts and coffee while the kids chased and played. Sunday morning started the week off right with church and lazy afternoons spent with our grandparents at Sunday supper. So many traditions woven into a lovely life.

I am sitting amid boxes of our treasures ready to move to South Carolina, a new place with new friends to be made, new sights to be seen, and the thought of the Brownie song my mom taught us as our leader in the basement of Crestview Methodist Church. "Make new friends, but keep the old, one is silver and the other gold." When I was eight and singing that song, it really was just words and a fun song. Now, at sixty-two, I fully understand the colors of our friendships, gold and silver. I will be humming that song as I leave the many faces of golden friends here.

The pep club uniform… Election year and I think back to when I was elected as vice president of the pep club at Capper Junior High. The girl who had won suddenly moved with her family and the election was held again. Mom said to put my hat into the ring. I won and was so excited to come home that Wednesday afternoon and tell her. I had an amazing patch with my name and the Capper Jayhawk on it that was to be sewn onto a green wool suit. I spent the evening doing homework, and my mom said she had errands to run. I went to bed both excited and disappointed that I would be the only girl at the football game not wearing my pep club uniform the next day. I woke up early and went in to have breakfast with my family, and there in the doorway to the kitchen, hung a green wool pep club suit with my patches attached, a new white blouse, and new saddle shoes. Mom and I both started crying. She had secretly gone out to buy the material and sewed until 4:00 a.m.

The surprise pep club uniform.
Vice President of Pep Club, Capper Jr. High

so I would have my uniform. It remains one of the most beautiful memories of love from my mom.

My bio dad was an All-American football player for Washburn University. I relished hanging out with him. When I was four, he had an affair, and my parents were divorced. My bio dad was granted weekly visits, which he did for about a month. His visits became monthly, and then whenever guilt must have prompted him to call. When I was eight, he called one October day and said he would pick me up to get a Halloween costume. I sat on our front steps for two hours waiting for him. Mom kept peeking through the curtains, and I am sure her heart was breaking for me, but I stubbornly sat there. Then, at some point, I realized he was not coming. I went inside and told Mom, "Call my dad and tell him

I don't want to see him again." Mom made the call. That was the first time I truly realized I could make my own choices, and it was also the first time I realized you can let someone break your heart or not. I also realized that day that you only need one good person in your life and you'll turn out all right.

How I learned to become a good aunt... My mom had three brothers and one sister, Ona. Ona was an accomplished woman, a nurse for the Navy in WWII and a nurse at the University of Kansas Medical Center. She went on to become one of the first female hospital administrators in the United States. She had one major flaw; she was an alcoholic. She lived for many years in a magnificent cabin on Lake Lotawana, thirty minutes past Kansas City. She often invited my mom, my brother, and me down for a weekend of skiing, fishing, and swimming, and as kids, the week could not pass quickly enough. With our clothes packed in paper bags, we made the two-and-a-half-hour drive to the lake. Some weekends were perfect with steaks grilled on the BBQ, hours of skiing, catching the big ones, and never out of our swimming suits until bedtime. By the time I was ten, Aunt Ona was drinking more and more. My mom had a routine that we came to know all too well. We would pull in her driveway and go in with our bags of clothes left sadly in the car. If she had the martini shaker out and was drinking, my mom would say, "Oh, we were just in KC and thought we'd swing by to say hi." After thirty minutes, we would drive the long trip back to Topeka. I never thought about how painful those short visits must have been for Mom. My brother and I were thinking only of swimming and a weekend at the lake. As a kid, I did begin to realize that she was not a good aunt. I vowed that if I ever became an aunt, I would do everything the opposite of my Aunt Ona. And so many years later, I have been blessed with my nieces and nephew that know I love them unconditionally. I learned many positive lessons from having a bad aunt. It's funny how you can sometimes learn as much from the negative as from the positive.

How you know you've found Mr. Right... When I was dating

Vann, we were at a restaurant, and they served yellow squash. I didn't eat mine and told Vann I didn't like the mushy seeds. About a month later, we were at a restaurant in San Diego and our food was served. I wasn't really paying attention, but I saw Vann cutting the middle out of all the yellow squash, and then he put them on my plate. Wow, a guy who remembered I don't like squishy seeds and cut the middle out for me. If you find someone like that, you have found your Mr. or Mrs. Right.

Finding that perfect look ... One of my best friends growing up was Linda M. When I was in junior high, I was late for dinner many nights because I was at Linda's house, and we were exploring our beauty enhancements like rolling our hair up in orange juice cans. One night, we were desperate to get that "ninth grade" sophisticated look. We were in eighth grade, and I told Linda, "Let's shave our eyebrows and then pencil them in." I was sure that was how the ninth-grade girls got that look. We took my mom's shaver with its double-edged blade and shaved off our little eyebrows. When we went out to show my mom, she was startled by our appearance as you can imagine. At the time, I had light blonde hair and my eyebrows grew back like pale yellow caterpillars above my eyes. Linda had dark brown hair and hers grew in like brown spikes straight out. Another time, we decided to enhance our hair with two bottles of Sun In. After four hours, my hair had turned a lovely shade of tangerine and Linda's hair looked like tiger stripes. We never quite achieved the look we were going for, but it was always good to have a buddy ready to try a new look.

School days... When I was packing my beloved "Tip and Mitten" books from first grade, I closed my eyes and remembered Mrs. Fallon, Miss Tull, Miss Thompson, Mrs. Beatty, Mrs. Anderson, Miss Morgan (fifth and sixth grades) and Mr. Timken, our principal at Crestview. Every one of my teachers was like Lewis and Clark to me—each day showing me a new adventure, something exciting to explore and learn and always wanting me to come back for more. I had perfect attendance certificates for all those years, too, as school was truly my second home. The two long hallways were pathways past rooms filled with colorful artwork, pulldown maps, handwriting samples above the chalk boards, the smell of wooden desks and lunches in cheery lunch boxes (I had a farm with a silo thermos), the sounds of the kindergartners belting out newly learned songs, and colored glass block squares at the end of the halls that put rainbows on the floor when it was time to go home. Recess with its myriad of playground equipment … four square, jungle gym, swings, monkey bars, all waiting to be enjoyed, and the occasional whistle from a teacher to send a quick warning to knock it off. On rainy days when the kids were fidgety or maybe the teachers just needed a break, we marched down to the stage and sat on the pine wood floor polished by years of little behinds and watched exotic science movies. Many afternoons, we headed back to school as if it were our private backyard and played on the equipment until dark. Almost always, there was a welcome light or two on from the room of an extra hard-working teacher making something for the next day's class. Crestview was all you could ask for in learning, and all those teachers filled me up with knowledge and confidence.

I have been reading my grandpa's journal again (yes, I should be packing for the move) and I am so taken by the thought of him writing about his life every day. The journal covers several years in the 1940s—long before "journaling" was made popular. The book is in pencil, with evenly written cursive and occasional small drawings of plants, calves, and other farm things. It is a peaceful story of daily weather reports, what my grandma was doing and cooking, their plans for the garden when they got the seed catalogue in the cold of winter, and the many visits and visitors they had for coffee and cinnamon rolls. Probably more than any aspect, it is the rich life they had with family and friends just stopping by for a visit, something that does not exist in our world of texts and day planners. My grandma seemingly always had something baked at the ready and coffee on for those lucky folks who pulled into their long farm driveway.

My grandpa was born in the late 1800s in Minnesota. By age fourteen, he was working for the railroad. He was a handsome man with shocks of white blonde Danish hair, blue eyes the color of cornflowers and always had a bag of orange slice candy in his pocket. He carried his railroad watch and pulled it out for us kids to listen to the strong tick tock. I have that watch now and like to hold its firmness in my hand. He smelled like new-cut hay, pipe tobacco, and pine soap. He was a good man, and I'm grateful to hold his journal and read about what mattered to him each day in his life on a Kansas farm.

Tennis... Our countdown to moving to South Carolina November 7 is on and only three more weeks of tennis at my beloved Wood Valley. I have played tennis for fifty-eight years, in lots of places, too many pros to count, and it all started when I was four. We lived on Parkview, across the street from Hughes Tennis Court. In the 1950s, the courts were a mecca for tennis with kids and adults playing seven days a week, tournaments, lessons, and a pro shop. I went there and watched and told my mom, "I want to do that." She sawed off the handle of her Jack Kramer racquet, wrapped it with tape, and said to have fun! And fifty-eight years later, it remains my passion. Tennis is a beautiful thing.

I am thinking of all the places in Topeka that as a kid made my life into a nubby soft blanket. So here goes... living on Burnett Road and playing with all of the neighbor kids, crossing 21st Street on my own to go to C&W Market, learning at Crestview Grade School and Capper Junior High, walking to Fire Station Number 8 on 21st Street to buy candy from the very nice firemen, shopping at White Lakes Mall for the first time and being dazzled by so many stores, riding our bikes to Tastee Freez on 21st Street, going to church at Grace Cathedral with the beautiful stained glass windows, riding our bikes to the top of Burnett's Mound, being a page in the Kansas Legislature, playing putt putt and jumping on the trampoline at the park on 21st Street, going to the Chief Drive-In, seeing movies at the Jayhawk and Orpheum theaters in downtown Topeka, and attending Topeka West High School when it was still out in the country and almost new. Thanks, Topeka, for being a great place to grow up.

Ann Anderson

I have a strange hobby—watching our neighbors go about their lives. First off, we have truly wonderful neighbors, but here is a snapshot of the past week. I see Vickie and Chase scrambling after their puppy. They get within two feet and the little rascal puts on the rockets. This almost always occurs when Vickie is very dressed up (she always looks FABULOUS) or when it's ten degrees and Chase is in jammies and bedroom slippers. The cats seem to be smirking as they watch the race.

Our next-door neighbor boys are in high school but play on a basketball hoop set at about seven feet—I guess because it's more fun and they can dunk. I like to hear their boys-to-men voices playing until 9:00 p.m. on these late summer/fall nights and grateful they're not inside on something electronic.

Our neighbors across the street have two wee ones in kindergarten and second grade. Every morning, their dad plays catch with them, and when the bus comes, he helps with their backpacks (as big as they are) and on the yellow bus they go. It's nice to see parents doing things with their kids and always being there when the bus comes and goes.

These last fall nights… Sitting on the porch with the cats on bug patrol and cradling a cup of hot chocolate with the warmth like mittens in my hands. Listening to the sounds of the day winding down and hearing the train from the river tracks like the call of a distant whale. If we are lucky, the mama deer will bring her two yearlings near, and they will make their gentle little snorts while they eat the last of the perennial flowers that steadfastly continue to bloom. The bluebirds have been vying for the boxes, which makes me think that we will have a true winter again. We will be on our porch in South Carolina by then, but I will remember this night, black velvet like an Elvis painting with stars dotting the canvas and a lone plane headed to land at KCI.

The survivors, the pink… October, the time of year to remember our "breast" friends and boobs! My mom died from breast cancer at the age of fifty-six, and I was thirty. It was a long four-year battle of many good days and then the awful months at the end. One day when we were sitting together, she said, "We're lucky."

I tried to laugh and said, "Mom, you have breast cancer. How is that lucky?" She replied, "Well, we've had all these months to sit together and talk that otherwise would have just been regular days." I have always remembered that when I see my favorite survivors: Sheri, Gwenna, and Nancy, and others spreading their love, donning their pink, and making otherwise regular days into spectacular memories for us all. Here's to all the survivors, their families and friends who have made that journey with them, and for those whose journey ended but taught us all that we are lucky to have these beautiful days together.

My grandma's quilts are better treasures than any pile of diamonds to me. Today I spread out the two I have and marvel at the many scraps of fabric, weathered like a pale water color painting, snips of my clothes from when I was little, all sewn with perfect, tiny stitches that have held together for sixty years. My grandma had a Singer sewing machine with a foot pedal, and I can't imagine for the life of me how she made everything. I was in junior high before I had "store bought" clothes as my grandma could whip out a cute outfit for me in a couple of hours. At Pelletier's Department Store, we picked out the perfect fabric and then back to her farm where I would impatiently stand as she cut a pattern using newspaper. Once, she made me a bright red dress with a big bow and layer upon layer of petticoats to go underneath so I could twirl. One of my favorite things she made was a pair of flannel pajamas. We picked out fabric with little kittens on pink flannel.

On fall days like today, my grandma and I would sort through the remnants, as she called them, searching for scraps from my dresses, shorts, and pajamas that would become a new quilt. Sometimes she would add in the soft blue denim material from my grandpa's work shirts. We laid out the pieces on her bed and they made a fine display of memories. I always asked for the Sunbonnet Sue pattern and Grandma would take care in picking out the sweetest fabric for the bonnets. My grandma lived through the Great Depression, so nothing went to waste.

The quilts are packed away and will spread their pale colors and many memories in our new home soon.

Ann Anderson

Stop....be still...don't miss it. The quiet sounds of fall returned this morning. I heard the ping of my phone signaling the first frost warning, and sure enough, the neighbor's roof had been painted with pale white glitter.

Sitting on the porch this morning, coffee in hand, and the cats sniffing for what would soon come—the first V of geese flying overhead. They are lazy geese but smart, wintering at Lake Sherwood and vacationing in the summer on the tepid ponds that dot the farms around us. Their call to each other is like a flying whale song: "Come—It's Fall, let's get to our new home." The cats know the weather is turning, too, through some ancient coding they still have. All three have grown stately, thick manes which they will soon not need in South Carolina, but they are quite elegant. Sumac paints the drives with crimson burnt red; the deer blend into the browning of the countryside, ready to rest from its big summer show. So, stop, be still in your place, and watch what Mother Nature shows us this time.

Cousins... Our cooler, wiser, and different-than-siblings... I had lunch today with my favorite cousin, Linda, who is three years older than I am. She explained the "birds and the bees" to me when I was eight and she was eleven, including the revelation that babies come out of your belly button when they're born. She gave me my first and only cigarette to smoke, took me out to drink beer when I was sixteen (yes, I got sick) and also gave me all of her grown up hand-me-down clothes to wear.

We have spent years apart at times, but when we're together, time melts away and we are back giggling and thinking of something devilish to try. I will also admit that when our grandma made homemade ice cream, Linda and I switched our brothers' servings for store-bought and they never knew the difference. We also played "bears" with our brothers. We put quilts over my grandma's furniture, and Linda and I were the bears. Grandma made cinnamon rolls, and Stevie and Mike fed the bears. It sounds kind of awful now to think how they never figured it out, but they always liked feeding us, so I guess they were having fun, too.

Cousins... good for the soul and an endless source of incorrect information.

Teaching my bunny to say prayers

The famous fireplace where we burned the
Christmas tree and mom repainted the house

SEA PRAIRIE

You can't chase two rabbits and catch one.

Cats... Ogden Nash wrote, "The trouble with a kitten is that eventually it becomes a cat." True, but I have loved cats all my life, and while kittens are so fun with their boundless energy, jumping at every mysterious noise, I do enjoy my cats as they grow into their personalities and find their inner cat.

Muffy, Jazzy, and Queenie will love their new warm home in South Carolina, and like us, they will not miss the porch covered in snow. I suspect they will become great hunters of chameleons and sniff the breeze for dolphins.

Queenie is our alpha kitty and seems to sense when we both need an extra purr. When my brother was dying, she stayed by me each night and was truly comforting. Jazzy is my soul kitty and follows me like the shadow that goes in and out with me. Muffy marches to her own kitty drummer and only wants to be babied by Queenie. The three of them came from different places, but like us, made their own special cat family.

Lasts and firsts... As I wandered the house this morning to change the two clocks that are left unpacked, I thought of life's

Ann Anderson

tides. Nine years ago, we moved back to Kansas from San Diego to watch my nieces and nephew grow from grade school kiddos into amazing college students and to reconnect with my brother. Now I notice the everyday normal—like changing the clocks on this windy fall morning. Two more last dinners with good friends, last goodbye lunch with my twin nieces and nephew, and the last week on our prairie.

Now we begin the many of new firsts. Our first adventure of driving with the kitties to South Carolina, the first morning to waking up in our new home, the first sounds I will hear from the little pond behind us, the first time my toes set foot on our beaches, the first people who will become new friends, and the first of many days in our new low country home. Life comes in big boxes which are fun to open, but I like the tiny boxes that hold little bits of lasts and firsts.

Unplugged... Those of you old enough to remember MTV, might remember their Unplugged series. That is what's happening around here today as coffee maker, blender, refrigerator, and the Apples are getting unplugged. All the cats' necessities are being lavishly displayed in the Jeep in readiness for the trip. A few more goodbyes with my BESTIES and then we hit the road. Plugging in to South Carolina will be fun, and I'll be ready to catch up with a myriad of Facebook posts and all that I'll miss in just a few days. I am feeling grateful for the love that has surrounded us here, and we take everybody in our hearts with us. You cannot unplug friendship.

Watching a white egret on the pond behind our new house in Bluffton, South Carolina. A hectic week of setting up the new "right size" house after literally cutting our possessions in half. The cats were troopers on the trip with Queenie and Muffy literally lying on my feet and Jazzy lying on my lap for two days while Vann did all the driving. We are fortunate to have several new neighbors stop by to introduce themselves, and one of them helped us move some stuff around. It is a time of missing all our Topeka pals and a time of settling into a new beautiful state of mind and place. We are going to the farmers' market this afternoon as our reward of non-stop unpacking since Sunday. Hugs to everybody back in OZ.

It is a miracle to see the stacks of boxes shrink and slowly pile up for the recycling center. We have been judicious in making more offerings—this time for "RE-Tail," the local resale shop that helps homeless pets. I have promised certain friends (Nancy) not to make weather comments, so I shall only say that the cats are quite pleased with lounging on their southern porch and coming and going as they please. We are happy to be in the land of local restaurants and have made a pact to avoid all franchise restaurants going forward. The farmers' market was a dazzle of vegetables, and who knew you could grow six kinds of okra. In my honest opinion, one kind is quite enough. Local cheeses, honeys from around the area, fragrant breads with rosemary and other herbs pressed into their round tops, and enough shell necklaces and beach stuff to make me happy. Well, I am supposed to be hard at work so more updates to come from the low country.

There is a tall pine forest behind our sea prairie house. Tonight, with a breeze blowing, I hear a strange mixture of sounds of the palm tree fronds rustling mixed together with the boughs of the tall pines. The duck couple in our pond snuggle together at night and seem to be whispering sweet nothings in each other's ears. The cats are on point as they see new sights like the lime green, mini lizards that zoom by outside our porch. The tidal marshes here remind me of the Flint Hills but are filled with water as the tide comes and goes. It is time to put ourselves to bed and dream of ancient oceans, pine whispers, and palms shimmering in a new moon.

"Yes ma'am." I have heard those two words every day since moving to South Carolina. Southern hospitality seems to be indeed an actual way of life as everyone has been so cordial and helpful, including several people showing us pictures on their phones spontaneously. When I taught tennis, I had the little ones learn the word "manners" during their session, and the older kids learned the big word "tennis etiquette." I think part of my passion for tennis is that it remains one of the few sports with decorum. "Thank you," "you're welcome," "yes ma'am," "yes sir," and "please" are so easy to say and yet, have diminished from our everyday hustled lifestyle. So, thank you for reading this and try it out on somebody today. Yes sir! Too early to fix myself a mint julep. Guess I'll fix a cup of coffee and watch this day unfold politely.

Lists and cords... Day five of the move and almost everything in its place and a place for everything. . . I have always been a person who thrives on making lists (and checking them off) and there are sticky notes and lists on almost every surface of the house. But slowly with a bright pink sharpie, they are being marked off. I am mystified how we quit our service in Topeka over ten days ago, and Vann is still able to send and receive email on his computer but not on mine. Anyone care to make a guess how that is happening? We are off to hit Best Buy for cables, the Dillon's of Bluffton, and try a new place for lunch called The Sippin Cow. Mikey, my nephew, is playing football for Ft. Hays State University in frigid Warrensburg, Missouri, today, so I am thinking about him and hoping they ice out their opponents. Then I'll mark that off my list, too.

Lost and found... The low country of coastal South Carolina makes the Topeka area look positively high altitude. We are surrounded by very tall pines and palms and my left handedness adds to my "wandering" wondering where are we. Vann has a gift for finding everything and can turn down any random road and arrive at our destination. After twenty years of living in California with the ocean to our west, I must also now learn that the ocean sits nicely to my east. I am not going to get the Lewis and Clark award for finding things, but rather I will get an award for "even a blind pig occasionally finds an acorn."

Left-handed compliments... One of my dear friends commented about my left-handedness. I have never felt any different as I play tennis right-handed. I guess that's how somebody showed me to play when I was four. Being naturally left-handed has also been a great help when teaching the occasional left-handed kid or adult player. But everything else, including how I think, is left-handed. When we are inside a big building, I have a never-ending desire to turn left. Vann has learned to use this to our advantage by asking, "Which way do we go?" and then he proceeds the opposite way. He has wondered if there is a support group for spouses married to lefties. Ha ha! When I was in grade school at Crestview, Danny, Kathy, Terry, and I were made to sit at a special left-handed table during handwriting sessions. As kids, we thought it was great. We usually goofed off and never saw it as being set apart. Mom came to school in the fourth grade and put an end to the "left-handed segregation" table. Over the years, I have adapted to right-handed tools, desks, stick shifts, using the mouse with my right hand, and all other things made for the "normal" right-handed world. But I am glad to be left-handed.

Southern food groups update... We took our first true break from unpacking and went exploring to the sea islands that sit off the coast of this area. Yes, of course, they are gorgeous and very natural. We went to a wildlife preserve that looked like a jungle in Costa Rica. There were butterflies, deer chasing about, and the occasional "beware of alligator signs." Dining at a local restaurant that sat on the edge of the Beaufort River, we had a fine seat by the window to look at the egrets, pelicans, and other sea birds. I had "she" crab soup, which is beyond delicious, and Vann had a mystery gumbo. We walked across to another little local place that offered breakfast, lunch, bait, bad tee shirts, and GRILLED donuts. The owner proudly explained that you take fresh Krispy Kreme donuts, grill them on the hamburger grill and then cover them in whipped cream and syrup. My mouth is still hanging open (and watering) but we declined as Vann and I both enjoy our open arteries. Anyway, we passed on the grilled donuts and boiled peanuts and settled on a sweet tea. Later this week, we might try a possum poor boy. Always a new eating adventure around the next palm tree.

Ann Anderson

Fixin'… Some of you may know this quaint Southern term which I now hear daily. I am not an impatient person by any means, but I have come to learn that "fixin'" means anything from it will get done, to I'm just putting it somewhere in the back of my mind for future reference, or maybe not even that. I have added "fixin'" to my new Southern vocabulary. When Vann asks when I'm going to do something, I now respond, "I'm fixin' to do it." Quite a handy term. Think I'll go fix me a sweet tea….

Tennis equals new friends… We have just moved to South Carolina where we know NOBODY! We left Topeka where we seemingly knew everybody. Hmmm, that part does not sound too smart, but anyway, I went to tennis here on Monday at our club and have had two emails and one phone call since then inviting me to play. I always noticed how people new to Wood Valley found an instant home with other tennis players, and now I am finding that same thing here—the first people I know are tennis players. I miss my Topeka pals and family and that will not change. I am grateful to have tennis to instantly start meeting some fun new people here in the low country. Tennis is the universal language of welcome: come play with us.

Across the miles… Since moving to South Carolina, I have missed all my Kansas friends so much. While I occasionally get irritated at Facebook for its "updates," I am also grateful that any time of day, I can click on Facebook and feel like we're all sitting around the table having coffee and showing pictures and catching up. I see everybody's kids, their pets, prayers for friends and family, funny cartoons, and just the random small comments that make our lives intertwined wherever we may roam. Good morning, friends. I'm always happy to see you every day.

Southern sides… My good husband, Vann, grew up as a Florida boy and is also about five generations of South Carolina. We went to a place today for lunch called Cahill's, and it was right out of a storybook. It is kind of a farm, and the restaurant is a barn with screened porches (and, yes, cute little geckos), concrete floors, vinyl tablecloths, random flowers, and lots of over-the-top country decorations for sale (yes, the wooden cutouts of peoples' backsides—my favorite). Their menu is everything out of the ocean plus every part of a of chicken you could want, including the inside parts, all fried. We got the "Field to Fork" special, which was four sides of veggies. It was delicious. I had fresh green beans, black eyed peas, mac n' cheese and homemade applesauce that someone thought needed a scoop of brown sugar and candied pecans. Why not? Vann was in piggy heaven eating "greens" which looked like something that sat in the back of the fridge too long. Oh well.

Cahill's is also the only place I have seen where you can order deviled eggs, which I love! The restaurant has a farmers' market attached, and you can buy all varieties of pecan pie, pecan brittle, pecan divinity, and pecan pralines. So that's Cahill's.

Thought this might be a good time to remind everybody that Thanksgiving and the holidays are about being with friends and family, being mindful of all we have, doing random acts of kindness for people and pets, and relaxing. It is not about whether your Thanksgiving table qualifies to be a Pinterest picture. Happy Holidays!

Southern comfort… Just booked my dermatology appointment with my new low country doctor. While on hold, I had the lovely advantage of listening to all their services which I will not be getting (chemical peel, face lift, eyebrows enhancement, tummy tuck, etc.). They said they offered freezing fat cells as the new alternative to weight loss and that got my attention!!! When Vann gets back, I'm going to have him help stuff me in the freezer and see if it works. By the way, greatest irony ever, the dermatology center is across the street from a Dunkin' Donuts. Guess if you're not happy with your tummy tuck results, you can go over there and get replenished.

New sayings… I heard two new low country sayings today that bear passing along to my OZ friends. "Butter my butt and call me a biscuit" and "You can't chase two rabbits and catch one." Hmmm,

Ann Anderson

I had heard the first one, but the rabbit one is a new to me. But I ponder it and wonder: How would one chase two rabbits and why would one do that anyway? I guess if your butt had butter on it, you might think you could run faster and catch the critter. Anyway, I think low country folks have a lot of time sitting around drinking sweet tea to come up with these charming little ditties. Just passing them along.

Thankful in my heart for my perfect husband of twenty years, my nieces and nephew who are lights in my life, for our three kitties who always bring a purr to me, for my friends who wrap me like a warm fleece blanket, for growing older with good health and zest, and for all the blessings I take for granted many days, but are always there. Happy Thanksgiving to all.

The snowy egret is silently landing on our low country lagoon (aka "pond" in Kansas). She walks on her tippy toes around the edge and catches flashing silvery fish in her beak. She is a bird diva. On the other end of the scale are the turkey vultures that sit like prehistoric hulks up in the trees waiting for something to croak. Along with the crows, they keep everything clean and spiffy on the roadways. I should not want to act sick and have one of them circling me. We also have a bald eagle I have named Arnold Palmer as his head resembles a bright white golf ball. I hope he finds a mate and they make little ones in the spring. Birds remind us there is another nature world out there far more serene than ours.

Christmas gifts... I shipped a special box to my cousin, Linda, today. She is the keeper of family history and the one who continues to make the family recipes. I sent her one of my two quilts with the sunflower pattern from our grandma. It is probably eighty years old, but still the carefully-placed stitches hold the colors together happily. I also included our grandma's Searchlight cookbook which is a true cookbook complete with how to cut every type of meat, measurements, and all other information one needed back in the early 1900s to be a successful chef. I have Mom's copy which I treasure, as it has her notes in it of recipes she tried, which relative or friend served the meal, and little variances she made to improve it. I also sent Linda the walnut picks and cracker which were our grandma's. The walnut picks have been with me for over thirty years in the drawer. She is a black walnut fiend, and I know they will quickly be put back in service. Lastly, I sent her a ring that her dad made for my mom long ago. He was a man of many talents and hobbies, including jewelry making. It was fun to wrap up family treasures that she has not seen for decades, and I only wish I could be sitting at her kitchen table in Kansas when she opens the Christmas box.

I am sick. I thought I was just exhausted from our move, but a visit to the doctor revealed I have hypothyroidism. I am so sad. I crawl into bed and tuck into a ball. I cry because I am used to feeling so healthy. I am so homesick.

The tall, dark pines and the overhanging live oaks covered with Spanish moss are overwhelming to me. I close my eyes, and my heart and mind go out to the tall grass prairie where I can breathe and see the horizon.

I cry. I pray. I lie with the cats for many days and sleep. I feel sad for Vann who loves this new place as much as I do not like it.

A box of scones… The hardest part of moving for me is getting all new people, but especially getting new friends. I look at the people on the tennis courts at our new home and wonder who will become my new fun friend. There is one lady who wears two different colors of shoestrings, so, of course, I see her as pal potential. Our neighbor brought us a box of scones and a welcome note, and she also gave us a much-appreciated list of her favorite places and services in the low country. I would make a very poor military wife as I want my nest just so and lined with all my familiar people, places, and things. Vann is my gypsy who would be happy with a big Winnebago and pulling into a different spot every night. Fortunately, the cats vote with me, so it is always four to one. I pronounce this National Friend Day. Give your friends a call, a hug, take something sweet and leave it on your neighbor's doorstep.

Ann Anderson

Oh, Christmas... I saw trees tied to cars this week, and it made me think of one of my favorite memories of Christmas and my brother. When I was twelve and my brother was ten, my mom, in a burst of holiday spirit, told us we could go out in our grandparents' pasture and select and cut down a tree for Christmas. Our grandpa obligingly loaded us up on his tractor with his cut-off Ford truck bed trailer pulled behind. He allowed my brother to carry the ax for the holiday deed. My brother Mike and I wandered the pasture, sizing up all the various cedar trees, and finally picked one that just seemed perfect. Taking turns, we whacked it down, and Grandpa kept saying, "Don't you think it's a little big?" No! We thought it was magnificent! We loaded it in the trailer and hauled it back to be loaded onto our car. The big tree was hefted on to the top of our 1962 Cadillac, and it did seem to somewhat dwarf the car. Undaunted, we went back to our house on Burnett and carried the Christmas tree inside. When we up righted it, about three feet bent at the ceiling. With a swift clip of the hedge clippers, the tree soon stood magnificently—though missing its point. Almost immediately, Miss Kitty, our Siamese cat, began a vigil at the tree. We just assumed she had never seen such a splendiferous tree. On day two, a bird emerged, and she chased it until Mom got it out the door. For the next two weeks, Miss Kitty watched over the flat top tree in hopes of another bird. It was a tree that we would all laugh about for many years. From then on, my mom took us to the Christmas tree farm.

My niece Reagan's nighttime prayer which I have been saying:

"Five little angels around my bed,
One at my feet, one at my head.
One to watch over me, one to help pray.
One to take my cares away."

The best gift... Most of us can't name very many Christmas gifts we have received through the years. My favorite gift I ever received was a doll house made by Mom when I was eight. On Christmas Eve, the doorbell rang, and I discovered a very large present with my name on it. I tore off the wrapping paper, and

26

there stood a magnificent, six-room doll house almost as tall as I was. It was made from six wooden boxes, painted pink with trees and flowers, windows and front door adorning the outside. There was a living room, dining room, kitchen, two bedrooms, and a bathroom. Each room had a special covering on the floor with real carpet, felt, and little tiles in the kitchen. There were tiny dressers, couches, chairs, lights, itsy bitsy artwork on the walls, and a family and, of course, some cats. This doll house would have many makeovers, many hours of fun for my friends and me, and it sat proudly in my room until I went to college. At Christmas, I think of my pink doll house so lovingly made for me by Mom and delivered on a snowy Christmas eve.

Wow, Rock Chalk! Found the KU/Georgetown game on TV only to discover it was ALL Georgetown announcers. I turned the sound off and did my own color commentary, sang the school song, and did the "Rock Chalk" chant at the end of the game for them. Great road win, mighty Jayhawks!!!

The cats sit by the back door at 10:00 p.m. to go on their "hunt" in the screened "bird cage." What they must imagine lives out there I can only wonder, but occasionally they are rewarded with an errant moth or a lime green gecko. Four thousand years of domestication has done nothing to diminish their thrill of the nocturnal hunt. But, of course, at 10:30 p.m., they will be crowding me out of bed.

I took a nap with my cats today. They snuggle around me, especially when I pull out the pink fleece blanket that is an instant magnet for cat biscuits. As they settle down, I love watching their secret cat life of touching noses and the way they tuck a paw around each other in some magical kitty embrace. To say that is not family and love, is not to see what God has given all creatures—the need to love and be loved. And purring, well, that's just the best sound in the world.

Ann Anderson

Blessings, living in gratitude, prayers, hugs... Words we share and say every day. They must work. They must send out little auras of goodness. I read the posts of illness, a death, a lost pup, and everyone gathers round to offer words of comfort. On those good days, a cheerful, happy, lighthearted post or picture to bring a smile, an LOL, and a little sunshine to carry us through the day. While we may have downsized our ability to sit face to face, we continue to yearn for words between us, the interaction, the understanding, affirmation, and joy. Tonight, I send all of you my thanks for filling up my life spaces.

I take my pills. I sleep under my KU blanket. I am so tired. Vann sits with me and brings me mac n' cheese. I think of the prairie.

The naughty list... Yes, I know it is hard to believe, but as a kid, I could be naughty. My grandma gave my brother and me each two $2.00 bills every year on the Christmas tree. After about a week, I would lure my brother into my room and tell him I would give him three $1.00 bills for his two $2.00 bills. He always fell for it thinking he had made one dollar. This Christmas "tradition" continued quite nicely until my brother proudly displayed his "extra" dollar to our mom. My punishment was removing all the ornaments and vacuuming tinsel. From then on, I have stayed always on the nice list! Well, mostly.

The Christmas skirt... Holidays are gingerbread cookies, presents happily wrapped and placed under the decorated tree, family traditions, Christmas carols on the radio, and many childhood memories. As you know from my posts, my mom was my "queen of hearts" and dazzled my life in her short fifty-six years. When I was in kindergarten, she made me a red felt skirt for the Christmas show at Crestview. I had the distinct honor of singing a solo "Up on the Housetop" complete with the hand motions. My red skirt was cut in a full circle, so it made for a natural twirl. But the best part was Mom covered it with felt Christmas decorations: a bright green tree covered with sequins and satin ribbons, Santa with a cotton beard, and a snowman family with silver glitter and two coal black buttons. Along the hem, she sewed a silver edging that hung like little tinsels all around my skirt. I wore the skirt until I outgrew it, and it became our Christmas tree skirt for many years. I can close my eyes and go back to all those years of so proudly putting that skirt on and singing the song with such joy in my heart.

For the first time in my life, I do not put up a tree. I do not watch "A Christmas Story." I miss home. I sleep through Christmas Eve.

The good deed… Now that Christmas is winding down, I will start seeing trees discarded here and there. One Christmas when I was twelve and my brother was ten, my parents went to Kansas City for lunch and left us alone. Like in Cat in the Hat, I felt quite "large and in charge" and decided that we would surprise our mom by taking the ornaments down for her, and then, why not chop up the tree and burn it in the fireplace? My brother and I chopped the tinder dry tree into chunks and crammed it into our fireplace, lit a match, and a small jet rocket explosion occurred. At first, we were delighted with the magnitude of the Yule tree burning, but suddenly, the living room filled with smoke. Though I was twelve, I had not thought to open the vent. After donning oven mitts, I got the flue open, but by then, the house was filled with the fragrant smell of burnt Christmas tree. Not to worry. I had the great idea to open a window and turn on the attic fan to get the smoke out. A minute later, the house was filled with smoke and ashes. Our mom and stepdad walked into Christmas "treemageddon," and the next week, Mom picked out a lovely new color of paint for the living room and kitchen. She was pleasant about our putting the ornaments away, but from then on, we were both banned from lighting the fireplace. So take your tree to Lake Shawnee!

Well, retirement means trying different things and places. Vann and I landed in South Carolina, and after being here, we have made the big decision to head back to our beautiful prairie home in Kansas. We look forward to seeing everybody in late March.

Ann Anderson

Biggest retirement lesson learned by me: it's impossible to replace family, friends, and indoor tennis. Dorothy was right. "There is no place like home."

I feel better. I am going home.

Things I did not learn in kindergarten… The beach is beautiful, but it does not replace family, friends, and for me, the wide open spaces of Kansas. Finding a good partner can help you solve just about any mountain of a problem. The Geritol commercial from long ago was spot on—If you have your health, you have everything. Cats (and pets) are wonderfully comforting if you are lying in bed feeling crummy. Never forget to call/write/text your true friends. They will listen, encourage, and cheer you up. And always wear something pink—at least once a week.

Hypothyroid tennis player update… My first days back at the gym riding the bike, lifting the weights with visions of tennis balls dancing in my head. I ate vegetables for the first time in two months. Funny what tastes good and what doesn't and how that changes. My mind keeps wandering to the prairie, to my nieces and nephew and friends. This bout of hypothyroidism has crystallized all that matters and all that doesn't matter. Luckily, we get do-overs. Onward!

Daybreak on the east edge of the coast… Another nightly frost coats the ground like sparkling glitter. Two snowy egrets land so elegantly on the little lagoon behind our house. Their pencil legs are pale yellow, and they walk the edge of the water to catch silvery tiny fish. As my niece would say, even "global colding" has visited South Carolina this winter. Time to dig out my KU hoodie. I have opened the door to the porch twice for the cats, but they shake their heads and go back to their fleece beds to dream of catching geckos.

Training wheels… In our "fifty-five and up" community in South Carolina, I see lots of people on bikes, beach bikes, racing bikes and even three wheelers. I remember when I was four years old, my mom took me to Western Auto and bought me my first bicycle. It was yellow with a red seat and red training wheels. I was on it from after breakfast to dinner. As I watched the bigger kids in the neighborhood on their bikes and received some good-natured ribbing, I realized it was time to ditch the training wheels. Mom obligingly removed them and on to the next phase

For my sixth birthday, I became the proud owner of a Schwinn Stingray bicycle with a banana seat and high curving handlebars. It was AWESOME! I literally parked it in my bedroom at night. The first ride, however, was a near death experience. With my family watching from our front steps, I pedaled down our steep driveway on my blue beauty, around the corner onto 23rd Street, and then, just like I had seen the big kids do on their English bicycles, I started pedaling backwards. You cannot believe how well those new brakes worked on that little Schwinn and how amazingly far I flew over the front of the handlebars, landing with a skid on my chin (four stitches) and the bicycle fortunately fell over unharmed. With as much dignity as I could muster, I rode back to our house with blood dripping off my chin and Mom frantically running to me. I rode that bike for many years and remember feeling super cool when I saw it waiting for me to climb aboard and take on a new adventure.

Grief… I received a kind letter today from Midland Hospice in Topeka expressing their care for me and my brother's kids. I read it and it made me sad as it brought home again the fact that my brother, Mike, is no longer with us. While we have been in South Carolina, my heart and mind have willingly pretended that we were "just away" and we will see him when we get back to Kansas. And yet that is not to be. Grief is like a smell from our grandma's attic that triggers something intense and unexpected. I saw our neighbor using duct tape this week and thought with a smile of how often Mike would dig out his duct tape to finish something.

I thought of the conversation Vann and my brother had on the way to Colorado to celebrate my nephew Mikey's thirteenth birthday. Mike and Vann started naming the layers of limestone found in Kansas and had an enlightened discussion of each type. Mikey and I were cracking up listening to them and making faces. My brother knew something about everything and could put almost anything back together. The Hospice letter said they could not take away our pain but could help on the "grief journey." That journey is as long as I-70 across Kansas, familiar and filled with all the memories we made with Mike in his short fifty-nine years. I hope my nieces and nephew find that journey to be filled with more good memories. I look forward to seeing the little glimpses of my brother in them as they grow up.

Heart Day... Valentine's Day is one of my favorite holidays. I am enjoying the love I feel for all my sweethearts: Vann, my nieces and nephew, friends, and the kitties. When we were kids, I loved making the shoeboxes adorned with crepe paper, glitter, hearts and a slot cut in the top for the many hoped-for Valentines from classmates. The cards were all small and had cute sayings, and occasionally I'd get a homemade card. After school, Mom and I would dump out the cheery contents on the table and look at each one.

She had heart cookies baked and frosted for us when we got home. Is there anything better than a frosted sugar cookie cut in the shape of a heart? Happy Valentine's Day to all my pals and glad you all live in my valentine shoebox year-round!

It is a day to be a tourist at the Cumberland Island National Park in north Georgia. There are only remnants of two mansions left and the rest of the island is all Mother Nature with miles of pristine beaches, shells, wild horses, armadillos, and other critters. It was soothing to walk and just hear the ocean, see no people, and be with Mother Nature. But also, grateful to get back on the boat, back on the mainland, and take a shower back home. We saw people in their twenties loading their camping stuff in wagons for "wilderness" camping with the snakes, scorpions, and such. Oh, I shall think of them as I drift off to sleep in my bed tonight. I am so tired but happy to be in nature again.

Mindfulness… With my recovering efforts from hypothyroidism, our return to OZ and other events, I have been trying to stay "in the moment" and be more mindful of all the joys, gifts, friends, family, cats, and blessings that have been laid on me. I have tried the ancient breathing meditation, using words and other meditation practices, and sadly, my mind seems to scatter like wheat chaff in the Kansas wind. I watch my cats who seem like ZEN yogis calming themselves with purrs and sun and resting instantly at peace. It is a lifelong practice to be present in each moment. My kitties are mentoring me. Purr Om.

SlowVannah… A tourist day in Savannah, Georgia. Mansions dating back to the 1700s, cobblestone streets, and the majestic Savannah River is forty feet deep. We saw the spot where they filmed several scenes from Forrest Gump and discovered LOTS of fried food - even green beans.The world is a marvelous place to explore and not to be missed. We returned home to find a gecko on the lanai, which Muffy promptly caught and Vann promptly rescued and released out the front door. We are a catch and release house. This week we are off to see a bird sanctuary north of Charleston. Our winter "vacation" before we head home to Kansas is filled with exploring this beautiful and very different part of the country. Well, that's it, y'all.

Vann. Everything I wished for in The Husband Book

Mom and me, ready for Easter, patent leather
and organza on Parkview Street

Chapter Four

EDGE OF GREEN

The cool breeze smells like the edge of green spring
and yet today, the north wind has a faint scent of
ancient snow from the Dakotas where the wind
blew yesterday.

Sex education… Thinking about my high school reunion, and I have been drifting back to school memories. Back in the day, we did not have sex education taught in school. We were self-taught! My cousin Linda told me when I was eight, that babies come out of your belly button and that seemed reasonable to me. In Miss Fallon's kindergarten class at Crestview, Miss Fallon obligingly read to us every day after naps. On one early spring warm day, she began reading, and as she was reading, she started to unbutton her stylish cardigan sweater. We all watched in amazement as her brassiere (as they were called in the '50s) started showing, and then we all gasped when we realized she didn't have a blouse on! Forget the story—this was "sex ed" at age five! The girls were as intrigued as the boys. She must have noted our faces and felt the breeze on her bare skin as she quickly jumped up and announced a special recess. The rest of my sex ed occurred in fifth grade by looking at the much-read issues of National Geographic showing the naked and partially naked tribes around the world. At one point, I also decided that only the "birds and the bees" had sex, as I would overhear Mom and my stepdad discussing who was going to tell my brother and me about the birds and the bees. Ahhhhh, sex ed. Somehow, we all figure it out along the way.

The cats and I are silent partners to the beginning of low country mornings. This is the first warm morning that we all go out at 7:00 a.m. and watch the sun starting to rise higher in the south skies. The pines are in full "bloom," meaning a soft, powdery yellow dust lies on the concrete like high tide marks. The pines here are over one hundred feet tall, and when the wind blows, it makes a sound like a Colorado mountain lullaby. The white egret swoops silently on to the lagoon and on tiptoes, selects her morning sushi. I am ready to head back to the tall grass, friends, my nieces and nephew, and our prairie home, but I am taking in these low country moments that I will not have in Kansas. I know my wild turkeys and the red-tailed hawk are waiting for me.

Rain... Eighty degrees today with sticky humidity to match. We have all been sitting on the "lanai" (southern for screen porch) watching the gray clouds roll in from the west. I picture them having traveled over Kansas, maybe where they were chilly and dropped some snowflakes. Now all plump again with rain to soak into the sandy earth and fill the swampy areas under the cypress trees. The egret has been snacking, and I never tire of watching her pale-yellow beak snag a silvery catch. I am a summer person and love the rain. When we were kids, my mom fixed popcorn balls with sweet Karo syrup and allowed us to drink icy ten-ounce Coca Colas that came in the six pack paper cartons. We sat in our breezeway in butterfly chairs, protected from the storm, and watched the rain. It was a simple pleasure made elegant by my mom's Rainy Day popcorn balls and Cokes. The wind has blown the rain onto us, so we are now inside. Tonight, with covers pulled up around all of us, we will listen to the sound of the rain that started out on the prairie. In the morning, the air will smell of grape pop from the purple crepe myrtles and sugary like a popcorn ball from the azaleas.

A soft spot... Vann just pulled out of the driveway for a three-hour drive to his homestate Florida to visit his kin. He will be gone for three days, and the cats and I will be quite busy packing, so it will go by quickly. After twenty years of being together, I notice the light and presence of Vann already missing. The house is quiet, and it is strange not to hear him at his desk, the Wall Street Journal opening, the coffee brewing, and the light smell of Old Spice drifting by. He is my one and only, a rock for me, a lighthouse to lead me on, and always with a word of encouragement. The cats, too, seem to know we're missing one as they have, at 7:45 a.m., already selected nap places and have no interest in my cat string. He will enjoy the drive down the Georgia coastline and visits with all his relatives, who can talk more than any family I know. They call Vann the "family guru," and I am sure they all have an issue for him to fix. I'm off to start packing and keeping Vann safely tucked in my heart until I hear him walk back in on Sunday.

Lions and tigers and gators! We saw our first alligator this morning, sunbathing so happily in our lagoon and giving ME the EYE. OK, thinking it truly is time to head back to Kansas before the critters really pop out here. Oh darn, we are going to miss live oak pollen season, the Palmetto bugs (two-inch flying cockroaches) and love bugs that cover your cars with love bug "love." Oh, and mosquitoes. Clicking my tennis shoes....

The circle of life... Mom used to say that anybody who grew up in Kansas always came back to Kansas. As a kid, I thought "No way, I'm outta here," and for over twenty years I did experience living in Chicago, Los Angeles and San Diego. Then back to Kansas to enjoy seeing my nieces and nephew grow up, and off again to South Carolina. We landed in the low country five months ago, a place that is drenched in beauty, azaleas, historical architecture, rich traditions, marshes, and the ocean. And yet, none of it could replace my love for Kansas, and that magical sense of the heart knowing where it truly belongs.

Ann Anderson

I am lucky to be married to Vann, who finds any place home and adapts his ways as quickly as the geckos here change their colors. Life is a nice basket of tradeoffs, and I will gladly put on some mittens to be back on the prairie, see those faces that swell up my heart, and listen to the gentle south breeze that inspires the people of the south wind.

It's a good thing... As Martha would say, the last couple of days have been full of "good things." First, many sweet birthday wishes, including cards from my beloved nieces and nephew, with my nephew correctly pointing out that five months is too long to be apart. I could not agree more! The flowers are blooming here: orange day-glow azaleas, dogwood trees bathed in pale pink and white blossoms. Different birds with new songs to be heard, alligators, and 90% of the house neatly packed and labeled. Our neighbor had us over for "cocktails," a term I haven't heard since my parents' day, but very much in vogue here in the south. She had a spread of lovely foods and a cocktail bar set up. The most interesting part of the evening was hearing about her mom working as a librarian on the South Carolina islands in the '60s when most of the blacks were Gullah and spoke a language developed during slavery. She wrote a Gullah dictionary and also several children's books. Wonderful people and stories are all around us if we stop for a moment and enjoy them. And now a day of steady rain which washes the bright yellow pine pollen into lines like a long pale snake. Tonight, I will watch the KU Jayhawks and, win or lose, it is another one of life's good things.

First sun on the east coast... Bluebirds have appeared to call dibs on the neighbor's bluebird boxes. My egret slides into the lagoon for her silver fish breakfast. The pine trees are quiet this morning as if to let everyone but me sleep in on a Sunday. The cats are stretched like link sausages, side by side, in the quiet sunlight. They try to be interested in the birds, but are too happy to be sunning. My coffee sends a cloud of mist like the dew that sits on everything each morning here. Next Sunday we will wake up in Kansas on our prairie porch, and I will watch the bluebirds there look for their boxes. And that same coastal sunlight will make its way to welcome us back home.

Lions and tigers and bears, oh my... South Carolina is a place where we are NOT at the top of the food chain. When Vann was off visiting his Florida kin last weekend, I saw my first (and hopefully last) coral snake. They are one of the most poisonous snakes (factoid—South Carolina has the most poisonous snakes in the U.S. and produces most of the country's anti-venom shots) and there is a rhyme that Vann taught me. I see the snake in our backyard and try to remember the rhyme as there is a "look alike" snake with the same colors in a different pattern that is harmless. In my state of mind, I cannot quite remember the poem: was it "red, you're dead," or was it "yellow, watch out, fellow." What the heck! I'm getting the kitties, and we are going inside! We watched the coral snake slither across the backyard. Now a neighbor boasts that he caught a black bear on his critter cam. What? We've moved to the wilds of South Carolina!

First day of summer... Today feels like a hot windy day in August with 86 degrees and the wind blowing. The pine pollen literally floats like yellow glitter in the air. Spring break has begun, and the beaches are loaded with out-of-town cars, people toting 100 pounds of stuff for the beach, and the smell of coconut sunscreen and shrimp hangs fragrantly in the air. It does not feel like St. Patrick's Day, but I do see a few green swim suits. Our celebration of the day is packing.

I hope for a long spring and wait for late summer for the 86 degrees and warm winds to find us again. I am daydreaming of our Kansas porch, the wicker chairs with cheerful cushions parked on the patio, the cats curled about like sun snakes, and smelling the heat lift the fragrance from the lavender and rosemary plants.

Familiar... As we settle back into our Kansas home, all five of us seem consumed with the feeling of familiar. Familiar is comfort to me. When I moved to Chicago many years ago, I did not know ONE single person. For the first couple of months, I found myself going to the local mall as those stores were familiar to me—Gap, Old Navy, Eddie Bauer. Familiar here is seeing our backyard yawn out from the prairie to the edge of the forest, waking up with the sunlight streaming in the windows and the gentle rain that falls here at night in the spring. The cats have found all of their sun puddles just as they left them. Vann has set up his command post (desk) downstairs, this time with views to the west. Familiar is a hug that wraps around us with a place in our hearts and people we love. I can't wait to see Marilyn, Nancy, the J's, Ronda and my family. Home!

Treasures… We are unpacked again. Unpacking is more fun, and re-discovering our treasures is a reassuring feeling. I am amazed by the little whatnots that have survived the moves since I graduated from KU. To name a few…when I was eight, I had eye surgery. To entertain me, my mom bought a kit to make a beautiful mosaic wall hanging of a Roman gladiator with three horses, complete with jewels, thin rope, and glitter. For over fifty-five years, it has moved with not one drop of glitter or jewel falling off. I have the minature people from my brother's train set, a pair of Indian moccasins on a safety pin that my friend Debbie and I have shared back and forth since we were in kindergarten, my grandma's well-used thimbles, Colorado rocks we picked up on family vacations, all of my school books from first grade (Tip and Mitten, The Big Show), and the patches from my Brownie uniform and Brownie pin. They are markers on my life map of what I've done and what has mattered most to me. Treasures that connect me to my life.

People of the south wind… The doors open wide, the wren inspects her new home, robins swim joyfully in the filled bird bath, buds of cotton-candy pink magnolias are ready to pop, the cats settle in their sun puddles, a Midwest rainstorm promised in the night will lull us all to sleep. Go slowly with this beautiful life. Do not wish for tomorrow to come quickly as today is here to savor and melt over you.

It is officially spring in my heart. The kitties have found all of their special places, and the house now happily beats again with five hearts. The wild turkeys are gathering in our back prairie, and the whirlygigs are spinning down from the maples as they leaf out. Today had no boxes to pack or unpack. Vann and I treated ourselves to a trip to Lawrence through the glacial hills, sprouting with greens and shoots of new growth on an ancient calendar we do not know. I had not seen cattle for five months, and they look sturdy to the land, their white faces down on the good earth finding the new grass. Lawrence was the usual Rock Chalk of KU tee shirts, the honk-for-hemp guy on the corner, and the hum of activity on Mass Street.

The Easter dress… Easter is one of my favorite holidays from Palm Sunday and the glorious waving of the palms to Easter Sunday and pews filled with the regulars and the "irregulars" who all feel God on this day. As a child, I wore my Easter clothes to church, my best shoes and hat, and I carried a small, white patent leather purse. One year, Grandma made me a pale lavender Easter dress with a pink sash ribbon and tiny flowers stitched on the front. It was made of organza and was perfect for twirling, though I thought better of it on Easter. The best part of the dress was the lavender petticoat that Grandma made to go with it. It was sewn in layers, and with the petticoat under it, the dress flared out at a girly angle. I wore it so proudly to Easter service, and at our family dinner, I put extra layers of napkins on my lap to protect the beautiful dress. Grandma held my hand as we left church that day, and I could feel the love passing from her to me on that special Easter long ago.

Aromatherapy of spring smells in Kansas… With the door open, tomorrow's rain is scenting the air with warm wet smells. Our lilac is just opening and mixing with the perfume of the delicate magnolia. The earth that I turned yesterday while planting wildflowers still hangs in the air with its Kaw Valley richness and maybe an earthworm mixed in. I am grateful for all of the scents that fill our space with the promise of the Kansas spring and the warm fresh scents of a summer that waits in the wings.

41

Ann Anderson

Somehow over the years, I have become my mom. Not in a duplicate sort of way, but I laugh when Vann and I plan an afternoon of driving around to look at houses (no, we're NOT buying), admiring the ornamental trees, and swinging by Gage Park to check on the opening of the tulip garden. Hearing the words, "Let's go for a drive!" was routine Sunday afternoon kid torture. Oh Lordy, Mike and I knew that meant sitting in the back seat for two to three hours while my parents drove around Topeka looking at houses and admiring trees and maybe a new business that had opened. Mike and I were left to torment each other with the "finger over the line" routine and anything else we could do to shorten the trip. Occasionally, we were rewarded by a stop at Bachman's ice cream store where I was allowed a double scoop of tutti fruitti ice cream.

I also find myself waking up early, fixing a cup of coffee, and watching the birds—just like my mom did. In fact, for over twenty years, she kept a record on the calendar of these daily comings and goings. (I have all of these.) Maybe as we grow up, the simple pleasures become what we enjoy the most. I am entertained by the tidal changes of the day in our backyard, the first bluebirds finding the mealy worms, the regal cardinal and his mate daintily nibbling at the sunflower seeds, and the sky changing from slate gray rain clouds to a bank of sun and pink clouds. Today our simple pleasure is an overnight visit from Vann's cousin, Beth, an artist from St. George Island, Florida, and her husband, David. And like our parents, we will take joy in spending the day talking about family and those things that seem to endure through the generations. Oh, and a drive to Gage Park to see the tulips now in full spring bloom.

My grandma was the spirit of us. She filled the rooms with hot smells of cinnamon rolls spread with white frosting like a sugar blizzard. She led me through the greens of her garden like a Paris guide. Her well-lived hands would push me forever in the elm tree swing. Late in the afternoon, she would spread a quilt made of my dress scraps for a nap near the lilac row. There I would sleep with the south wind blowing the fairies in from the golden cornfield that surrounded their farm.

✿ ✿ ✿

Grandparents... Part of the fabric of my childhood. I did not know my bio dad's parents, but Mom's parents lived on a farm on California Avenue south of Topeka, and my brother and I spent most of the summers there. Summers were always the special time of our year when Mom packed paper sacks full of cutoffs, flip flops (called thongs in the day), a pair of Keds, and one set of good clothes—just in case our grandparents decided to take a rare trip into town or visit one of our relatives.

We played tractors in the garden, building tall mounds of dirt from the rich soil and almost always ruining at least one row of new onions. We pushed each other in the rope swing, walked to the pond with cane poles, and watched anxiously for the red and white bobber to go under. Grandpa would say, "Set the hook," and we'd bring in a bright sun perch or bluegill. We also played fort, hide and seek, and sometimes just lay in the hay bales with our cousins and watched the Kansas sunshine stream like golden dust through the cracks. If we were lucky, we'd find a kindle of new born kittens just opening their eyes to the world.

At lunch, Grandma would lay out a spread of cold fried chicken, vegetables from the garden including one of my favorites, cukes and onions soaked in a sugar vinegar bath, and fresh red and black raspberries.

In the evening, we sat in the big front yard, Grandma always rocking slowly and swatting real and imaginary flies off of our arms to our delight. We counted the cattle across the road as they went to feed. There were always the same number, but we always counted—just in case.

Grandpa kept a bag of pale orange, circus peanut candy that would jam up our teeth pleasantly. Sometimes on a Saturday evening, we were permitted to stay up late and watch Gunsmoke and eat Neapolitan ice cream.

We slept in the spare bedroom under sheets that had flown on the line all day. They smelled like gladiolas, lilacs, and the sun. Out the windows, we could see the sky glow from the far-off lights of Topeka and the brighter lights from softball games at Lake Shawnee.

Down the hall, we listened and fell happily to sleep as Grandma and Grandpa talked about how nice it was having the kids in the summer.

Ann Anderson

This spring night takes me back to those spring nights as a kid on Burnett Road. I have to laugh that there is furniture named for when I was young—Mid-Century! Our after school routine was a snack, homework done, and whatever we pleased until dinner at 6:00 p.m. Then OUT THE FRONT DOOR I went to a buffet of things to do. Our neighbor's Brady Bunch-looking house had a TENNIS COURT! I thought they were the luckiest people in the world. They were generous about letting all the neighbor kids hop onto the court whenever we wanted. There was always somebody ready to hit some balls until dark. Linette's house was filled with activity—her brothers, Steve and Dave, making their latest scientific experiment and Linette listening to Beatles music in the backyard. Three houses down, our neighbor had built a baseball diamond in their large back lot. We spent many evenings with a pickup game of softball, sharing the gloves that a few of us owned. Sometimes we snuck out to Kenny and Debbie's house and watched Saturday night midnight wrestling. We had a tetherball in our yard, and I can still hear that familiar clang clang of the chain gently hitting the pole in the evening. We were always outside. When we came in, Mom would march us into a shower with Dial soap and Prell shampoo and into our pajamas.

Occasionally, on a very lucky night, we would come in the door after playing and Mom would have plates of warm German chocolate cake cut into huge slabs with a snowball mound of vanilla Sealtest ice cream just beginning to melt into the cake. Mid-Century kid—unplugged and forever grateful for those wonder years.

Joe College… Vann and I spent part of today in Lawrence, just flat out the coolest, hippest, and neatest town anywhere! I have gone there all my life, including my KU years, and some things remain pleasantly and eternally the same like a place permanently stuck in the '70s. Some of my fondest KU memories are afternoons spent in my dorm rooms at Corbin Hall and Ellsworth listening to the music of Crosby, Stills, Nash and Young, Fleetwood Mac, Moody Blues, 2:00 a.m. outings to Joe's Bakery to carb up on hot pastries after supposedly pulling an all-nighter, Thursday night, heading to the "Mad Hatter" with my roomie, Leslie, for ladies' night, and, oh yeah, sometimes I'd even go to class and get good grades. It was a keen place and still is full of whimsy, tradition, memories old and new, the smell of the limestone buildings, the goosies you get when you enter THE Allen Fieldhouse and realize you're actually at a KU basketball game, and the joy in knowing Lawrence is always there for a visit to never-never land, one of the happiest and coolest places on Earth. Rock Chalk.

Jazzy and I have been porch sitting, which we have both elevated to an art. It is my meditation – looking out over the prairie which yawns behind us toward woods and hills. Right now, the forest is dotted with native redbuds, delicate trees that look as if someone glued bright pink flowers all over their branches. Other trees are pushing out their new yellow green leaves like paintbrush strokes on a canvas. Jazzy stays tucked around my neck like a purring fur coat, and we both relish each other's closeness and warmth. Her blue eyes drift shut, and her purring slows down as she dreams. Then a bird lands on the roof and whiskers twitching, she makes the cat chatter bird sound. We have seen the shimmery blue swallows making their erratic elegant circles, catching bugs and finding crevices for their nests. The cool breeze smells like the edge of green spring and yet, today the north wind has a faint scent of ancient snow from the Dakotas where the wind blew yesterday. The crisp clean smell of last night's rain hangs like tiny blue ornaments shimmering still on the branches and plants. All the riches do not compare to our kitty meditation times on our porch overlooking our prairie.

Alleys and roly poly bugs... Doug, one of my favorite artists, posted a painting of an alley. It brought back the memory of the alley behind our house at 720 Parkview. I would guess most people don't know or think about alleys anymore, but as a kid, it was like having a playground at the edge of our backyard. Across the street, out our front door, was Hughes Tennis Courts, which were bustling with activity. When we stepped out our back door, the alley beckoned with a quiet place to explore, to find lost coins and keys, and to see our neighbor's lives through the back of their houses. A line of swing sets, play houses, and trees for climbing all magically appeared to us just by crossing the alley. We held

"Cats leave paw prints in your heart,
forever and always." —Unknown

many kids' meetings in the alley to plan our day, decide where our bikes would take us, find roly poly bugs, and maybe just rummage in our garages and look for buried treasure. During the daytime, our alley became a dirt freeway of kid fun and a grand place to sit on the ground and play with our various cars and trucks.

We had a stone wall that ran along our alley in our backyard. Mom told my brother and me that roly poly bugs were made into butter brickle ice cream, our favorite. She said the little bugs were toasted and tossed into vanilla ice cream. Sometimes she would tell us that if we went out by the stone wall into the alley and caught a milk bottle full of roly polys, she would take them to the store and bring back the butter brickle ice cream. My brother and I would go about the three-hour task of filling up a milk bottle with the bugs and presenting it to my mom. She would take it and then return with the promised ice cream. I was probably ten before I figured out she had just found a way to keep us busy for the afternoon.

Next time I'm out driving, I think I'll go drive down my old alley and see what changes time has brought to it since the 1950s. And I think I'll stop and get some "roly poly" ice cream.

Stop and smell the springtime… Vann, the kitties, and I took "paws" this afternoon to drink in this spring day. After a morning with my lively, joyful tennis kiddos, it was soothing to wander our quiet house, stopping now and then when a place beckoned "come sit here for a while." In the sunroom, Jazzy stretched out full length on my legs, and it looked like my tennis shoes grew out of her bunny-soft brown ears. Her purring was like ocean waves or a thunderstorm, so soothing and calming, and I could hear and feel her slowly going to a cat nap. Nearby, Queenie moved with the sun puddles and occasionally flopped over on the cooler tile until she was ready for more sunbathing. Her fur glistened in the sun like sparkled sand on a beach. In her dreams, her feet move— perhaps she is chasing one of the wild turkeys that lives on our back prairie. Muffy is our "creature of comfort" as Vann has named her. She finds the fleeciest blankets, the softest cushions, and the "loungiest" places for her daily snoozes. Even Vann was spotted dozing on the porch as the afternoon sun drifted out to Colby for an orange and pink sunset. I am dazzled and drowsy from an afternoon of Kansas spring.

Endless love... If there is anybody reading this who is hoping for a perfect mate, let me reassure you that it does happen. In my case, I had to wait forty-two years to find him, but someone is out there for you. Vann is the most intelligent, kindhearted, generous and loving husband I could ever imagine. When I was in my twenties, after a night of some Boone's Farm Strawberry Hill wine drinking, my co-worker and friend, Tonnie, and I (we were single and no dates) made a "Husband Book." It was quite elaborate and featured pictures cut out of magazines of what we "demanded" and "deserved" in a husband. As the bad wine poured, it became even more detailed, down to a page of what kind of underwear was unacceptable (fishnet) and no proper husband would own an El Camino or bunk beds. That became our Husband Book, and we showed it to all of our friends at work, including our boss, Bill, so they could help us find the husband as outlined in our book. Over the next few years, Tonnie found her husband (no doubt because of the book) but I remained steadfastly single until I met Vann when I was FORTY! We dated for two years, and then we were engaged, and he was everything in the Husband Book. Over the years, he has added qualities I couldn't even imagine with his sweetness and generosity. Here's to the Husband Book that seemingly worked. I married the dearest man ever with no fishnet underwear, no bunk beds, no El Camino, but twenty years and going of fun, happiness, sharing through thick and thin, and a happily ever after.

Fledges... Summer is my favorite season, but spring is no doubt a close second. The kitties and I put on our fur hoodies and sit outside this morning at 7:00 a.m. with a cup of steaming coffee to watch the remnants of last night's thunderstorm drift overhead. Clouds that look like whipped marshmallows and some gentle thunder give way to Kansas blue skies. It is fledge day on our bird campus and every bluebird box, sparrow nest, turkey cave, and other bird homes have spilled out tiny cartoon yellow beaks of joy begging for another bite of bug or worm. The cats sit transfixed by all of the bird goings-on, almost as if to not disturb the show. There are always the two or three fledges who aren't sure about leaving the womb and sit with their bobbing, little heads poking out of the hole or over the nest. The mama bird does her best to make this world seem inviting by chirping, holding bugs, and flapping her wings. Just like people, some of us come a little later to the party, but in the end, the late-blooming fledges find their wings into this beautiful world. There is an early morning magic in Kansas that is over by the time people come out in their robes to sleepily pick up the Sunday paper. But the cats and I saw it— fledge day on the prairie.

Buggy whips and such… I came across one of the last 33 1/3 records I still have. It is Peter Pan from the 1950s, complete with the art cardboard case and story book. It's a pleasure to hold in my hands and smell the warm scent of its age, and I love the story. I had to smile thinking about the things that no longer exist…the buggy whips of our lives. As a kid, we were so proud when my parents extravagantly bought THE entertainment center with a television AND a stereo housed in a giant piece of furniture complete with little slots for records. We had it for many years, and I thought we were approaching rich by having an "entertainment center" in our home. In my bedroom, I was the proud owner of a small turquoise record player that started out playing my kid songs. Over time, I started playing my rock n' roll records on it. Many a night, my friend Debbie and I would listen to it. It was a perfect match to my turquoise Princess phone that I received for my thirteenth birthday.

Buggy whips, record players, 8-track tapes, rotary phones, and lots of things go extinct every year. If you want to remember some of these things, stop by the Kansas Museum. It is a good memory zone. I like that I am a child who grew up mid-century.

Unanswered prayers… This week I feel like my cells and heart and brain have been filled up to the brim with happiness, love, friends, family, kitties, husband, tennis, rain, flowers, and the precious beauty of this life. I got to sing the Beatles song "They Say It's Your Birthday" to my lifelong KU friend, Leslie, and we laughed through forty-five years of knowing each other.

I live in gratitude for all of the love and gentle ways that weave my fabric. I think of Garth Brooks' song "Unanswered Prayers." It reminds me of the not very thoughtful prayers I have sent up over the years to God, and God wisely put them in the shredder, answering the ones that truly mattered.

As a little kid, it was my nightly ritual to say my prayers with Mom, feeling like God was truly listening to only me. I have prayed for good health for many of my family and friends, and they were taken for reasons I cannot comprehend but must accept. There is a balance that spins the universe, and far be it from me to understand it. All I know is, I am thankful, and I feel like I am kneeling with my mom, saying my prayers.

The truest love... Happy Mother's Day to my mom. Though she has been gone from this sweet Earth for thirty-three years, she lives spontaneously within me, in my dreams, thoughts and deeds. A mother's love is the purest, and she is in Heaven, I know, with her daily pompom cheer for me to do well and have fun. My mom was a magnet to happiness. Friends would literally visit our house for coffee and be there three days later—still wishing to stay. Two of my favorite male cousins, Johnny and Spencer, spent almost every weekend at our house, playing cards, drinking coffee, and like my brother and me, just soaking up the aromatherapy of good that floated out from my mom. Johnny told me that my mom was like a second mom to him. He was convinced she held the sky up.

When she was diagnosed with breast cancer at fifty-two, I was twenty-six. I sat holding her hand in the doctor's office, and Mom comforted ME and said, "Well, what do we do first?" She was always unfailingly optimistic and stubbornly happy as my dear friend, Debra, said. She persisted and made life joyful for the next four years. She showered us with gold and silver glitter, spun us into young adults, and then had to leave. Happy Mother's Day to the greatest mom I could ever have dreamed of and love to this moment.

I have spring trapped in our backyard. Columbines are spilling over pink and purple and yellow blossoms in the shade, the birds flocking to the bird beach, the trumpet vine getting ready to sound off with bright orange blossoms, the wren maneuvering twigs into her red house, and the herbs perfuming the air as we sit on the porch soaking in this beauty called springtime.

Ann Anderson

My brother's best friend Mark sent me a special picture of the two of them all duded up, John Travolta lookalikes. I'm not sure of the year—guessing in the '80s. I was always trying to get my brother to be a model as I pictured us growing rich off his handsome looks and jetting away to the islands for photo shoots. He had curly hair and mine was pencil straight and we often thought God got that switched up. He's been gone from us for ten months, but I still feel like he's just gone on a photo shoot to a far-off island and will call me soon. My brother was a handsome boy who grew into a kind, funny, and loving man.

It's National Pet Month. I have been enriched and molded by all of the sweet animals we have had since I was a kid. My family, for some reason, always seemed to rescue Siamese cats. My grandma even had a Siamese cat show up on the farm. She named her Opus, and she was with kittens when she arrived on the back porch. She had five kittens, and Grandma named them after angels. Opus and the kittens were anything but angels and ran up Grandma's white sheer curtains—much to my brother's and my delight! Grandma had a barn full of farm cats, too, who were clever, uncatchable, and kept a check on the mice population. We rarely saw them, but they all appeared in a row when Grandpa milked the cows. He squirted the milk right into their waiting open mouths while my brother and I admired his aim and their catch!

May is like Christmas. Full of spring blooms, green grass, the first days on the porch, stretching out in the hammock in the rising southern sun, graduation parties, colors emerging out of closets of pinks, yellows and greens, birthday parties, and the promise of the sweet tastes of summer yawning out from the close by. Ready, set, spring.

KU buds for life... Two of my first friends at KU were Susie and David. We were instantly and famously the life of our own party with bike riding, watching KU basketball, eating oranges, porch sitting, fraternity schmoozing, and frequenting their house and mine for the weekend. They remain two of the most clever, kind, and fun friends I've had, and I am grateful that an invisible golden thread has kept the three of us woven together. They are frozen forever at their KU age, boundless, long hair, zooming, and making me forget to go to class. We are all grown up now, but in our hearts, we stay forever young and lounging around the KU campus wondering what mischief we might look to next.

Double the fun with twin nieces! Graduation weekend for my twin nieces, Jordan and Reagan, from Allen Community College. I blink, and they stand in cardboard hats at their kindergarten graduation with tiny hands gripping their certificates. Then we are applauding, as they send their smiles to us at their Topeka High School graduation. Two years of good grades, meeting new friends, playing on a college soccer team, and tomorrow another milestone as they graduate from community college. They are beautiful girls, full of gratitude, kindness, discipline for their schoolwork and sports, and an abundant love for their many friends and family. Now, Jordan and Reagan will toss their caps high into the air and dream of being Kansas State University Wildcats this fall. Make this time go slowly for all of us to enjoy, savor, and remember.

I think Kenny Chesney sings the song "Don't Blink" (and 100 years go by). With everybody's graduation pictures being posted, I am reminded of that song. I was fondly remembering going to my very own kindergarten roundup at Gage Elementary School. It has since become the Topeka Civic Theater, and I love being there as it still smells like a mid-century grade school. I remember my ninth-grade graduation and shopping with Mom in Kansas City for a special dress. We never went to Kansas City to shop, and she surprised me with the trip and lunch, just the two of us, at the Country Club Plaza. My dress had lace over white cotton, and I remember feeling exceptionally lucky.

My KU graduation brings back the sweet memory of being dressed up with pink pearl earrings Mom gave me. However, I topped off my outfit with "Baretraps"—the very popular sandal of the 1970s. They were clunky, funky, and I thought I was pretty cool wearing them. Mom said, "Years from now, you will look at your KU graduation picture and wish you were not wearing ugly shoes." Ironically, I look at that picture and smile hearing Mom say that.

I am blessed to be a part of my nieces and nephews' milestone events and the graduations we have enjoyed with them. The next one in two years will be from Kansas State University. In a blink of an eye, that time goes by. Enjoy it all, soak it in, don't wish for something to come too quickly and maybe follow your mom's advice on what shoes to wear. Or not.

Memory Day... Memorial Day—the official start to summer, and last night Vann and I watched the very moving tribute to the military, their families, and the poignant stories of kids losing their parents to war. Memorial Day was the last holiday we celebrated with Mom thirty-three years ago. Her favorite season was fall, but she reveled in the summers of Kansas with her garden big enough to feed the neighborhood, fishing, swimming, and every evening spent sitting on our patio surrounded by neighbor kids and our cat.

She was given six months to live in March 1982 and was feeling very poorly by Memorial Day. But she wanted a grand holiday, so we filled the house with red, white, and blue everything. Every room looked festive, and balloons floated around on the ceilings seemingly following Mom wherever she went that day.

She wanted a grand picnic. My brother engineered a fire pit in the backyard with bricks and chairs around it. We roasted hot dogs, made s'mores, and our big finale was breaking out the Black Cat firecrackers and sparklers that we always seemed to have tucked in a drawer. The sounds and smell and laughter of that day come back to me each Memorial Day. Mom enjoyed every moment, and for that day, life seemed so normal and full of the promise ahead. I learned from that joyous impromptu holiday to jump on the opportunity to celebrate—don't wait. Happy Memorial Day to everyone and God bless those that no longer are with us.

Oh, the places he'll go. I just had dinner with my nephew, Mikey. I look at him and see him all grown into a handsome young man, but my heart and mind float easily back to holding him for the first time and not wanting to let him go. Now he sits across from me with plans, dreams, best friends, a beautiful girlfriend, and his first apartment. He is so much more poised than I was at that age, serious but with a constant sense of humor and a way of brightening everyone's spirit around him. My heart is filled with gratitude for having him in my life, a blessing that never ends and only improves each day. You will go far, my nephew, and you are a wonder to watch as you breathe into each new experience.

My favorite car of all time—
Chevy Impala convertible

Chapter Five

SPARROWS

The height of summer, another two boxes of
sparrows have fledged, their yellow cartoon beaks
grinning from each beckoning flight.

I like a boy, five years old, Miles, who didn't mind me putting a
Hello Kitty Band-Aid on his knee. He is being raised right.

Tiny bits of beautiful life spill out around us when we stop. Last
night, the skies flashed and opened up a giant jar of fire flies and
silver bolts of light better than any fireworks display. Jazzy and I
awoke early this morning. Jazzy for a quick nibble of kitty bits and
me for a mug of steaming rich coffee laced with a splash of real
cream. My hands encircled it to shake off the 6:00 a.m. chill on our
porch. The last remnants of the rain clouds were torn around us,
like kids tearing navy construction paper, and left glued on to the
pale blue morning sky. The birds had long been awake and were
on batch two of their spring babies, jockeying for the best limb or
bluebird box. They landed in the gutter to catch the bug buffet in
the eaves. Holding Jazzy's strong warm body, I love to hear her
"bird" chatter and see her little filament whiskers dance with some
ancient desire. Yet she was happier to cuddle down in my hoodie

and drift in and out of a cat beauty sleep with her steady purr. A cicada was stuck on the screen, perhaps too drowsy to start the day or, like us, just enjoying the morning freshness. I tapped my finger in the air, and presto! like Harry Potter's wand, I woke up the lights in the neighbors' homes. But just for that thirty minutes, Jazzy and I had cornered the magic and awe of early morning, the beginning of a Kansas summer day.

Cicadas… Chainsaws with prehistoric armor. They buzz, they sing, they bump into our screens, they find mates, and then back under for seventeen years. Just think, we won't be able to enjoy them again until 2032! I'd make a helluva lot of noise too if I only got to come out every seventeen years to see what's going on!

Cicadas… Part two. As usual on this blissful early summer day, the cats and I take to the porch. This morning, we were rewarded by the hatching of hundreds of baby cicadas—something I have not ever seen. The cats ran for an hour trying to chase them through the screen. The cicadas bumped like drunken bumblebees against the screen, no doubt, being new to flying. Their sound was the ebb and flow that it was summer's end, time for last swims at Crestview Pool, a visit to our cousins' Alma farm, buying back-to-school clothes at McDonald's Department Store at 21st and Gage, and imagining all the excitement that lay ahead as Labor Day ended. Cicadas were a bookmark for the end of summer.

Planting the seeds… I am third generation Kansan, which is probably one of the reasons South Carolina didn't agree with me. I am forever tied to this Kansas River black soil and limestone. The ancient seas that were here still beat a tidal rhythm in me each day. Each firefly lights a spot in my native brain, each thunderstorm brings childhood memories of sitting sheltered on our breezeway, eating Rainy Day popcorn balls and drinking 10 oz. Cokes.

Today I planted native wildflower seeds and held their rough contents in my hands. My little shovel smoothly moves into the dark brown earth and turns over wiggling, fat earthworms who must wonder: What is this world with light and air all of a sudden? I gently and quickly tuck the seeds into their earth bed and ask the earthworms to watch over them and help them grow. I have pulled off my garden gloves as the touch of the soil is so much better, and the cool squirt from the hose waters the seeds and cleans my hands. Now I sit with my kitties and admire all the other good plants we have grown, the prairie cone flowers that attract the goldfinches, the daisies with their crisp white petals and party-yellow centers, the sage that seemingly drifts on the south breeze and waves its plumes of gray blue flowers, and the rosemary and lavender which perfume the air at night from the heat of the day. This prairie Earth, so plain to many people, but to me a never-ending season of growth, rest, and solitude. To sit and be still, watching the grasses and feeling the ancient waves on the tide of Kansas time.

Eighty is the new sixty and no one proves that more than my wonderful husband Vann! He will celebrate his eightieth birthday and Father's Day this weekend. He is my soulmate, a kind uncle to my nieces and nephew, a caring father to his kids, a friend to all who meet him, a magnificent cat dad, and someone who makes each day enhanced with his gentle ways, intelligence, support and love. Happy Birthday and Happy Father's Day to Vann!

Class of 1970... I saw a post this week for a classmate who died recently. With our forty-fifth reunion coming up Labor Day weekend, I shake my head and think it cannot be that people our age who walked with the original sixties swag, high water jeans, mini-skirts, go-go boots (mine were white) and long hair carefully rolled in orange juice cans to be pencil straight can leave us. It cannot be that we have lost classmates. I am forever frozen in my mind at that age in some ways, so it seems we all must be.

That time was perhaps the last of our carefree days and of this world spinning rather quietly as the Vietnam War would shatter the innocence of our college years and take older siblings off to a jungle a world away. High school days were spent at the new and beautiful campus setting of Topeka West. I felt so fortunate to walk outside between classes, even in bad weather, chat with friends,

59

sit in the grass, and watch the pep rallies by "A" building. We had a magnificent gym filled with kids on winter Friday nights, cheering for the Chargers, boys in button down shirts with a fruit loop on the back and girls in their purple and white pep club sweaters and pleated skirts. My brother and I walked home almost a mile in the dark with no worries of any safety issues after a basketball game. It seemed like all of southwest Topeka was our neighborhood and Topeka West was there to hold us each day.

The ten-year reunion was about "What is your job?," twenty-year was "How many kids?," thirty-year was noticing how people were aging and for the forty-year, we all shrugged off those things that kept us different. We truly felt like a group of people bonded for life by a single experience. I am already anticipating the warmth of seeing everybody Labor Day weekend, visiting the school, and being reminded of the youth and innocence we keep in our hearts.

Summer's middle... When we were young, the Fourth of July signaled the middle of summer, halfway to the start of school, which was then rightfully the day after Labor Day. It was also the biggest kid holiday of the summer and anticipated for several weeks. Families shot off their fireworks ON the Fourth of July, and I think for most, it was a simple fare of Black Cats, sparklers, snakes, Roman candles, and my personal favorite, the parachute guy. For a week, my brother and I laid our treasures out on the bench in the garage to be loaded up for the drive to our grandparents' farm. We meticulously unwrapped the Black Cats that were twisted together like dried spaghetti strands and put them in paper grocery bags—each bag carefully holding the exact amount for my brother and me. Our punks were tucked in to be lit on the Fourth of July.

The day of the Fourth was so joyful. Our grandparents had a beautiful farm with twin oak trees that framed the house and kept it cool in the hot summer. Grandma had her usual offerings of holiday fare: golden fried chicken, new potatoes just dug that morning, cukes and onions, bathed in a fragrant bath of sugar and vinegar water, green beans snapped from the garden and simmered for hours, homemade yeast rolls that we always snagged before lunch, and usually her famous lemon ice pick cake poked with holes and thin lemon icing poured over it, drowning the buttery yellow cake that happily lay underneath.

Of course, the highlight of the day was getting to shoot off our fireworks. Firecrackers and snakes were allowed during the day. It was my brother's all-time favorite holiday, and our cousin, Stevie, and Mike would find countless ways to tie the Black Cats together to blow up all assortment of cans. Our cousin, Linda, and I preferred to sit in the swing or on the big rock, drinking grape or orange Nehi's that my grandpa had iced in the large wash tub. My grandma made homemade ice cream with fresh fat cream, sugar, and some type of fruit: peaches, apricots, or raspberries that had hung on the branch before jumping into the creamy yellow mixture.

At the end of the day, we gathered as my granddad and our parents carefully lit the Roman candles and we ohhhed and ahh-hed at their colors and sound. We also carefully waved our spar-klers and shot off our parachute men (who usually were found in Grandma's garden in August, their parachutes worn white with the summer sun and clinging to a raspberry bush).

In those mid-century days, we knew it was our nation's birth-day, and we exalted in the anticipation, the joy of being with family, delicious food, and a day spent celebrating. We were "in the mo-ment" before "in the moment" became something people strived to achieve. Happy Fourth of July. Family, faith, country.

Manners... Today was the beginning of a new tennis session with my kiddos. On day one, we always learn the word "manners" for the three-to-six-year-olds and "etiquette" for the seven-to-ten-year-olds. Tennis is still one of the few sports that truly has sports-manship as its foundation.

As a kid, I learned from Mom that manners were as important as our words, and I was to use the best of both. The manners Mom taught me were to not interrupt (I always had difficulties with that one), to say "ma'am" and "sir" to older people, to not order the most expensive nor the cheapest meal when someone was nice enough to treat us to dinner, to use the correct silverware (work your way in when all else fails), to keep elbows off of the table, and her classic, to let one of us cut the cake or pie and the other one choose the first piece (my brother and I became virtual experts in that field), to share our colors with our cousins (even when they broke off the tips), and not to yell. Mom said you cannot get your words back once you have said them.

I can honestly say that Mom never once raised her voice to me. Vann and I have never raised our voices to each other though we have worked through issues many times. On the tennis court, it would never occur to me to yell at a child. It is the same as being hit and maybe worse when you are hit with a negative word. Those harsh, loud words stick in your brain for a very long time and can leave little tiny creases on your heart.

Manners and etiquette. They make my life calm, my interactions steady and healthy, and I love to see my kiddos' faces when they hear good words coming their way.

Ahhhh, those summer nights as only John Travolta and Olivia Newton John could sing. That song has been humming through my head this weekend. The height of summer, another two boxes of sparrows have fledged, their yellow beaks grinning with each beckoning flight. In the early morning and evening, the hammock calls to me to savor the smells of the prairie flowers and watch the cotton candy clouds daintily float over me.

Last night as we sat on the porch, the young, energetic neighbor boys played basketball until almost 9:00 p.m. There is something so "Kansas summer" about hearing the solid bounce of the ball, whoosh, and the boys cheering.

Then they were in the pool, and they are between boys-to-men—their voices alternating between young fifteen-year-old boys and the men that lay in front of them to become. They were a joyous sight and sound to hear for an hour, and I laughed every time they would call out "Marco? Polo!" I remembered being that age, never wanting to get out of the pool. Then finally stepping out and wrapping myself in the warm beach towel followed by a perfect night of sleep.

Today brought a belated surprise birthday party for Vann from our best pals Nancy, Marilyn, Jeannine, and Jeanne with offerings of sweet chocolate and vanilla DQ ice cream cake and a "Life is Good" tee shirt. Two hours of sitting on the porch with a welcome southern Kansas breeze, casual talk, and hugs until the next time. These are the days and ahhhh, those summer nights.

✿ ✿ ✿

Mid-century summer... It is July some time in the early 1960s. A hot and humid day like we're having, and life is happy on Burnett Road. My stepdad announces at dinner, after grilling steaks outside and drinking warm Coors beer (smuggled back from our summer trip to Colorado), that he is buying an air conditioner! My brother and I looked at each other in stunned disbelief. We had survived unknowingly our whole lives on Hunter fans purring in our bedrooms and the beast in the ceiling as we called it—THE attic fan—that no matter what the temperature, seemed to rush chilled air over us at night.

Mom kept us cool with quarters for admission to Crestview Pool every day. We were always riding our bikes to the pool, hitting the kick stand (nobody locked bikes in the '60s), and if Mom felt extra generous, we had another quarter to rent one of the neat metal baskets with a number on the front and matching key. For some reason, I thought it was the original pool "bling" to have that key safety-pinned onto my swim suit.

Mom mixed up all flavors of sugar-laden Kool-Aid in her yellow Tupperware pitcher and sometimes made Kool-Aid popsicle ice cubes in the metal trays. Mom did not seem to mind us being sticky all summer. She also kept cold washcloths in the freezer and put one on our necks or foreheads after we had played all evening. I can still remember that kind of pleasant, stinky, sweaty kid smell, and if we spent all day in the pool, we could sometimes get away without having a nighttime bath.

My stepdad went to Sears and lugged home the air conditioning unit. Some guy sawed a hole in our living room wall, tucked it in, and just like that, we had entered paradise! Mom cranked the new machine on its lowest setting and to celebrate the moment, started a small fire in our fireplace. Yes, we had moved up in the world. At that time, we only knew one other friend who had a window air conditioner AND a color television. She invited us over every Sunday evening to watch The Wonderful World of Disney in color. Our eyes were stupefied by the beauty of color television. But nevertheless, the window AC marked our move into high society, at least in our minds.

I still think of that trusty black Hunter fan and the gentle turns it made in its effort to cool me at night. If I had my choice, I'd still pick that happy purring fan over AC. Such were the times of our lives in the early '60s.

ZZZZZZ... On those rare nights that I cannot fall asleep, my sweet husband, Vann, has suggested that I "tour" my grandma's house. It is one of the most cherished places in my life, and it's a "sleeping pill" that always works. Want to join me?

I am fifteen, and my mom, my brother, and I are in Mom's 1967 Super Sport Impala Convertible, lemonwood yellow with black interior—my all-time favorite car. I was old enough to learn to drive, so she pulled over at 45th and California and, with much flair, I ceremoniously took the driver's seat for the ruler straight drive to my grandparents' home less than a mile away. My biggest challenge was making the right-hand turn onto their crunchy gravel drive. I tried to keep my eye on the driveway, but immediately, I was captivated by my grandma's one acre garden with perfectly straight rows of cucumbers, squash, tomatoes, rhubarb, and forests of black and red raspberry bushes. My brother and I ran to the rope swing that hung in the giant oak tree. We pushed off to see how high we could go to escape Earth's gravity. Sometimes, we sat on the cool limestone rock under the elm tree. It had a hollowed-out spot for birds to sip water from, and it served as a place for us to shuck corn or snap green beans. Even on the hottest day, its cool ancient stone was pleasant to sit on and daydream. It also had mysterious fossils that Grandma taught us how to find, and we imagined the ancient oceans of Kansas ebbing over our grandparents' farm. But on to the house we went, ever vigilant for Grandma's two most dangerous animals—her killer rooster with talons that were ready to stab us in the back of our legs as we ran for the door or the billy goat who seemed to always be lurking in the lilacs ready for a head butt to our backsides. We ran up the stairs to the porch and into the mudroom through the screen door festooned with freshly painted trim. The door made a proper smack as it slammed shut. The mudroom had grandma's washing machine, a sink for Grandpa to use, a closet where he hung his jean jackets, and a whole wall of 6" X 6" cubicles for all sorts of small farm tools and wooden pencils. There was no dryer as all clothes were gaily dried on the clothesline.

Then into the heart of the house, my grandma's kitchen. It never disappointed with some aroma whether it was the sharp, clean scent of cucumbers and onions swimming in a vinegar water/sugar bath, or a batch of cinnamon rolls that had just been baked and were drowning in pale yellow frosting. Everything was fresh, and we could not walk through the kitchen without sampling something. My grandpa had the other spectrum covered with ice cold Pepsis or grape and orange Nehis, Neapolitan ice cream and orange chewy Circus Peanuts that were kept in a bag just out of our reach. The first floor made a circle of the living room, the dining room, and the "parlor" where Grandma's rocking chair proudly sat. Many nights we were rocked with sweet old songs in that chair. After watching Gunsmoke, we happily climbed the sixteen stairs up to our bedrooms on the second floor. The beds were Jenny Lind beds with painted white frames, sheets that had flown like flags on the clothesline and smelled of gladiolas, and blankets that were stored in the quilt closet. I always chose "Sunflower Sue" with the little girls all wearing bonnets made of faded dress scraps and material that smelled like baby powder and yellow cake. A south breeze was gently blowing, and I was fast asleep, dreaming of the kittens in the barn I would try to see, riding the draft horse that made my legs stick straight out, or eating peaches that ran sweet, sticky juice down my chin. Good night, sweet dreams. I walk through my grandma's house to dreamland.

Did you feel it? Six-thirty this morning, the cats and I felt Mother Nature brush by with a trial run of fall. There was a hint of the football games to come, trips to Manhattan and Hays to see my twin nieces and nephew, the light scent of golden cut wheat still warm from yesterday filling the air, and butterflies hovering over the purple thistles in the prairie. Everywhere, there are hints of this season slowing into another.

Summer is my favorite season, and yet I am grateful for the changes we feel in the comings and goings of Nature upon our lives. As a kid, the end of summer meant our cousins from Alma would come spend the week with us. Mom permitted my cousins, my brother, and me unheard of liberties of staying up late to watch Twilight Zone, riding our bikes to Burnett's Mound with sack lunches, and our yearly tradition of seeing a movie at the Grand Theater the day before school started. Those were our mile markers telling us that fall and school were upon us.

Mom and Grandma spent a week sewing new dresses for me with strange fall colors away from the pinks and blues and yellows of summer. A new dress of dark checked gingham, navy stripes or forest green and purple paisley filled my closet each day. Grandma was a master seamstress and every year made me a couple of pleated skirts for proper twirling and starched white blouses with Peter Pan collars that I adored. My favorite day was buying our school supplies. Mom had the list for our grade, and I was bedazzled by going to Seacrest Drug Store on 21st Street. There on the wooden shelves, the wares and needs of our class were laid out like mind desserts, ready to be consumed. Shiny rulers, new paper, a handful of #2 pencils, a new box of crayons, and our workbooks, which I could not wait to open. Mom took us to Smaks Drive In on Huntoon Street for what my brother and I deemed the best hamburger ever for fifteen cents. That night, I would stay in my room alternating between looking in my closet at my fall wardrobe and laying out my school supplies.

This morning, fall touched briefly. Summer is at her glory, and much is left to be savored. I think I will make a root beer float today and read in my hammock.

Ornamental cats… A sad state of affairs at the Anderson house today. Muffy brought in a present, a little, grey field mouse, and proudly dropped it as her offering to us. And then she and the other two cats went to nap. Vann said, "Go get the cats. They'll want to catch the mouse." Reluctantly, I carried them each to where the mouse was hiding. They looked at us like "not our problem—we don't do work," and went back to their cat nests. Vann caught the mouse and put it out of the house. He is now calling the cats "ornamental cats" as they seemingly have lost all interest in the hunt, but I do have to admit they are very pretty sitting around.

Back to school… I drift back to the beginning of my school days which were always a glorious time at our house. School supplies, new dresses, and, as I entered the eighth grade, real bras (well, kind of) and my first "grown-up" looking shoes that weren't Buster Brown and Poll Parrot. Eighth grade also brought me my first boyfriend, Mark. He was a quiet, kind, sensitive, and talented boy who played the guitar, wrote me love letters, and rode me on the handle bars of his Sting Ray bicycle on summer and fall nights. I dated him off and on through junior high and high school, and we remained friends throughout our lives until his death.

Mark and I were in Cheaper by the Dozen, and I was able to memorize my lines only because I was so excited for play practice every day with Mark. For the eighth-grade dance, Mom bought me my first pair of "stockings," as they were called then, and sewed a wool dress of kelly green and turquoise to wear to the dance with Mark. He is missed in this world, but knowing him taught me to look for his qualities in the man I would someday marry many years later.

Ninth-grade graduation brought my first visit to a salon with girlfriend, Laura, and we both walked out with "mile-high hair." I always laugh at the picture as I think Laura looked like Trisha Yearwood and I looked like, well, not sure who I think I looked like, but I know I finally had to jump in the swimming pool to get my hair to come back to normal from so much ratting and hairspray. All of those magical times blended together to make up our junior high and high school years full of first boyfriends, first kiss, first grownup shoes, and beginning to explore this world as a teenager. My guides were all my friends, and together we made our way through it with support, family, friendship, laughter, and a lot of bad hairdos.

Hey, little brother... One year gone from us. A year ago, we were at hospice for your last great day, listening to you talk endlessly about everything and telling me you wanted Vann to take you on a trip to Camelot. You made it there, no doubt. We grew up catching lightning bugs, walking to school together, making Rice Krispie treats, playing with Kenny and Debbie and spending late nights shooting hoops. Somewhere along the way, you grew up and went off to Kansas State University to become an architect. You knew so much. Who else could name the layers of Kansas limestone and explain GMOs? You were always learning and teaching.

Sadly, you had such a short time with us to share all you knew and loved. I visit your limestone rock at the cemetery, and you'd be happy to know that we all leave you little gifts of this life, pictures of your kids and prairie flowers I pick from our yard, and some shells I found in South Carolina where you would have eaten all of the shrimp in the state.

You had the gentle soul, you knew no strangers once you walked into a room, and now that Earth room is so empty without you in it. But we are honoring you by shining bright, learning, and keeping your kind, gentle ways always going forward. Miss you, bro. Michael C. Vigola, December 1954–August 2014.

Pet vows... In sickness and in health, in good times and bad, 'til death do us part. Today, I was feeling the little crease of grief that lives forever in my heart for our three beloved kitties, Banndit, Leche, and Noche, who all died five years ago this summer from the bad food problem. Like our wedding vows, I think those of us who love our pets feel that same vow of commitment to them, and they are truly our "fur" kids, our family, and the soul of our homes.

My lovey-dovey Leche was the first to become gravely ill, and I took him to the vet on a Wednesday morning. They said he was so sick that little could be done. They waited until Vann got there, and together, we cuddled and held him for an hour as he reluctantly slipped from us. Even as I held him and as sick as he was, I could feel him trying to make some tiny biscuits, as if to let me know that he felt our love. Leche was a boy, but had the violet blue eyes of Elizabeth Taylor and was so pretty everybody thought he was a girl. I had to smile through my tears when I picked up his little box of ashes and his "pink" paw print.

A month later, we would lose Banndit, my rescue soulmate kitty, who we adopted off the street in San Diego. She ruled her world and ours, and every night would drape herself across me, protecting me from any harm. She had a fierce spirit, and as I held her, I shall never forget her two final breaths, as if she were willing herself back into this world.

Noche would die six months later as much from the illness as from a broken heart, losing his litter mate, Leche, and his Banndit who had claimed him as the ugly duckling kitten when he was little. Noche did not purr until he was five months old, scared of everything, but Banndit took him in and taught him the cat ropes.

Although Banndit was "fixed," she actually produced milk and nursed both of the kittens when we got them. They were a family, and when only Noche was left, he would cry and howl in the night with a voice that sounded my sadness. He took to staying in our closet and literally lost his will to live. And he was the last for us to hold as we put him to the rainbow bridge. He died peacefully as if he were more than ready to join Banndit and Leche, no longer the lonely kitty.

Vann got a pretty box, and we made a little shrine to them of their favorite toys, their clay paw prints, and their boxes of ashes so they would always be together. Though years smooth over the rough sadness of their loss, I still think I catch a glimpse of them— of Banndit draping across me as I doze off, of Leche stretched in the sun with his fur glistening silver, and of Noche looking for Leche to play and Banndit to love him.

That house was empty, silent, and so missing its heartbeat after they were gone. We got Queenie, Jazzy, and Muffy and renewed our "vows" to them. They bring us happiness, peace, and after a trying day, those tiny biscuits that melt our hearts and say "Love."

Summer vacations… This week is like Christmas on Wanamaker Street, with cars driven by crazed moms and saddened children realizing that school starts on Friday. Wasn't it just Memorial Day and the cool rainy June? Then poof, bang, boom! it was the Fourth of July. Now it is August, the cat/dog days of summer and the true sign that summer is fleeting—the closing of the pools.

Some brave families have taken to the road for that first or last summer vacation. When we were kids, our summer vacation ended with a trip to Colorado to visit our cousins.

Our parents would pile my brother and me into the '57 pea green Cadillac with four-foot fins and we're off on the highway to "Cool Colorful Colorado" as their border sign always proclaimed. However, the trip to Colorado in August across western Kansas and eastern Colorado was never cool nor colorful. Mom had several wet washcloths under the front seat for the sole purpose of keeping us refreshed. However, somewhere around Colby, they turned to a sour, nasty kid smell from "refreshing" my brother and me. Our Coleman cooler was filled with ice at 7:00 a.m. and sandwiches, chips, carrots, and chocolate chip cookies sat gaily wrapped in wax paper. Somewhere between 7:00 a.m. and lunch, they seemed to slowly sink like tiny ships into the melted ice, adding a chilly wet taste. But no matter, it was an adventure to pull over and eat at a rest stop or some historical marker that my parents thought would enlighten my brother and me.

Our sibling friendliness, in close quarters, usually ended about the time we hit Hays, three hours into our trip. Hard to believe but that car was so huge that Mom laid two suitcases on the floor and one of us could stretch out there. My brother enjoyed lying in the back window. He never seemed to mind it, but he was always sunburned by the time we got to Colorado Springs.

Back then, the Black Forest where my cousins, Linda and Stevie, lived was like the forbidden forest in Harry Potter, towering old growth trees, a few houses tucked in like treasures, with endless exploring for us. My cousins had a go-cart, and we would spend hours driving in a dizzying circle around their house. One time, Mom wrecked it into the fence.

Our excursions never varied. We never minded going to Cave of the Winds and feeling the constant chill of the cavern, walking scared to death across the dizzyingly high Royal Gorge bridge, visiting the "it's always Christmas" North Pole house, taking yearly pictures pretending to hold up massive red rocks at the Garden of the Gods, and at Seven Falls, running up the two hundred steps while our parents lingered at the bottom, shouting "Be careful!"

The first time we went to the Continental Divide, I could scarcely contain my excitement. For days, Mom had been telling us that this is where the river runs to the east and runs to the west. We could not wait to see this magical river running in two directions. We leapt out of the car and were met by a dreary "Continental Divide" sign with too much writing, not one river to be found, and certainly no magical river running in two directions to the Pacific and the Atlantic!

We loaded ourselves back into the car for the ten-hour trip home, sunburned, oxygen- starved, and filled with a head and heart full of new experiences. We had no cell phones, no iPads, but we had our imaginations. We played "ABC" of billboards, kept a list of the states of the license plates, and watched the scenery of our childhood go by on I-70. Summer vacation... back to school... the kid calendar of our mid-century lives.

Joy & Sadness... Last week I saw the lovely and most complex movie Inside Out. It has been rummaging through my mind ever since. It is at once a simple story of a girl moving from Minnesota to San Francisco and all that involves. It is thought provoking as the girl's "insides" factory, working all day to keep her joyful, becomes challenged by sadness, fear, anger, and other emotion "characters" that step up and try to override her joy.

The longer the little girl is away from Minnesota, the more "core memories" she loses. I have begun a list of mine. I am thinking that core memories—truly heartfelt—define us and are so important. Core memories are the bucket lists of our hearts.

Not to give the movie away, but the lesson was that joy and sadness belong together. Some of her best memories have the edges of both. So much joy and sadness in seeing my nieces and nephew growing up, heading to college and beginning their lives, loving our pets without limit yet knowing profound sadness when we ultimately let them go, savoring a summer season of flowers, pools, friends, and the tinge of sadness when the north wind comes across the prairie. Even in February, with joy, we begin anew to look for the first signs of spring, the first purple crocus poking boldly through the snow-crusted Earth.

Joy and sadness must touch our lives, and along with other emotions, they make a luminescent sphere with swaths of blue, our heart's core memories.

I heard the prairie sigh this morning at 6:40 a.m. as if to say "I've done my work for the spring and summer, time to rest. I've painted blanket flowers with crimson heads, all the shades of yellow that Van Gogh ever used, fragrant spikes of lavender and purple, and tucked them all in my native bluestem grasses."

The cool breeze blew one snowflake, or so the cats and I seemed to see in our early morning not-quite-awake state of being. Then it was gone in the warming morning air. The cats lay like fur pretzels in the chairs, their paws tucked under in fall mode and their tails wrapped around like a beautiful mink stole. I was barefoot and stretching out our seemingly endless days and nights of porch sitting. In the night yard, the deer have left their tiny heart prints with their hooves.

Ann Anderson

The red cedar was covered in azure blue berries as if festooned for a Dr. Seuss party. By 8:00 a.m., the secret show was gone, and the sounds of the world made the prairie retreat into daylight silence. She was ready to change her feathers to golds, browns, oranges and then wait for a warm winter blanket of white snow to sleep and restore.

But there was still more summer to squeeze like a big lemon, a few more pool days, shorts and tee shirts, a boat trip with friends on Lake Sherwood, root beer floats, and barefoot walks in the thick green grass.

Transformed… The cats and I blink our eyes as if to bring into focus the sight outside early this Sunday morning. Our world shrouded in a fleecy fog so thick that it drips like tears down the screens. Our neighbors' homes have seemingly floated away, they are not to be seen, and sounds are muffled like we are wearing ear muffs too soon in the season. We take our usual places around the wicker table, cats tucking paws into fur hearts, me with feet luxuriously stretched out and a mug of Earl Grey tea that adds its own fragrant fog to the air above it. The sounds are muted; even the bird calls seem quiet and faint to us. Our prairie has been repainted by Monet with pale shades of water colors. The blue gray sky merges into the pale green Earth as if they cannot decide where to start and end.

In San Diego, this was a daily occurrence with names like "May Gray" and "June Gloom." It was the same sight—the blending of ocean water and sky—and by noon on most days, it was but a foggy memory or none at all for late risers.

The cats and I are content with this gift from Mother Nature. She is stilling us a bit, ready to bring back warm ninety-degree days, but testing out her quieting skills.

Now Vann is up and says, "Was it foggy?"

I am sitting at the counter reading the Sunday paper and reply, "Yes, just a bit." I swear I saw a smile cross the cats' pink dolphin lips.

Deb and me, BFFF. Best first friends forever

Grandma and me on the sidewalk together

Chapter Six

LAY DOWN THIS NIGHT

Lay down this night which is settled by the smooth cool rain taking us from summer into fall.

Hammock thoughts on this forty-fifth high school reunion eve… I am lying in my hammock this evening, hefting my Topeka West yearbooks up from the patio and balancing them on my tummy. I stare so contentedly at our faces beaming at me with the promise of the late '60s, although they were tumultuous times in our country. We were cocooned in a shiny new high school with trees and grassy walkways. Our purple and white uniforms and pep club sweaters proudly displayed our gallant Charger horse.

I was an awkward high school kid, and maybe we all were, like Kevin in The Wonder Years. My parents got divorced my sophomore year, and I remember one of my teachers actually calling me in after class to ask why my A's had gone to C's. It was so caring. Then Mom married an alcoholic and my immersion to happiness was school activities, studying, being in my home "D" building, while always wishing to be one of the popular kids. I felt I drifted on the edge of that circle—some days in it and then some days not—and never quite finding the right combination, like a seventh grader with a new lock.

Ann Anderson

Always a tomboy. Off to swim team practice at Crestview Pool

It was a time where a snapshot of all of us was clicked, and we are tucked forever in each other's memories. At no other time in my life have I been connected to so many people at once, in one beautiful place.

As forty-five years have melted and drifted from us, we stand in that perfect moment of reuniting again, all of the pretenses, cliques, prejudices, and judgement dropped. Back to those sweet faces now aged with deserved wrinkles, laugh lines, cry lines, and all those things that make us love and feel life. Our long hair is probably cut short, and short skirts have probably grown long. We grieve for those who will not join us, those who were taken much too young. When I was fifteen, the Beatles released "When I'm Sixty-Four." I loved that song and at that age, I could not even conceive of what the words meant. Now we are that song—grandchildren on our knees, or nieces and nephews and families of our own.

This night I sifted through the three years that were high school at Topeka West. I am still that black-and-white picture all grown up, and I look at all of us with a smile that appreciates the time we shared and the memories that weave through me like purple and white threads.

I am a fat bumblebee, covered in the sweet nectar of heirloom friendships, buzzing from one classmate to another at my high school reunion. Some of these flowers are at once familiar, their petals seem the same on a stem just a bit weathered, and others are just as sweet but do not come to me so quickly. I am a hungry bee and wish to taste and savor them all, as I know by the end of this summer binge they will be gone in the wind.

I must rest, my wings weary from the flight to each one. Tomorrow night, I will again drench my wings in the rich taste of flowers that only comes every so often to be taken in fully, and I will be covered in this golden pollen of ageless ties to my childhood.

Lay down this night. The red-green-yellow shadow of rain on the TV screen bodes well for a night of sleep with the Kansas thunderstorm as my tonic. It is the ocean to my ears and pulls me to the dreamland where all is possible, like Dorothy stepping out of her house into the colors of OZ. I am sated from a quiet starlit night on Lake Sherwood with my champagne friends, the boat silently floating on the mirror surface, the water still warm to the touch. I am sated from celebrating the twenty-first birthday of my cherished twin nieces, Jordan and Reagan, and a visit from my first childhood friend, Debbie (now Debra), whom I have known since age five. It is still as if I see her bedroom light from our house and can run across the damp grass of our yards to find her there.

I must rest from the exhilaration of being involved in life so much. I will sleep tonight with so many poignant words, moments, hugs, and memories to mix in with the falling rain. My husband, my good husband, who prefers the sanctity of our home, always welcomes me with his love and constant heart. My cats tonight will make their familiar nesting turns and settle against me as if to protect me from the darkness. Lay down this night which is settled by the smooth cool rain taking us from summer into fall.

These late summer/early fall days are laden with opportunity for goofing off, sitting on the porch with an iced tea sweetened with huckleberry honey. I come from hardy pioneer farmers and gardeners, but I rely on the sturdy native grasses and perennials of Kansas to make my garden shine. I have taken the liberty of planting a deep pink hibiscus as I was sure something so tropical would simply not pop back up each spring after being covered in the snow. And yet, it is in its full glory and adorned with humming-birds, feathery ornaments that come and go, much to the cats' delight.

We hear much about mindfulness, which is simply being in the present moment, and this season seems to keep me there. Perhaps it is to savor fully the flowers and grasses which are in their moment always. The goldfinches come to our prairie every day for the sunflower feasts and strip the rich seeds with their dainty beaks.

This is a time to go slowly, to gently melt in the sun as it moves across the south for the fall, to put our feet up and have a chat, and to be still and notice until our memories are imprinted with this in-betweenness of summer to fall. How does my garden grow?

Lego girl... With last week's forty-fifth high school reunion, the season changing and the anniversary of Mom's death, September 22, I was thinking about how I am the essence of so many people put together, like little Lego blocks spilled out of their container and reassembled in me.

Mom left me the biggest and most colorful Lego blocks, my foundation, her legacy to me. She would be ninety this year, probably still hitting some tennis balls, and a cat or two curled around her legs. She would be absolutely smitten with Mikey, Jordan, Reagan, and Miranda, her grandchildren. She would have put her Lego blocks into them as I have tried to do. And in return, they would have filled up her heart with their dear sweet faces and love.

My friends have put their Lego blocks in me, little colorful shapes that are pieces of who I am and want to be. I have continued to surround myself with the best people, family, friends, and colleagues. One advantage of growing older is that one can "unfriend" those people who do not enhance us. Just like a Lego creation, I can pull out a little piece that on that rare occasion does not belong anymore.

I look in the mirror and see all of the Legos looking back, the colors, the shapes and the little spaces where I have more room to put more pieces.

Stay little… I whisper this to Jazzy, my "baby" kitten who is my constant fur shadow day and night. She lies against the back door when I leave, and when I return, I open the door gently as I know the solid feel of her body will be against it. At night, she finds her sleep nest against the back of my legs. Queenie, Muffy, and Jazzy are five now, and they have not adhered to my constant directive: "stay little."

I have thought of this "stay little" so many times this past summer as I watched my twin nieces don Kansas State University tee shirts, move into their first real apartment, and begin their junior year at K-State. Weren't they just little? I picked them up from school when I visited from California and they had a list of things to do on "Aunt Ann dates." It rarely varied—Maggie Moo's, museum, mall, and movie. Those dates seemed to have no end and yet—poof!—my nieces are no longer small, no longer waiting outside their house to get into my rental car to share an afternoon together. Sleepovers at the hotel, pushing the elevator buttons, calling shotgun, and making waffles in the morning only drift in the air like the smell of cinnamon rolls out of an oven. I drove past French Middle School on Thursday and smiled with a mixture of joy and nostalgia, thinking of all of the happy hours spent watching Mikey, my nephew, play football for Landon Middle School. They were suited up in one-size-almost-fits-all, but his pride of being one of the "boys of fall" transcended any uniform discrepancies. He played every game, watched every film, played another four years for Topeka High and then Ft. Hays State University. How was he once so little on those middle school, ragged, green grass fields? How was he just sitting in the Landon gym next to his best friend,

Ann Anderson

Garret, playing trumpet while we applauded the noble efforts and sounds that came out of a seventh-grade band? He is a young man now, but when I see his smile, he is at once still that "stay little" boy eager to be off on an adventure with me.

I know it is not possible to "stay little," but I will keep whispering it to my kitties, to my nieces and nephew, and to myself. Good life, please stay little.

Nature girl… The cats and I have the exotic hobby of porch sitting each morning. We have been watching a spider build a fantastic silvery web with threads so fine that at first, I did not notice it covered the whole screen. Yesterday, the web was adorned with crystals in the form of tiny dew droplets, the perfect spider bling.

In the night, the wind had torn part of it and he/she spider was joyously rebuilding the beautiful home this morning before we were up. The spider weaves and floats back and forth, intent on the goal and never stopping to complain.

When the birds were nesting last spring, I watched them in daily admiration as they worked tirelessly from early morning to dusk, gathering their supply of sticks and straw, some cat fur, and whatever else is needed to feather their nests for their babies. There are apparently no lazy birds as they work every day to accomplish this. Then the real work begins once they have hatched their chicks, with constant scouring of the prairie for bugs and whatnot to stuff in the open, bright yellow baby beaks. Again, the birds do not whine about their tasks but go about them diligently.

Somehow of all of the creatures, only humans have become "un-nature" like. We grow weary of our daily, weekly, monthly tasks, and we can choose even not to do them. How can I be more like the industrious spider, the intentional birds, finding that joy that comes from my purpose, my role in this world?

I embrace the work ethic of the itsy-bitsy spider, and I calm myself to be a part of the natural world.

I am proud of my adventerous husband, Vann. At eighty years young, he has taken up tennis! Vann strategically sees the tennis court as a big math problem. It makes me happy to be on the court with him, teaching him my favorite sport. I am proud of my guy. A lot of people much younger than Vann decide "it's time to be old"

and park themselves in the Naugahyde Barcalounger with a Boost cocktail. But Vann is all about planning our vacations next year, organizing a trip to Florida with his son, and keeping his eye on the prize—living life to its fullest.

Thank you, God, for all of the guys who passed on me and for all of the guys I let slip by. Thank you for making me wait forty-two years for Vann.

Dear Mom: Thirty-three years ago, tonight, I stayed at our home with you, sleeping lightly under Grandma's Sunflower Sue quilt and listening to your breathing, which was becoming like shallow pieces of air. I was only thirty and I did not know what death sounded like, but I somehow knew that I wanted to stay with you that night. You had been in a coma for two weeks, but you were there, your hand to hold so thin and frail, a hand that had held mine to cross the street, to wipe away a tear, and to stroke my head when I did not feel well.

Miss Kitty took up a spot on your hospital bed in the living room that whole summer, leaving your side only to eat something and go outside. That last night, I was so surprised when she jumped down and pressed against me. Her purr was as shallow as your breathing, and my heart sickened at wondering if she sensed you were about to leave us. And so, the night passed and in the morning, I kissed your forehead, whispered "I love you, Mom" and "I will be right back."

I had a meeting and was just at the turnpike gate when a highway patrol car pulled up behind me with lights and no siren. I knew he had come to tell me you had died, and in a quick moment, I grieved for him having to be the messenger.

I drove back to our home and said my final goodbye. You were at peace, no ridges of pain showing on your face anymore; perhaps you had floated away already when Miss Kitty came to be by me. She had gone outside and would stay under your tulip tree all that day as if she, too, were grieving.

You have now been gone from me longer than I had you. Gone at fifty-six years old when we should have just been starting a wonderful journey together as best friends, world travelers, and continuing to tell each other of our day's adventures. But oh, weren't we lucky to have had those thirty precious years! You graced us all with your gift of warmth, of being able to present a beautiful meal upon a moment's notice, to nurture a garden, to help me grow into a woman with a gentle soul and a sense of humor and to become a cat whisperer like you. I try to give the pieces of you to Mikey, Jordan, Reagan, and Miranda so that your beauty and strength goes forward in them.

I would reach across the sky to Heaven to hold your hand tonight and whisper again "I love you, Mom" and you would be right back with me.

Happy moment... Driving home from tennis last night, a box turtle, so handsome with his dark green shell and neon yellow squares, patiently and somewhat unwisely, crossed our wide street. I parked my car, and he quickly tucked his head inside his house as if I would magically not see him. I picked him up and carried him to my garden with a rock wall, native plants, a curved seashell that gathers water each day, and a supply of bugs. I love box turtles. We used to see them all the time as kids and now it seems rarer. Live long and prosper in our garden, my friend.

When my niece, Jordan, was four years old, she randomly announced at dinner that her "special grandma" came to see her at night. My brother and I looked at each other in disbelief as our mom had died years before Jordan was born and she had probably only seen a picture of her. But I knew she was telling the truth. I asked her what she looked like, and she pretty much described our mom. She said that her special grandma comes to help her with problems when she's having a hard time. I will never forget that, as I do believe that angels walk among us and angels come down from Heaven to intervene when needed.

Yesterday, when I was on the tennis court, a woman was watching and motioned to me. I did not know her, but walked over to the railing and said, "May I help you with something?" She said, "No, I come to watch you because you wear colorful clothes that make me happy and you are joyful." I was so stunned by this that I had tears fall down my face. I took her hand and said, "Thank you for making my day." When I turned to go back to the court, she had left, and I wondered for a second if I had imagined this. I thought about it the rest of the day. It was such a reminder of how we touch people for good or bad by our deeds and the way we live.

I have slowed to a crawl today, immersed in the message of forgiveness, love, understanding, gratitude, and appreciation.

✿ ✿ ✿

Sayings... I've been thinking lately of my mom and grandma's wisdom sayings. As a kid, many of them I did not understand, though I always gave a quick wink or head nod as to delay any further education on their part. It almost always worked.

My grandma, when talking about somebody who wasn't quite cutting it, would sometimes say, "You can't make a silk purse out of a sow's ear." My brother and I would roll our eyes and look at each other as we did not know first of all, what a "sow" was, nor why anyone would make a purse out of an ear. Now I have come to understand that quaint yet quirky saying.

When we were complaining about being bored, Grandma would say, "Idle hands are the Devil's work." Geez, mention the Devil and we got busy fast doing something. If we were being lazy about hoeing the garden, Grandpa would say, "Look to the end of your arm for a helping hand." Huh, that meant us working. Oh well, he was right.

"Don't cry over spilt milk." Again, my brother and I were told that saying many times when things didn't go our way. Once we decided that it should be "Don't cry over spilt chocolate milk," as that would be much more meaningful.

Mom did have two sayings that I have actually repeated. I used one tonight with a little tennis kiddo who is not athletic, but is enthusiastic and likes tennis clothes. She was missing most of her shots, and I could feel her mounting frustration. At the water break, I went to her and gave her a pinky high five and said, "You're do-ing great." She looked down and didn't say anything. I gently took her chin in my fingers as Mom used to do with me and said, "Are you doing your best and having fun?" She nodded, and the shine of a smile came back over her face. I said, "That's all we need to think about," and she went back at it. How often Mom encouraged me with those words: "Are you doing your best and having fun?" More often than not, I had to say "yes," and we were moving on from whatever potential disaster had been averted.

Ann Anderson

My friend Debbie was largely responsible for getting me through junior high math. I had never received a grade below a B until ninth-grade algebra. On the report card, I got a C and I was devastated. I trudged home, and Mom knew that some misfortune had come upon me. I told her I got a C on my report card. She just laughed and said, "Oh, Ann, in ten years it won't matter." Wow, she wasn't mad, and suddenly I thought, "OK, I guess a C is not the end of the world." I have used that saying many times to get me through a particularly undesirable time in my life, and you know what? It's true. Except for losing someone, in ten years, most bad things are not even a memory. My first C is actually now a pleasant memory, so many years gone by of Mom standing in our kitchen on Burnett Road, stirring a pot of chili, and saying that to me.

My prairie has taken a beau. I have not noticed him coming to see her, but today, I see that she has done up her grasses in loosely woven brown and golden braids, and he has brought her some new white and lavender flowers to lay down with the last of her native sunflowers. He has turned her cheeks a pale shade of pink, perhaps a blush from his cool breath that I could feel coming through our window this morning. No doubt he is wooing her away from the upcoming chill to a place that is warm where she can rest until spring. She has done much this year, more than most, bringing us flowers since early spring until now. She has grown her grasses as tall as the bluebird boxes whose little roofs now stick out like small red balloons.

My prairie has nurtured a thousand birds: squawking blue jays so handsome in their blue and white tuxedoes, the majestic shiny black crows chatting high up on the cedar tree, the sweet, fat bluebirds working tirelessly to raise their broods while protecting their prized boxes from sparrows, and the crimson cardinals ever whistling their resplendent brightness.

So, she has found someone. The woods behind her seem to blush as they, too, are watching the courting of the prairie by Winter. Their leaves drip golden rings and pink roses to celebrate this new courtship.

I know this fellow who loves my prairie, and I know he will bring her back next March. Until then, I am their chaperone to make sure she stays with us as long as possible, watching her braid up her grasses and blush at Winter's touch.

Yes, this is me. Pollyanna. I like the story; I like the thought of one person being able to make a town "glad." That is my happy thought on a Friday night. And by the way, I still have my Pollyanna doll that Mom gave me after I saw the movie ten times. I have the two prisms Mom gave me to splash rainbows on the walls. Think I'll go hang some prisms and watch rainbows all weekend.

The porch days... When we were kids, we had a breezeway. I thought, even at the age of five, that it sounded so enchanting. It was basically an eight-foot space between our house and the garage, concrete with steps on each end. Later on, my stepdad would wall it in and claim it for an office, thus ending the allure. Until then, it was an endless space to create chalk gardens, play outside even in the heat of summer, take a nap on quilts with a cool breeze and watch thunderstorms with Mom who always fixed us popcorn balls so sticky and sweet with Karo syrup that the Cokes we drank tasted sugarless.

I guess I have "porch sitting" hardwired into me as I am on our porch every day, even in the winter if the sun is warm and no wind. It is a quick step into nature. This afternoon, Vann and I did our screen porch vigil. Jazzy knew it was a sure opportunity to hop onto my warm jeans and nestle in for some cat dozing. Queenie and Muffy poured themselves into the pale sunlight and snoozed, their tails wrapped like furry mufflers around their paws. Vann and I were quite comfortable with the perfect silence, no need to chatter, and we shared in the prairie that yawns out from our house. Today, we were rewarded with monarchs and two hummers partaking of the buffet in the grasses, lavender penstemons, crown vetch and pink cosmos, sweet sugar for the long vacation to the South. It was so still, we could hear the swooshing wings of the hummer who will soon be vacationing far away. There was a hooty owl that called for a mate somewhere out in our dense forest. It was too late to mate, but perhaps he called to find a friend or just to share his song. Two turkey vultures caught the thermals and flew in lazy circles so high up that we could not see their ugly necks. They instead looked like lovely prehistoric birds spinning in the cloudless pale blue sky of eastern Kansas.

A porch day afternoon. We are the better for it.

Mid-century kid... I am up at 6:30 a.m. on this fall day in 1959. Like a Folger's commercial, Mom's percolator coffee pot is puffing the smell of rich dark coffee down the hall to our bedrooms. I am in second grade and don't drink coffee, but it smells good. It smells like a family starting their day, and it smells like Mom will have pancakes or eggs and bacon sitting at our gold-flecked Formica table after I get dressed.

Our house was a 1957 ranch and probably 1,500 square feet, three bedrooms, one and a half baths, and a tidy unfinished basement. I wonder what year we all decided that bigger was better. The four of us shared the main bathroom with its black and pink plastic tile, with never a thought about it being too small. I was already a little germophobic at that age and insisted on my own towel. I could not bear the thought of using my brother's towel covered in "boy cooties"! We took thousands of baths with Mr. Bubble, and we each had a small drawer for our toiletries.

My bedroom got a new coat of paint every two to three years, depending upon Mom and her best friend's interest in decorating. For my twelfth birthday, Mom painted my room a cozy shade of gold, as if the sun were constantly rising in it, and bought me a matching floral bedspread and curtains from Pelletier's Department Store. We were not a family that getting "sent to your room" was used, but I would have found that to be no punishment. My room was cheery, windows to the north and east, a bed all to myself, and a massive desk with secret drawers and cubby holes my stepdad bought me at an estate sale. I also had a beautiful and cherished record player for my 78s, 45s and 33 1/3s.

Walk-in closets did not exist, but we did not need them either. My closet was five feet long with a shelf. I had my school dresses hanging gaily on wire hangers: plaids, stripes, checks, flower print, and two good dresses for going to church or to someone's house for dinner. We each had a dresser full of underwear, shorts, tee shirts, a sweatshirt, and we would move our "winter" clothes to a cardboard box in the basement in the summer and vice versa.

I had a pair of Keds, flip flops, a pair of dress shoes, and maybe an old pair of tennis shoes stuck in the back for muddy days. On the shelf were my treasures: a scrapbook Mom made for me when I was eight years old, my troll collection, my Nancy Drew books, and other items that looked nicely arranged up high.

Mom would sometimes have me sit in front of her on the ottoman and put bobby pins into pin curls in my long hair while watching TV. The next day's result was truly transforming as my thin blonde hair would puff out and sometimes she would cement it into place with her Aqua Net hairspray. I loved being in my home as a kid. It was my castle, the source of my renewal, and I always seemed to be smiling when I walked up the driveway. I would open the door and see Mom turn from the stove and ask, "How was school today?"

Meet Muffy. Muffy is a creature of comfort as Vann describes her. She is the tiniest of our three kitties, the most fur, but all little bones and body underneath. Muffy sees herself as the mighty huntress and has caught two voles and several bugs to bring in as gifts. She could easily be alpha kitty but prefers to be Queenie's kitten, so she can lap up Queenie's motherly affection, daily grooming sessions, and nuzzling. She and Jazzy are all about being play cats, chasing, kicking, and then some cat kissing that restores all. After a big day of admiring herself, Muffy usually finds the best place in the house and molds into the sun like mercury poured out in the form of a little cat. She is a constant reminder of what relaxing and a good nap look like.

My grandparents waiting to have
a slice of lemon icepick cake

Chapter Seven

PERMANENT PINK

*The roses by the mailbox are stuck in permanent
pink as if they are not ready yet
to step into winter.*

When I am old… Jenny Joseph's poem, "When I am an old woman, I shall wear purple," has been on my mind this week. I have taken two of my friends, who are both in their late eighties, for holiday lunches. One of my friends I have known since junior high. She cannot weigh more than ninety pounds and holding her elbow to help her walk is like holding onto the wing of a humming-bird. Her mind is clear, and she talks through the whole lunch while I eat. She never fails to say to me, "You eat fast. I still have all of my food." Ha, I have to smile as I do not eat fast—I just do not get to talk. So we pack her food in a to-go box for later.

Today I was with Mom's best friend, age eighty-seven, Marge. She has known me since I was born and was like a second mom to me. She has very poor eyesight, and her apartment is adorned with two huge clocks and a remote control the size of an iPad. She has found ways to adapt and still can walk her path near Gage Park. I look at her and both of us are frozen in my mind—me as a kid and she as someone in her thirties. In her younger days, she could outrun me, played a sweet game of tennis, was always in some mischief with my mom, and they were together almost every day in their lifelong friendship.

This morning I played tennis. Strong, running, chasing, smacking balls, and pleased to have a mind and body that can do those things. I am already wearing purple, but I read that poem and think I do not want to wait until I am old to do those things. Old creeps up on you so you better be doing all that stuff right now. When I am old, I hope I have a younger friend to come hold my elbow, to share some time, to talk about fun days gone by. Loneliness seems to be the hardest part of growing old. I will grow old, but I'm putting on all the colors I can right now. Like saving the good China for only special occasions when every moment could be a special occasion.

If you know someone older, give them a call. The only cure for loneliness is hearing a familiar voice.

Mid-Century kid Christmas… As the day draws near, I love the decorations on people's homes, the plates of sweets that seem to arrive daily at our tennis club, and the cheer that surely floats in the air for all ages.

As a kid, the days leading up to Christmas were almost as good as the holiday itself. Perhaps anticipation is as good as the real thing. Mom kept our presents secured in her bedroom closet, but my brother and I would nearly wear the door off sliding it open to peek in. We knew Santa Claus brought our other presents and always made sure Mom kept the fireplace clean the week before Christmas. No touching but just looking at the growing heap of brightly wrapped treasures was enough to incite a holiday swoon for the day. One year, we begged for the board game, Casper the Ghost. We accidentally saw Mom buy it, and we secretly opened it and played it quickly when she would run an errand. Being all grown up at eight, I would carefully adjust the tape but I am sure she knew we had played it. Oh well, it was Christmas and as long as we stayed off the real naughty list, we could have some pre-Christmas fun.

It is funny what presents I can truly remember as a kid, and some of them I still have and treasure. My grandparents were frugal, not cheap, but were depression-era people who did not waste money. Every year, all of their grandchildren could expect an en-

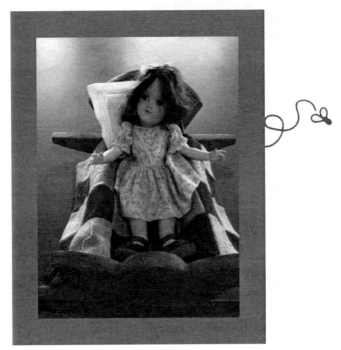

The Christmas cradle and dolly.
Patchwork homemade love

Halcyon days at the farm. Homemade benches and love

velope with a two-dollar bill in it on their tree. As two-dollar bills were a thing of curiosity, it always was a good present, and I usually hesitated to spend it until February. My grandma always made me a new pair of flannel pajamas, so soft and warm for the winter months. She would magically cut out a pattern with newspaper, hold it against me, and voila—new pajamas that would then be wrapped and under the tree.

One year, my grandparents made me what would become a long-treasured gift. My grandpa built a small cradle with designs carved into the sides and my grandma sewed a small patchwork quilt for it. It was graced with a new dolly wearing a flowerprint dress, ribbons in her hair and stockings. I still have that cradle, the quilt and the doll.

The nights before Christmas were spent at our Baldwin blonde piano. There was usually someone who could play Christmas songs, and we loved to belt out our favorites. Mine were "Up on the Housetop," "Jingle Bells," and "Rudolph."

Back in those days, there were no travel miseries as only the rich could afford to travel by plane. It was also a time when most families all lived near each other, so it was a simple car ride. At Christmas, we didn't wish to be anywhere but our own home or our grandparents' farm.

On Christmas Eve, Mom would read my favorite poem, "'Twas the Night Before Christmas." Though I knew every word, I thrilled to hear her voice, and she would accentuate just the right lines. I would nod off to sleep with visions of sugar plums dancing in my head.

In the morning, all those presents from the closet appeared magically beneath our Christmas tree.

The best gift... As a kid, getting Christmas presents was the feast for all senses. But when I was ten, I learned for the first time the sweetness of giving a special gift to someone.

Next to Mom, my grandma was the most important person in my life. She was in her early fifties when I was born and she was the fragile link between the bygone days and the new emerging world. She held steadfastly to the old ways and that is what she taught us. We were unfailingly taught good manners, to let others go first, to share, to work in the garden (I drew the line at picking tomato worms off with my bare hands), to thread a needle, to tie a hook on a line on a cane pole, and, of course, all manners of cooking. She never raised her voice in the twenty years I had with her, yet her presence commanded a respect and reverence with our whole family.

When I was about ten, Mom and I were in JC Penney's and I saw a snowflake pin. I begged Mom to buy it for my grandma, so I could give it to her. My grandma owned fewer than six pieces of jewelry: her wedding ring and several brooches that she wore on her good wool coat. The snowflake brooch fairly dazzled my eyes with its fake tiny diamonds, shiny pearls, and gold sparkle. I could already picture it on my grandma's black wool coat.

The saleslady told us we could put it on layaway and have it paid for by Christmas. I gave her my two dollars and Mom gave a small amount. Then the race was on to get the rest of the money to pay for my grandma's present. I think it cost about thirty dollars, a huge sum in those days, especially for a kid. But I set about earning the money, and my stepdad let me take ten dollars out of my savings account as he allowed it was for a good cause.

On the day we went to Penney's to pick it up, I was nearly dizzy with excitement. The lady was especially nice and had wrapped it in their most dazzling paper with a sparkly green bow on top of the small box. I held it like a treasure on the way home and placed it under the tree with a label that said "To Grandma—Love, Ann." It was the first time I had ever given a gift except to my mom that was just from me and picked out by me.

On Christmas Eve, our grandparents came over. I fidgeted through the oyster soup, ham sandwiches and skipped the Christmas cookies. Finally, the little box with the green bow was given to my grandma. I'll never forget her exclaiming "Oh my" and giving me a kiss on my head. She promptly put it on and pronounced it the prettiest pin she had ever seen! For many years, she happily wore it on her winter coat.

Before she died, she gave me her small wooden jewelry box. It contained a watch, her three brooches and nestled in the Penney's box, the Christmas snowflake pin. I wear it and I am still dazzled by its beauty and the love I felt for my grandma and the special gift.

The sounds of the season... Sitting here drinking a cup of coffee and automatically hitting play on whatever Christmas CD is in the Bose. Yep, old school with an actual clock/CD player. But anyway, I thought of how much music, movies and performances are a part of this Christmas season.

My first memory of a Christmas pageant was kindergarten with my dear friend, Debbie, at Crestview Grade School. Somehow, the teachers had all patiently taught us songs. The kindergartners were to sing "Up on the Housetop" complete with hand motions. Our parents and families were jammed into that sweet multipurpose room, and we sang our hearts out. I still love that song and remember all of the hand motions for it.

At some point Mom decided that my brother and I needed more culture, and we attended The Nutcracker. Well, maybe we weren't ready, as we thought it was quite dull except for the dancing mice and mushrooms.

Over the years, I have attended many Christmas plays, and some of the best ones have been at our own Topeka Civic Theatre, sharing the evening with family and friends. We just saw A Christmas Carol, which I have probably seen ten times. Each time I see it, it makes me think differently about my life. Perhaps as we grow older, we come to understand better how we are truly living our lives and treating people in the past, present, and future.

When my nieces and nephew were in grade school, I decided they might benefit from seeing The Nutcracker. We all dressed up, dinner at Red Lobster, and with much anticipation, we took our seats at the theater. About twenty minutes into the show, my sweet eight-year-old nephew, Mikey, leaned over and whispered, "Aunt Ann, when do they start talking?" Oh my, the look on his face when I told him it was all dancing and the music was unforgettable. OK, so maybe The Nutcracker is not for everybody.

I did take my "little sister" when I was in Big Sister/Little Sister to see The Nutcracker at White Concert Hall. I got front row seats, and she was positively dazzled by the production. Suddenly she jumped from her seat and went up on stage and started dancing with the cast. There was much laughter, and they were very kind about escorting her back to me. She was so lost in the beauty that she had to go be a part of it.

So 'tis the season to listen to Bing Crosby, Mannheim Steamroller, Mariah Carey, and all those songs we love. I will be watching a list of Christmas must movies: Elf, Little Women, White Christmas, A Christmas Story, and a bunch of cheesy Christmas movies on the Hallmark Channel. 'Tis the season. With a song in my heart: "Up on the housetop, click, click, click; Down through the chimney with old St. Nick."

The last Christmas…. 1981 was the last Christmas we would celebrate with Mom as she would die the next year from breast cancer. It is a strange feeling when you know something is officially your "last" and I guess in some ways, it is a gift. That Christmas is forever imprinted in my heart and sealed in a place deep inside of me. The tree went up Thanksgiving weekend—not December 15th as was the usual date. We did not worry nor discuss the dry needles by Christmas.

For probably the only time in my life, I hung the tinsel with such care that Mom actually kept nodding her head and did not make one adjustment. As you might know me, I was one of those kids who thought tossing tinsel was much more fun than individually hanging them like Mom did.

Our gifts were simple that year. I framed pictures from my mom's grade school collection, my grandparents' wedding picture and several of Mom, my brother and me. It was as if those pictures could permanently keep us all together forever. It still hangs in our home as homage to that last Christmas.

Our dinner was simple, too, that year as Mom did not have the energy to do her usual flurry of baking cookies and pies and making peanut brittle and divinity. Our table was spread with her Christmas tablecloth, and we joined hands for the last time around a lovely feast to be shared.

As I often did even after I had my own apartment, I stayed at Mom's that night. She and I stayed up after my stepdad and brother had gone to bed. We had a tradition each year of sharing a final gift when all of the living room was strewn with tissue and ribbon. And so, at the table, we exchanged our gifts one last time. I could not dare to speak as tears hung tightly to the edges of my eyes. My gift to Mom was a stuffed animal cat, a Siamese, who looked just like our real Siamese, Miss Kitty, who never left her side. She would hold that stuffed animal in the months ahead, and I believe it brought her comfort to feel its soft plush fur.

Her gift to me was her worn Timex watch. She said she did not need to look at it anymore as time was what she wanted and did not want to keep track of it. It is still in the box she gave to me, stopped long ago as I never took it out after that night.

I see the moon and the moon sees me... I stepped outside to walk to the mailbox and the clearness of this Kansas chill night caught my breath. I stopped halfway and stood dazzled by the lights from the neighbors' Christmas decorations, each house offering a buffet of reindeer, twinkling white lights, old timey big bulb lights, and in the windows, the joyous Christmas trees weighed down with their ornaments and treasures.

I looked to the sky and said, "There will be a full moon for Christmas."

The mailbox willingly gave forth its contents of Christmas cards, and they feel like heartfelt love in my hand. The roses by the mailbox are stuck in permanent pink as if they are not ready yet to step into winter.

I like to stand outside at night and see the far-off city lights of downtown and then turn to the west and see only the edge of dark dipping down behind the Rockies.

Then I turn back to our house. I see a cat in the window, probably Jazzy, always worrying that I won't come back quickly enough. I see the glow of our Christmas lights framing our home, and with a lifted heart, I push open the door, all the better from standing in the midst of this Kansas night.

Tennis fairy tale—kids at heart

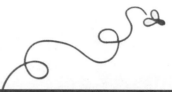

Cotton candy sweet twins, Reagan and Jordan

Chapter Eight

SEED CATALOGUE

...the seed catalogue was a much-anticipated arrival, especially for my grandma.

Nature's child... I wake up this morning and instantly think that I need to be with Nature. My favorite place is our back prairie and the limestone rock that sits under the red cedar trees. Our rock is just like the one that sat under my grandma's tree, the rope swing tree. In the rock, Nature has carved its own little bird bath where there is always a gathering of birds after a gentle rain.

Bundled up, I walk out on grass that is sprouting green for spring and find a place to sit on my rock. At first, I busy myself with thoughts of the people world until, as if by magic, Nature floats a net down around me and I become as still as a rabbit. My breathing is slow, my heart beats like the small south wind that has drifted in over the past few days, and my fingers trace the ancient fossils that are forever fixed into this rock. My hands calm as I touch the mysterious little creatures which once, too, sat or swam by this rock and somehow found it to be so lovely, they stayed.

The red cedar is a green umbrella over me and its boughs whisper ancient tales. Perhaps some Native Americans camped under it for a season or wild horses grazed on the grass that surrounds it. I can feel all of this absorbing into my too-busy body. I am calmed.

Ann Anderson

I can hear the wild turkeys down in the draw. I cannot see them, but I know they see me. Their turkey voices are sweet and chatty, and I feel a smile fall onto my face.

A red-tailed hawk circles above me and realizes I am not suitable for him. But still he is kind enough to show me his fat white and tan belly, full from a mild winter, and his burnt orange tail feathers spanned to catch the warm thermals of this spring day. In the cedars, I hear the crow family discussing me in their nosy, chatty voices. The blue jays throw in their mimicking opinion too, and then it is silent again.

The blue skies soak up my cares. How does one live in a noisy city high-rise and not be able to sit with you? After a while, the late afternoon chill pulls me back into our warm house. I stand at the window and look at the western sky gathering in its dark gray clouds for perhaps a rain tomorrow. The sun slants onto my rock where I was sitting. Oh, Nature, you are my church.

❁ ❁ ❁

Signs of spring... The seed catalogue arrived unexpectedly yesterday. I admired each page with its bountiful offerings of fruits, vegetables, award-winning flowers, and seeds for everything one could hope for in a garden.

As I touched its pages, I thought about my grandparents and the arrival each winter of the catalogue. Long before nurseries and the internet, the seed catalogue was a much-anticipated arrival, especially for my grandma.

She would walk the long gravel driveway, hold my hand to cross California Avenue, and exclaim with delight, "It's the seed catalogue!" We would hurry back to the house, and she'd always put on a fresh pot of coffee and pour my milk generously into a cup and top it off with just enough caffeine and sugar that I was slightly loopy for an hour. Then the joy began of sitting side by side at her kitchen table and studying the seed catalogue. She had a thick yellow carpenter's pencil, probably from my Uncle John. She would study and then circle her choices of seeds. It was unheard of to buy plants as I guess they cost a lot more and probably seemed extravagant to my frugal grandma.

Half of our time was spent simply admiring the pictures of the flowers, a light blue iris, a dark orange daffodil, a yellow sweet onion, and Grandma would ponder where she might plant the flowers and vegetables. We savored looking at the catalogue together, and it was kept for several months for more viewing enjoyment. With her order form carefully filled out, she would write out a rare check, and we would walk back down the crunchy driveway to the mailbox. On the way back to the house, we usually stopped and surveyed her garden. She would point out where each vegetable would go, and we were always so happy talking about the coming of spring.

My grandpa would be in his shop, sharpening the hoes and shovels and cleaning the Rototiller. On the first warm March days, they would both be out in the garden, hoeing ruler- straight lines and filling up muffin tins with dark Kansas soil ready to nurture the new sprouts. Each time I visited, I ran to check on the seedlings with their spindly green stems growing to the sunlight in the south kitchen window.

Soon the wintering robins returned to the yard, and it was time to plant the now strong seedlings so carefully selected at my grandma's kitchen table on a winter day.

Bumper cars… One of my tennis kiddos came to class sporting a new Disney shirt he got on a recent trip to Disneyland. He excitedly told me about enjoying all of the rides and meeting the Disney characters. I nodded appreciatively as Disneyland is a truly magical place. When I lived in Los Angeles, I took visitors to Disneyland probably three times a year and never tired of its "happiest place on earth" feeling.

My kiddo's shirt made me think of Topeka's version of Disneyland that we had as kids growing up. Boyle's Joyland was on California Avenue, and for a mid-century kid, it was every bit as good as Disneyland and in many ways better. On a hot summer evening, Mom would spontaneously announce we were going there and I would zoom to the car.

It was built in a wooded area so that even on a hot evening, the big shady trees cooled the pathways and rides. One area had a ride for kids with giant fat boats that floated around in six inches of blue water. They also had a very small Ferris wheel with enclosed cars.

But we were on to the big stuff. Our two favorite rides were the bumper cars (we never tired of ramming our cars into each other) and the roller coaster. Although not big, the roller coaster gave us all a proper thrill as we mounted the height of its hill and zoomed down around its corners.

The go karts cost extra, and occasionally Mom let us ride them too. Our five laps had us dreaming of a career as racecar drivers. Then we headed to the carousel and picked out our favorite pony to ride, gliding up and down and straining to catch Mom's face at each circle of the ride. It was joyous to wave and yell at her and see her waving back.

Boyle's Joyland had an arcade with different games and three giant mirrors that distorted our image into tall, skinny, and super wide. We never failed to look in the mirrors and laugh at our transformed bodies.

Usually, our last ride was the little railroad car that we hand churned. I loved it. It was on a small track that curved down into the cool, shaded woods. I would slow down and listen to the quiet.

Happy, tired, ready to go home. But one last treat. Boyle's Joyland offered soft serve ice cream. We ordered vanilla ice cream cones, licking the drops as they melted in the warm evening air.

Boyle's Joyland is now long gone, but it was one of the "happiest places on Earth" for a mid-century Topeka kid like me.

Mom's advice… Like most kids, I heard advice from various family members, teachers, and random people in my childhood. But the person I paid the most attention to was Mom. She was not wordy, and when she offered up some motherly advice, I was usually quick to soak it in. Even in my junior high years when most young girls become at odds with their moms, I took the other path of leaning into her for guidance, support, and wisdom. Perhaps it was because she was constant and happy, and I wished not to drift from that wonderful space.

Mom gave me advice that I sorted and filed, like how to do ironing. She thought all material was enhanced by ironing; her iron seemed to constantly be on and at the ready. Our ironing board was like a prized piece of furniture and most of the time was set up just off of our dining room. To my utter disbelief, Mom ironed my stepdad's boxer shorts, his handkerchiefs and, Lord help me, our sheets. We had several discussions about this, but she said it made everything neater. I could not imagine why my stepdad would want neater boxer shorts but that was Mom's passion—ironing. I did grow to be fairly proficient in it and especially liked to iron the back pleat on the oxford cloth shirts with fruit loops that we wore in our teens.

Most of the time, Mom saved her advice for life events and situations. She was not into women's lib but yet was already liberated. She taught me how to fix everything in the house from checking the electrical panel to turning off the water and showed me how to build things with nails and a hammer.

She told me not to be defined by a man, but find someone kind to share life and never expect to change that person.

She gave me advice about being a strong young girl and to stand up to boys. She said never let a boy win just to get him to like you. That seemed reasonable to me, so I always tried to run fast and play hard. She also told me that cheating in sports or cheating at anything was only cheating myself. I learned that lesson a few times. She was right.

One of the best pieces of advice Mom gave me was to surround myself with good friends. I have had times in my life where I forgot that advice and chose some friends that took more than I could give. I have had a few friends that I thought would be for life, and for reasons I do not still know, they chose to drop away from me.

As I approach sixty-four, I know I can say I have surrounded myself with the cream of the crop of friends. Friends who are interesting, fun, adventuresome, nurturing, always have my back, and make me a better person. Some of them have become the family I have longed for—the brothers and sisters we get to choose for ourselves.

Thanks for the advice, Mom. It still works.

Fierce wind… You are a strange lullaby, like the oceans whose waves are crashing onto the shore. Did you start across the vacant, vast plains of the Dakotas? As I lie in our bed, I tuck my head under the covers to soften your voice and yet, it is still a hypnotic sound. The cats press against me as if you are a stranger outside our windows trying to get in.

I hear a wolf's howl in your voice and the cold snort breath of a buffalo herd still roaming free. We are the people of the "South

Wind," so you must not stay. You are but a visitor and must go back to your Northern home.

You have kept our birds from their feeders. They are nestled in the red cedar as if they, too, fear your power. Our tree limbs shake from your breath and the tall grass waves for you to leave.

North wind…winter wind…you must go home. Bring our south wind back from the Gulf, the scent of manatees and saltwater and a gentle breeze to warm the air and to open up spring's awaiting flowers.

Be my Valentine… Next to Thanksgiving, my favorite holiday is Valentine's Day! Like Thanksgiving, it is a holiday that you can share with everybody from your sweetie, to your co-workers, family, and friends. Anybody! It is commercial, but still retains that homemade feel of long ago.

I treasure the valentines I received when I was young. When I was a kid, Mom and I would be busy finding the perfect shoebox, adorning it with construction paper, crepe paper, doilies and glitter in red, pink, and silver. Mom would carefully write my name on the side and cut a generous slot in the lid for the much-anticipated greetings to be slipped into the awaiting heart box. We all brought our boxes to school, and with stealth and sneakiness, the boxes were filled up with valentine cards from classmates and the teacher. I would carry my treasure home like a box of diamonds. Mom and I would spill out its heartfelt contents on the kitchen table. Most of the girls wrote hearts and kisses, xoxoxo, and usually one or two of the boys would write them, too. Oh well, it was exhilarating to get all of those love messages.

As I grew into a teenager, Valentine's Day became the "oh no, I don't have a special boyfriend" dreaded holiday. Too bad we didn't keep making the shoe boxes for our friends to stuff with good wishes. One year I was lucky. Mark, my first boyfriend, sent me flowers. The flower man came to our front door and offered up the most gorgeous, small vase filled with pink roses, baby's breath, and a card from Mark with a poem. Yes, I was swooning and in love.

When I was at the University of Kansas, my roommate, Leslie, and I found ourselves without boyfriends as the big romantic holiday approached. We still laugh about sitting at Mass Street Deli, designing cards that our "would be" boyfriends would be sending.

Now I have my own sweetie, and each year we exchange heartfelt messages of love. Happy Valentine's Day to everybody!

Thoughts on a cold spring day... I was thinking about the little gifts I used to make Mom and my grandma for Valentine's Day. Most of the time it was my "go-to potholder" with colors to match the holiday.

I thought it was like making a Monet. Mom graciously accepted them for almost every holiday. Of course, for Valentine's Day, I would select pink and red loops, and she always acted surprised when she opened the handmade gift. When she died, I laughed and cried at the drawer full of potholders I made for her.

I was thinking that most of us are kind of like those potholders, handmade, lots of colors or a little plainer. Some of our edges are perfectly tied up, but more often than not, we get frayed around the edges somewhere. But no matter, we still function and look good.

Chanel No. 5... My parents had an active social life, and on many evenings, I would park myself on their bed and marvel at their getting-ready rituals. My stepdad had a drawer full of laundered shirts starched so stiff that you could flick your finger on the beautiful material and hear it click. They were wrapped in cardboard bands. He would don one and then select a tie from his big tie rack, knotting it just so with usually a quick adjustment made by Mom. I learned how to tie neckties by watching this routine over twelve years. He slipped on his suit jacket and carefully tucked a brightly colored handkerchief into the pocket. He had a man's jewelry box that housed his cuff links, several large watches, and tie tacks.

My mom's getting-ready routine required makeup first. She sat at her small dressing table, applying pancake makeup, blush, eyeliner, eyebrow pencil, mascara and Avon red lipstick. Then the wrestling match with the girdle and hose would begin. I always stifled a giggle. Watching anybody struggle into a girdle, especially with no AC in the middle of summer, was a sight to behold. But she won the girdle wrestling match and would select an elegant dress to slip on.

Her dressing table held a jewelry box filled with her Timex watch, flamboyant rings, earrings of every color, and elegant bracelets. She had a comb, brush, and mirror matching set that was cream colored with delicate pink roses painted on the back of them. I thought she looked like Scarlett from Gone with the Wind when she sat at her dressing table. Her finishing touch was a squirt of her favorite Chanel No. 5. My mom and my stepdad were ready for a night out.

I thought they looked marvelous, like Grace Kelly and her prince. They would kiss us goodnight and the smell of Chanel No. 5 would wonderfully stay on my cheek.

So cool... Vann and I have been away for ten days visiting our old home in Southern California. Though we have been gone since 2005, Southern California is instantly familiar and feels like a happy place. We saw Vann's son and wife, Keith and Janet in Orange County, my childhood friend, Debra, and her husband, Steve in Los Angeles, my good pal, Jill, from my American Cancer Society days, our old houses, and the place where we were married at stunningly beautiful Torrey Pines State Beach.

One of my favorite movies is LA Story. There is a line in it about Los Angeles, "It's a place where they've taken a desert and turned it into their dreams." I think that has always been true, and I know when I moved to Pasadena in 1990 from cold, gray Chicago, it was a dream come true.

Southern California is not the golden place it once was, as you cannot cram 25 million people into that part of the state and have it turn out well. There was never quiet in the ten days we were there, and most things looked overused. The beach is still as breathtaking as ever, and the Pacific Ocean continues to provide that perfect infinity pool off the edge of California. To see the palms waving and the birds of paradise with their beautiful bright orange and blue flower blossoms is dreamlike.

But we are pulled home, to this plain Kansas prairie with the red-tailed hawk circling high, no noise from her outstretched wings, the cedar rustling with a slight sound, and the tall grasses whispering in the south wind.

It is the place where I create my own dreams.

Prairie dawn... A still moon, dark outside and the slants in the bedroom shades float cool air across my face. I have no cows to get me up to feed and milk, yet my Kansas DNA seems to wake me. Or maybe it is Jazzy, who loves to come up with her pink nose and touch my cheek and then lay a padded paw on it. She is better than any alarm clock, and I always feel her lightly land on the bed with her wake up call.

I lie there under my blanket and peer out through the blinds to daylight dawning. The cedar shows the first crest of golden pink sunlight playing in its furry tree top. A lone blue jay jumps out to get the early worm. The tree suddenly rustles as if saying to me, "Come on, get up!"

I am kind of claustrophobic, so I have to sleep with the blinds partly open as if to always let some nature float in. Last night, the first sweet spring rain lulled me to sleep with its plop of drops on the window, dripping down like Christmas silver tinsel. There is no better sleep tonic than rain.

I hear Muffy and Queenie stretch and turn in their beds, doing their cat yoga stretches to settle in for one more hour of sleep. But Jazzy and I know these early mornings are to be savored. The eastern sun is rising on its journey from the Atlantic Ocean and spreading light and soft colors. Mr. and Mrs. Bluebird are already selecting their box as if they are filming a Bluebird House Hunters in our back prairie. I do not want to miss all of these nature sights. Jazzy sits at the window and makes her bird chatter, whiskers eagerly twitching. The grass leprechauns are weaving green threads into our yard, and I see the beige giving into green.

There is that magic hour while most are asleep, yet the world is very much coming to life. That is the world Jazzy and I wander every morning together.

Mid-century kid school days... I watched our neighbor kids belching out of the yellow school bus this afternoon and thought of Crestview Grade School days so long ago.

As our parents used to say, "We walked to school uphill both ways." Well maybe not, but we walked. Only in frigid snowy weather would Mom load us into the Chevy for the four-block drive to school. We thought nothing of it as walking and running to school was fun.

Always in my arms were my Big Chief tablet, my school workbooks, and my treasured farm lunch box with matching silo thermos. It sits proudly on our counter sixty years later, and it is a testament to the simple life we enjoyed. Mom would neatly stuff it with a sandwich, a small bag of chips, whatever fruit we had, and fill my silo thermos with chocolate milk. On very cold winter days, I would have a nickel taped inside my lunch box to buy the small half-pint of milk and my thermos would be filled with hot Campbell's tomato soup. It was fine dining, and I rarely wanted to trade with other kids for their lunches.

I have often wondered how we did not all die of mayonnaise food poisoning, as our lunches sat happily unchilled in the coat closets. By noon, the faint aroma of warm bologna, liverwurst, and tuna salad would be wafting out from our closet. With a quick snap of its trusty lock, I would open my farm lunch box to see what sandwich Mom had made. She often tucked a note of encouragement inside, a funny face or something to get me through the second half of the day.

Back in the fifties, a prayer at lunch was commonplace. I was always nervous that the lunchroom teacher would call on me to recite the prayer, but somehow I escaped that duty throughout my Crestview years.

The other chore I did not enjoy was being the "pencil sharpener monitor." It required staying after school for about thirty minutes, cleaning the chalk boards, smacking the dark gray felt erasers together, and then, gulp, taking the pencil sharpener to the boiler room to empty. I never quite understood why we had to take the #2 shavings to the scary boiler room, but we did it, no questions asked.

At 3:15 p.m. the bell would ring, signifying another day had successfully been completed at Crestview Grade School. We exited our desks (names taped on the front) and grabbed our coats. I retrieved my red barn lunch box and walked with no cares in my heart to our home with lights in the windows and Mom waiting to ask me, "How was your day?"

Gecko me... My reptilian brain is alert today. I am lying gently on a flat rock soaking in the rising southern sun. I look at the Kansas sky and land, and it is as if Mother Nature has painted a new spring picture with her black box of Prang watercolors, with so little left in the green and blue squares that she mixed in extra water. Pale blue sky and faint green meet at the Earth's crest.

The cats, too, seem caught in meditation, purring the sun into them after a winter's nap. We look at each other with a silent wink of understanding that this is a special day worth savoring, not moving, just lying on that ancient gecko rock with eyes half closed.

This morning, three hot air balloons floated over our home breathing their distinct dragon's breath, and then I looked, and they were gone. I wonder, did I imagine it? There is no vapor trail, just the whisper of the dragon floating down to the grass.

Gecko me. I lie still in this early spring-warmed air. A crocus pops through with purple, just now.

Senior Night KU Basketball... First of all, I AM going to senior night next year if I have to beg, borrow, or buy a ticket. I watched the whole event on TV, and it was so moving and poignant. One easily forgets that these are young men who are not used to speaking on center stage to 16,000 plus fans. Athleticism does not necessarily prepare a young person for all of the attention and glamour that comes with playing ball in a place like Allen Field House.

I heard a compelling speech by Coach Self several years ago. I will never forget him telling about having his team, including a young freshman, over to his home for the first time. After everyone had left Coach Self's party, Mrs. Self discovered the young player standing in the living room and asked if he needed something. He replied, "No, it's just the first time I've ever been in a house." Even though you are playing D1 basketball and famous, people really don't know and understand your background.

Each of the four seniors who spoke on Senior Night were thankful: first to their families, then to their coaches, staff, players, faith, and their fans. It was clear that they had experienced a safe and nurturing environment during their time at KU. Hats off to Coach Self and the young men who all will graduate with a degree. Rock chalk, KU. Next year, I will be there.

Spring spots… March 5th and it is here! Spring! A herd of robins plop down unexpectedly in our backyard and begin pulling up fat worms. A crow, beak full of grass, prepares a nest. Forsythia blooms by the lake. Girl Scouts in front of Dillon's sell their Girl Scout cookies and sing. Kids in tank tops and flip flops. Our first trip to the nursery with a small section of blooming lavender and yellow pansies, a feast for the winter eyes to behold.

The red buds with furry pink branches just waiting for a spring rain this week and then bursting out with color. There is nowhere prettier than Kansas in the spring. The thunderstorm gathers its dark clouds together in the west. Tonight, we will sleep with a spring window open.

✿ ✿ ✿

"When I'm sixty-four"… On my birthday eve, thoughts about this exquisite life that has unfolded for me and hearing the lyrics of the Beatles song. When that song came out, I was a teenager and thought, "Wow, sixty-four sounds really old." And now it sounds really just right.

I think of Mom as a young housewife, twenty-seven years old, in Stormont Vail Hospital, waiting to give birth to her first child. The night I was born, my grandparents and my mom's best friend, Marge, were at the hospital with her. My bio dad was missing in action already. But Mom, always surrounded by the love and support of her friends and my grandparents, was more than up for the task of raising me.

My earliest memories are of our five years living on Parkview Street. It was a quiet, post-war street with airplane bungalows, big trees, the wonder of Hughes Tennis Courts across the street, and the roar and sounds of the Gage Park Zoo just blocks away. In our backyard, I had a small playhouse built by Grandpa. Mom painted it pink and installed pink gingham curtains in the two windows. It was my own "Barbie Dream House," and I spent endless hours in there preparing pretend tea parties for the neighbor kids and more often, quietly reading my books with the west light coming in from the small open door. Behind our house, we were lucky to have an alley, the meeting place of the neighborhood kids, our private ball park, football field, and dirt road.

Our home had two bedrooms and one bath. No one thought of it as a small house, it was just like everyone else's home. We did not need granite counter tops, stainless steel appliances and walk-in closets as we owned just the right amount of play clothes and one or two outfits for church or a special occasion.

Mom was an amazing seamstress, and her treadle Singer proudly sat in our living room. From it, she would whip out a summer wardrobe of Crayola-colored shorts and tops or a sundress, and from time-to-time, she would be creative and make us matching mom and daughter outfits. As a kid I wasn't too sure of this, but we always got lots of compliments, so she continued this practice until I was about seven.

When I was little, my favorite food was stewed tomatoes. I remember sitting in my red wooden high chair in the mid-century kitchen and eating tomatoes while Mom did dishes. I had a small silver salt shaker that was mine, and felt quite content with my bowl of tomatoes. I remember hearing Mom and Marge discussing whether I could survive on eating stewed tomatoes and hot dogs. It seems like it did not deter my growth.

I have no memories of my bio dad being at our house. I guess he was already in the process of being elsewhere, and by the time my brother was born in 1954, he was gone. My brother used to tell people that he died in a forest fire. I guess that was his way of settling our dad's absence in his young mind.

I feel so happy that I was born to my mom, Irene. I feel so lucky I grew up in a little house with a screen door that smacked soundly when I raced out to the tennis courts each day. I adored sharing a bedroom with my little brother, our bunk beds next to the windows letting in cool thunderstorm air and the cooing sounds of mourning doves.

Moon beams… A birthday so filled with fun, sugar, and all those things that make life sweet. Yesterday after leaving my twin nieces, I drove happily through my Flint Hills that were getting their grasses burned for new green growth. The hungry fires were like burning sidewinders slithering across the grasses. The warm, rich smoke drifted into me and mixed with the sweetness of early spring air. I treasured that hour drive, just me and so much empty beauty. Overhead, the red-tailed hawk clutched a branch, his beautiful golden head turned to hear a critter running from the flames.

The small herd of bison seemed to nod as I passed them as if to say, "You are almost to Buffalo Mound." I have seen that landmark all of my life, and it always makes my heart jump, thinking of the ancient peoples and how they too must have been gladdened at the sight of it. Off to both sides, the great banks of the Kaw River rose up into the pale blueness of a late afternoon sky.

All of the Kansas sky and earth seem born of watercolors this time of year, pale in palette and soothing to the eyes.

I stand outside. I see the crooked smile of the moon eclipsed as if it, too, is giving me a birthday smile.

A moveable feast… Lucky me to have lunches this week with my twin nieces and nephew. I always try to pick a place that is quiet, so I don't miss a word they say or a smile they share. Since they have gotten older with college and jobs, it's harder to herd them into one place, so I'm extra grateful for those little feasts with them.

As a mid-century kid, dining out was a very special occasion. Most of our shared meals were at home or at our relatives' homes. Mom fixed breakfast, lunch, and dinner every day. If she were tired of cooking or perhaps if we had a very good report card, she would announce with great flair that we were going "out" for dinner. Back in those days, that meant going to Smaks Drive-In on Huntoon and getting their fifteen cent hamburgers, Allen's Drive-In on Topeka Blvd., or if we were very good, going to the first Pizza Hut in the concrete block building on 21st Street. Dining out seemed so exotic and sophisticated.

Mom frequently made us hamburgers at home, and when we were at Smaks, my brother and I would go on and on about how delicious the Smaks hamburgers were. Mom would say, "Don't you like the big thick ones I make?" No, we liked those greasy quarter-inch things plopped on a bun and smothered in ketchup and mustard.

I would say most of my favorite meals were at our house. Mom was always decorating our table with something of the season… some bunnies and eggs at Easter, fresh flowers from our yard in a cut-glass vase in summer, or red and orange leaves in the fall. We also had a picnic table outside that was full of splinters but received a fresh coat of shiny green paint every year. It was fun to eat there with a flowery tablecloth spread on its surface, transforming it into a fine dining experience. Fried chicken, new potatoes, asparagus just cut from the garden, and chunks of German chocolate cake spread out from end to end. There was the constant chatter from all of us—school, sports, Mom's bowling team, summer plans.

It is a happy occasion to sit around the table with loved ones and share some good food and chat.

7:00 a.m. to 8:00 a.m.... After a late night of watching the KU Big 12 Basketball Conference win, I willed myself to linger in bed this morning and not spring ahead with daylight savings time. But my circadian clock and my Jazzy kitty both woke up early. We are always rewarded by what Mother Nature has offered. The fog shrouded our back prairie down to the lowest tree branches. It seemed to stretch a quiet net over the "spring ahead" world to hopefully slow us all down.

In the front yard, Mr. and Mrs. Mallard waddled through to nibble on the offerings under the bird feeder. They are resplendent in their coats of iridescent green, brown, white and tan feathers. Mr. Mallard is a good husband and always keeps watch to let his Mrs. eat. I often wonder how he stays fat as he is always on protection duty. I called the cats to the window with my whisper "bird." They were intrigued by the big ducks, but then just as quickly, they have retreated to their cat nests for paw licking and a spring ahead snooze.

I stay at the window. I see the magnolias waiting for tomorrow's eighty degrees to open their buds of lavender pink. The red bud seems fairly quaking in its desire to blossom out. We have set out the hammock and the porch chairs, and the colorful pots stand ready to be filled with rich dirt, herbs and bright flowers.

It is time to spring ahead to the renewal of spring.

Training wheels... I witnessed one of life's little big passages this afternoon. I was sitting on the front steps watching with a smile as our neighbor's little girl mastered riding her bicycle without training wheels.

Training wheels are kind of one of those things you forget about unless you have kids. But I immediately was transported back sixty years to my little yellow and red bike and its training wheels. I was content with them until one day some of the older kids—probably eight or nine years old–said, "Only babies have training wheels." Okay! I was so over my training wheels and pedaled straight back to my house in a huff.

I asked Mom to help me take them off, and she did not question me. I guess I had a look of set determination on my face. She maneuvered the wrench and voila! I was without training wheels. I hadn't quite thought that through. "Now what?" My mom said, "Are you ready?"

We went in the yard first, and she steadied me with her hands, one hand on my back and one on the handle bars. I got the hang of balancing, she pushed, and then down I went. On about the tenth try, success! I was doing it.

Despite a few skinned elbows and knees, she pronounced me "training wheels free," and I never looked back, pedaling everywhere as fast as I could go. My first destination was a speedy run by the older kids with a smile on my face and my ponytail trailing straight out behind me.

The next day, Mom obliged my request for streamers to put on the end of my handlebars—pink, of course. Then she showed me how to clip playing cards to the spokes with clothes pins for the most amazing click-click motor sound. What? Could it get any better?!

Congratulations to my little neighbor. After thirty minutes of trying, frustration and falls, she, too, is riding up and down our street. I can feel the smile she is wearing as she experiences that little big passage in her life.

Peeps... I cannot go to the store without walking down the Easter aisle at least once. Maybe because I love spring and the pastel colors, it is just a joy to look at everything. Of all the holidays, it seems to have the happiest candy and treats and many fond childhood memories.

All holidays were BIG at our house, and Mom was a "holiday cruise director"! Although we did celebrate Easter for its religious significance, we also embraced it as a time to be with family and friends, good food, and the coming of spring. Mom and I made place cards for the table with pastel shades of construction paper: lavender, pale yellow, grass green and petal pink, and I carefully cut out the bunnies and eggs she drew onto the paper. We sprinkled on glitter, buttons for the bunny eyes, and my favorite, a proper puff of cotton ball firmly glued on the bunny's behind with our ever-present jug of Elmer's glue. In my most expansive cursive, I would write out our guests' names... Grandma, Grandpa, cousins, and our family.

Easter weekend was for dyeing our Easter eggs. Mom was generous with the eggs and the sharp clean scent of vinegar delighted my nose. My brother dipped his eggs randomly in all the colors, usually resulting in a pale gray or brown egg. But my eggs were carefully dyed with various colors and then gently set in the cardboard holder they provided. After we had finished, they were proudly placed in the straw baskets lined with the fake Easter neon grass to be admired on the table.

Mom got up early on Easter and hid dozens of Easter eggs, chocolate bunnies, little plush chicks, and some plastic eggs with money tucked inside—a dime, quarter and one or two with a dollar bill as the prize. I would fidget through church and Sunday school thinking of the Easter egg hunt that would commence when we got home.

Going to church meant wearing our good clothes. I liked putting on my petticoats, a pink or lavender dress, little white gloves, and a proper hat with small flowers on the side.

The Easter egg hunt was great fun with my brother and cousins racing through our house and outside. Mom tried to keep track of all that she had hidden, but almost every year, a hard piece of Easter candy would be discovered in the couch in late April.

After the hunt, we sat down to a table laden with Easter food. Ham drenched in mustard, spice, and brown sugar, asparagus bathed in browned butter, new peas and potatoes floating in a white cream sauce, rolls with butter and apricot preserves from my grandma's root cellar, and for dessert, Mom usually made a coconut cake so tall it looked as if it would fall over from frosting and coconut. Peep bunnies frolicked on the top, and we were quick to snag those first.

Easter was a special day at our home filled with the traditions and feeling of belonging to a happy place. It is nice to still see the bright colored Peeps winking back at me from the aisle.

Home Ec... As I was making my daily breakfast smoothie, I thought of Mrs. Girotto and seventh grade home economics. She might frown on my breakfast of almond milk, fruit, and protein powder dumped in a blender and served straight up in a glass.

She was a delightful and caring teacher. Her room was right off the gym and was a magical environment. While Mom and Grand-ma were always trying to urge my tomboy ways to become more domesticated, it seems like Mrs. Girotto had a knack for turning young girls into chefs and worldly women.

I remember the first breakfast she taught us to make, and I served it to my family, bursting with pride and anticipation. The appetizer was a "daisy" which consisted of orange slices arranged elegantly around a mound of powdered sugar. The entree was "toad in the hole," which consisted of a piece of white bread with a hole cut out in the middle, an egg in the center and the whole thing fried in the skillet. Mom appropriately applauded my culinary skills and my stepdad probably stopped at Hanover's later for a real breakfast but nodded his approval.

We learned more than just fine dining. Mrs. Girotto was also tasked with teaching us to sew. While my grandma and Mom could sew or knit anything, their DNA did not extend to me. We started with a simple apron and matching hot pads. I selected a lovely golden gingham material and made the apron for my grandma. While cross stitching the pockets with what was supposed to be sunflowers, my friend Linda and I became engrossed in conversa-tion about the ninth-grade boys we could see going into the gym and industrial arts room. When the bell rang, I stood up and real-ized I had cross-stitched the sunflower clear through to my skirt. I heard Mrs. Girotto "tsk tsk tsk" as she kindly snipped all of the tiny x's so I could make it to my next class. I finished the apron and hot pads and proudly bestowed them on my grandma. She said they were "too pretty to use" and kept them in her dining room drawer. I still have them and smile when I think of her saying that they were "too pretty to use."

Undeterred, I tackled our final project—a navy blue pleated skirt that, gulp, we had to wear to school when finished. Did you know you can make forty pleats all a different size and sew the waist band on backwards? Well, I wore the skirt with the longest blouse and sweater I owned, and I do not remember its demise.

Anyway, thank you, Mrs. Girotto, for your valiant attempts to turn junior high girls into the women of tomorrow. It was a fun class and I learned a lot. Way better than algebra.

Nature is beautiful. As much as I love a warm spring day bathed in sunshine, I am equally happy to lean into a late fat-flake snow day. Our magnolias are pushing out deep red and lavender blooms and seem to quake with wonder at the white flakes.

Down in the prairie, the wild turkeys have grabbed a cracked corn snack and are back in their turkey draw, a thick nesting of bushes and tall grass. I stand on the porch bundled up and soak in their chatter. It is as if they are all talking about the weather and wondering if they should start making the baby turkeys or wait another week.

The cats run on sun time wound by their ancient coding to light. They open one eye each, eat a snack on auto cat pilot and find dark warm corners to sleep out this late March dusting. Vann, too, has pulled the spring blankets over his head and sometime this morning, snagged mine too.

I like this quiet snow. It will not stick to the green grass earth that has already been warmed. By noon, it will only be a memory in my head. But sitting here with my hands wrapped around hot tea, it is a soothing wonder. I like seeing things that are only here for a moment—the last snowflakes of winter, a butterfly landing on the prairie coneflower, and the blue Russian sage that is poking up through Mother Earth.

Second home... I gave myself an afternoon of spring break with no kiddos to teach. And where did I go for my break but love-ly Lawrence, my second home, and instantly felt like I dipped my toes in some familiar sandy beach. I drove the back ways, and I am always astonished how the high tide of the west edge of Lawrence now laps at the east edge of Shawnee County. The

Ann Anderson

My grandparents' farm and the walk to
the mailbox for the seed catalogue

roads are as friendly and the same as when I drove them as a
KU student. Old houses and a few new ones, a two-lane winding
blacktop with groups of cows and horses to wave to, Stull, Kansas,
frozen in time with the old cemetery, the foundation of the limestone church, and the spring break island songs of Jimmy Buffet
and Zac Brown, Izzy singing "Somewhere Over the Rainbow," and
Ziggy Marley giving me that "no worries, mon" feeling.

Although there was a spring chill in the air, I did not feel it with
a KU stocking cap on and my KU hoodie. I sat by the window at
Zen Zero and just felt my constant smile watching March Madness
up and down the street. An endless array of KU apparel and even
two dogs with KU ball caps on.

I have spent hundreds of hours on Mass Street in my lifetime.
As a KU student, my roommate, Leslie, and I would wander the
shops, the Hodge Podge, Sunflower Surplus, Mass St. Deli, and a

few bars that are still there like Louise's, frozen in time with their yard-tall beer.

I remember sitting at Jayhawk Tower and watching KU in the "dance" with my forever college buddies David and Susie, eating oranges and rice and caught in the joy of our friendship.

The sounds of Neil Young, Gordon Lightfoot, and The Moody Blues still float out to me when I walk that street. And I swear the scent of patchouli hangs in the air from all of the incense burned in so many dorm rooms long ago. I thought of going to The Wheel, which still exists, to watch a few of the games. But I wanted a quiet afternoon to soak up the so-cool vibes of Lawrence. When I am there, I am no age, just Annie leaning against the 1970s, and all is good.

Some people fly to Florida or Mexico for spring break. I'm lucky. I just float over to Lawrence. The smells, the music and the rock chalk vibe take me anywhere I want to go like a time machine always parked ready and waiting.

The best gifts… I have managed to stretch out my birthday until almost Easter, with weekend celebrations and lunch with one of my Besties. Yesterday, Vann and I went to my cousin Linda's lake home in Gardner for dinner.

Linda and I have been like sisters since birth although she's a bit older (only in age). She has been my role model and has taught me everything from where babies come from (out of your belly button) to the taste of beer—one too many. She was my mom's favorite niece and, unbeknownst to me, my mom gave her several treasures.

Several years ago, a box came in the mail, and when I opened it up, I had tears of happiness for its contents. It was the plastic Santa Claus with a small light inside that was my mom's number one Christmas decoration during all my years growing up. Sometime after I had moved to my apartment, Mom had given it to Linda. In a most generous act, Linda gave me the much-loved Santa Claus who, to this day, is carefully displayed for Christmas and plugged in with its 1950s cord and light bulb still working.

Last night after a delicious home-cooked meal and birthday cake with glitter and pink roses, Linda again gave me a gift of my mom's pitcher and matching bowl with dainty fruit and flowers painted on the side. That set was in our house for as long as I can remember, not to be touched, one of our pieces of "fine" art. Where Mom got it, I'll never know. I did not know that she had given that treasure to Linda many, many years ago. And now it is back with me, displayed beautifully on our kitchen table, and I cannot go by it without delicately touching its pastel fruit so beautifully painted. It was an heirloom gift which is one of the best gifts you can receive.

Wrapped in tissue was also a yellow plastic diaper pin that was my brother's. Why anyone thought to save it is almost beyond my comprehension. Linda said her mom saved it because she used only plain diaper pins and my mom had "fancy" diaper pins with colored plastic on the end. I love to have that little piece of my family back with me and think about it holding a diaper on my baby brother.

I have been lucky to share back with Linda a couple of rings her dad made, my mom's walnut picks, my grandma's book of poems and other family items that she and I still care about. We are like two Native Americans carrying the "tribe's pack" of the most cherished items with us through this life.

Vann did not go home empty-handed. He admired Linda's butter dish with the cutest little cow as the lid. It is now happily chilling a stick of butter in our refrigerator.

I'm lucky to have my cousin Linda. She is quick with her generosity, her laughter is contagious, and she can cook circles around all of us.

Bucket list… Just read an interesting article in the Wall Street Journal about bucket lists for retirees. Most people when they retire envision world travel, moving to exotic places, and doing things they have only dreamed of doing some day. Well, we did that too, moving to South Carolina. As we kept getting farther and farther east on I-70, my heart and mind kept realizing that I should not be going, but we were on our way. I call it our five-month vacation to South Carolina when we took all of our stuff with us.

One year ago today, we were pulling into the driveway of our home that had not sold in Topeka (karma/destiny), seeing the beautiful "Welcome Home Vann, Ann and Kitties" sign in our yard, and being met with the best friends anybody could ever imagine.

My bucket list is enjoying our home with Vann, watching the kitties move from sunspots to sun puddles, lying in my hammock while the south breeze ruffles the pages of a good book, playing tennis with my pals, getting my hair streaked pink, watching my nieces and nephew on their perfect paths, and feeling surrounded by love and contentment. Happy Anniversary. There's no place like home.

✿ ✿ ✿

Wait fifteen minutes… Holy cow! Watching the Weather Channel and seeing the Colorado blizzard, I-70 closed out west, fifteen degrees in Goodland, and I have been outside in the gale force wind spray painting my garden art. Probably not the smartest day to spray paint, but who can pass up an eighty-degree day with sunshine in late March?

Midwesterners are all fond of saying "Don't like the weather? Wait fifteen minutes." Maybe every state has that saying, but it certainly seems true here in the heart of the nation. I have lived in beautiful San Diego where there is essentially one weather, and I never heard anybody say, "Wait fifteen minutes." It was almost always seventy-two and sunny or occasionally seventy and a marine layer. I remember one El Niño year, the local meteorologists were almost giddy with the excitement of promised rain. Vann and I laughed out loud at the weather man pronouncing that the coast could get up to an inch of rain. People were literally going to the stores to stock up.

I also lived in Chicago, which I think has some of the worst weather anywhere. It was either gray, windy, gray and windy, gray, windy and snowy, or hot and windy. When I lived there, I was mainly interested in finding biscuits and gravy and wearing sweat pants. One time at work, a co-worker offered me his Chicago Bears tickets. Oh MY Gosh! I was beyond excited. On the day of the game, it was ten degrees. It was the year of the Super Bowl '88 Bears, and I will never forget they were playing Tampa Bay. The Bears players literally had rolled up the short sleeves on their uniforms exposing more bare skin. When Tampa Bay took the field, you could tell they wanted to just say "You win, put us back on the plane." I stayed until half-time and that was my one and only Chicago Bears game.

Ann Anderson

I love weather, the four seasons, the big, dark gray wall clouds that build to the south and west in the spring and summer, a drenching rain with thunder and lightning in the night, our clear blue sunshine days, and even the quiet blanket of snow covering the prairie in December.

Eighty degrees today with a chance of snow tonight. That is my kind of Kansas forecast! Kansas weather is like a "box of chocolates"—you never know what you're going to get, and in fifteen minutes, it might be different!

The family God gave me—Wyatt (left),
Sadie and Miles (right)

Chapter Nine

ROCK ME

After a bath, playing, or lunch, I would watch my grandma like a red-tailed hawk to see if she were going to pass by the rocker.

The cats and I went out to the patio early this morning. There is something about a cool, summer morning that seduces the senses. The air is still scented, sweetly wet with the night's fierce rains. Our herbs float out their smells of lavender, basil, lemon thyme, and mint. The cats are stretched and not bothering to groom, but just enjoying the cool concrete, taking another siesta. I am stretched between two chairs and pleasantly realize that I need my hoodie. Digging quietly in the drawer so as not to wake Vann, I triumphantly pull out my oldest KU hoodie, cottony soft from years of use, the fleece worn flat. I slip it on and it feels like a touch of fall. It will not stay on past 10:00 a.m. when the summer creeps back onto us.

But for now, I savor its warmth and feeling against my skin. My hands are cupped around a coffee mug with birds on it that Marilyn gave me, and it is filled with graham-flavored coffee. I could be sitting by a morning's campfire at the lake as the world is so still this morning.

Ann Anderson

The sky is not sure what color to pick. It is a pale sun-washed, denim blue color in the west and a pale pink, party cellophane color where the sun is regaining its reign over the day.

I touch my hoodie sleeve and close my eyes. Happy for summer, but a touch of a fall dream in the air. A maple leaf turns gold and then back to green. Magic.

The salmon run… Like salmon, our family will find its way back to our ancestral river, the fragrant, beloved prairie and hills that wander from Alma to Volland. My grandparents found their way to Kansas, worked hard and had "a litter of kids" as my grandma used to say. Five kids who grew up to be successful with cousins for my brother and me. The Volland Hills, west of Alma, will once again hold us as we gather at my cousin's childhood home, now transformed into a beautiful bed and breakfast, The Mill Creek Lodge at Volland Point. It is different, and yet, it is as familiar as my childhood home. I remember its paths down to the creek with its deep, quiet pools that invited us in as children. I can close my eyes and smell the sweet scent of summer strawberries and hear Uncle John telling us kids to go pick some for dinner.

I can see the upstairs where Linda and I will stay once again. She will stay in her old room and I will be next door in my older cousin's room. Just like kids, we will talk and giggle about this and that until we fall asleep.

Saturday, we will travel that well-remembered river back to Alma and gather. It will be a day of storytelling, sharing the foods our family has loved and, once again, being reminded that we are all connected.

Won't you be my neighbor?… Just back from a trip to see our friends, Kim and Don, in their cozy home in the Red Rocks of Littleton, Colorado. They live by a stunning rock that towers over their home and is more beautiful than anything in the Garden of the Gods. I am always plotting how I can bring a big chunk of it back to Kansas.

It is so lovely to have friends who are like family, and we can drop in there without even calling and stay in the "Anderson Suite" as it has been named. Don always sets my side of the electric blanket to eight, so it is warm and cozy as even on a summer night, there is a Colorado chill in the air. He makes us his famous "bottomless" lemon pie that is so delicious!

I taught Kim how to play tennis. At first, she was like all new players, one hit for every ten tries. Over the years, she has become an accomplished player and loves it. Kim is like the sister I never had, and we laugh and call each other "twins" though we are seven years apart. She is smart, kind and throws the best birthday parties of anybody I know!

Mom and I used to watch Mr. Rogers' show on PBS. I especially loved Daniel, the tiger, and had a stuffed animal of him that I cherished. The concept that stuck with me the most was wishing I could create the "neighborhood of make believe" where all of my favorite people live like Kim and Don.

I wish they lived closer, but it is always nice to think of Kim and Don just at the far end of I-70. Just down the street in my neighborhood of make believe.

Our Town... The play by Thornton Wilder has been drifting through my mind these fall days. Our high school put it on, and even as a teenager, I was connected to its message of how precious our life is and how little moments weave together the fabric of us. This week has been a whirlwind of activities, being on Ralph Hipp's 'red couch' WIBW TV show, spending every night on our summer porch with the cats, and finding a sunflower bouquet from my friends at the door.

In the play, the girl must choose a day to come back to visit after she has died. Many might quickly choose a magnificent day such as a wedding, a cruise, or something special. But I would choose from those days spent quietly with my mom. Perhaps a day that we were making a new pair of summer shorts on the Singer sewing machine while humming a song together. I might pick a day cruising with Mom in her Chevy convertible, top down. Maybe a summer night on our patio looking at the stars and talking about school, family, and our cat, Miss Kitty. Those simple days are more special than any special event. I would give anything for just one more normal day to spend with my mom.

"Oh Earth, you're too wonderful for anybody to realize you."

Ann Anderson

✿ ✿ ✿

Rock me… As long as I can remember, my grandma had her rocking chair sitting in the "foyer" as it was called. It sat on a rug she had hooked with long soft pieces of wool, and in the summer, the front door was open, and a southeast breeze floated in like corn fairies over us. In the winter, the rocker sat near the floor heater above the coal furnace that was kept constantly toasty by my grandpa shoveling pieces of the jagged shiny, black coal into its hungry mouth.

After a bath, playing, or lunch, I would watch my grandma like a red-tailed hawk to see if she were going to pass by the rocker. I would run to her and say, "Rock me." And just as quickly, I was in her lap, my legs tucked into pretzels, my head resting against her housedress that smelled of something fragrant like lilacs or lemon cake. This would be a piece of paradise, wrapped in my grandma's arms, a summer breeze cooling us, her humming one of her grandma songs, and I was so dizzy with happiness that I had to make an effort to stay awake. I did not want to miss a moment of my grandma. Such a feeling of safety, time standing still and being tucked so closely into her that I could feel our hearts beat together across a generation.

Sometimes she would rock me if I didn't feel well. First, I would get a bowl of milk toast, a strange concoction that was warm milk, butter, and a piece of toast floated on top. I can still smell that warm rich remedy as it always seemed to cure my ailments. Then we were off to the rocker and she would hum "The Old Rugged Cross" or "Rock of Ages" as I felt my cares drift away.

The rocker is almost one hundred years old now. When she died, she gave it to Mom and said it would be mine someday. As a kid, I could not imagine having something so precious. When Mom died, I did become the keeper of the rocker. I have sat in it during my sad days, happy days, and all the in-between days. I can feel my grandma's soul in it, and I can whisper "Rock me," close my eyes, and feel its gentle rock bring back those arms around me.

When I was three, Mom gave me my own little rocker. I rocked my baby dolls and my cats when they would let me, and it turned sixty this year. I have given it to my Florida niece, Anna, for her new daughter to enjoy. I hope it is a rocker that Anna's daughter will cherish and give to her child someday.

It is a good night to pause, rock in my grandma's rocker, and let those corn fairies in on this cool fall night. I shall perhaps let myself doze off and hear my little voice saying, "Rock me."

Title IX... As kids, we knew nothing of "sports equality." Every day when we got home from school, we grabbed a snack, put on play clothes, and with a proper smack-slam of our screen door, we yelled to Mom, "We're going outside!" Where else would we want to be? At one point, Mom decided that I was becoming too much of a tomboy and that piano lessons would right the course. Oh dread for both me and the poor piano teacher. The worst part was mandatory practice for an hour every day after school. I was awful and agreed to wear dresses more and comb my hair and thus escaped more piano lessons.

Our garage looked like a vintage sports store. It was an unfinished one-car garage circa 1950s which made for excellent storage of everything that involved large nails and hooks. We had every assortment of sports equipment, including our prized baseball mitts with our names written proudly on the thumb, wood bats, and a small sack of baseballs and softballs, three wooden tennis racquets in their presses with white balls that we tried to keep clean, some hula hoops, playground balls, a basketball, an always under-inflated football, and some jump ropes. We invented cross training as every day a different sport would call to us. With our mid-century neighborhood, including Debbie, Kenny, Ricky, David, and Linette, we could quickly field enough kids for a game of baseball or basketball. Our neighbors across the street had a real basketball goal mounted on their garage. They generously allowed us to use it even if they were not outside. We never tired of playing "HORSE" and would shoot hoops until Mom hollered "Time for bed." On fall nights, we would come home, sweaty, happy, and usually with the start of a sore throat yet elated with our just-finished game.

Our neighbors down the street had an actual tennis court. We thought they were rich and maybe they were by our standards. They were friends with my parents, so we had the great benefit of being able to play tennis on their courts when we were invited over for a BBQ. When that court wasn't available, we strapped our racquets to our bikes and pedaled to Crestview Park and played there for hours, and then if we had a quarter, we kicked up the kickstand on our bikes and headed for Crestview pool. Sometimes, when our mom was not watching, we jumped off our bikes on a slow roll and let them career to the ground. We never had a lock as no one ever thought to steal someone's bike.

We were always tired at night, full of the day's sports challenges, the thrill of victory, and readiness for the next day's adventure.

We were pre-Title IX kids who knew that it was just fun to go outside and play.

An affair to remember... I sorted through a box of letters last night and found with utter astonishment, a letter Mom had written in 1955 to my bio dad. He had an affair with the wife of their best friends, and the letter was his acknowledgement of this. Mom found out when my bio dad said he had a Santa Fe Railroad training in Denver and would be gone for a week. She called them to come over for dinner while he was gone, and the husband said that his wife was at a training for Santa Fe Railroad. Mom's intuition told her that something was "rotten in Denmark," or Denver, and she called Santa Fe and found out that sadly, there was no training. My bio dad and the wife had gone on a trip together. And so this letter, acknowledging what happened, old and folded, with my bio dad's faded signature and date. At the time, with two kids under the age of four, she got a divorce. Not easy to do in the mid-fifties, but I am sure my grandparents were supportive. I barely knew my bio dad, and even at four, I did not really miss him.

Mom married my stepdad in 1957. He was an attorney, and I believe they were both very much in love for half of their twelve-year marriage. But he had a "wandering eye" as my grandma said, and sadly, he had an affair... actually, many affairs, that doomed their marriage from the start.

He and Mom were the toast of the town in the early years of their marriage. They loved to host elegant parties at our house and go out to celebrations. I loved watching them both get dressed up, he in his fine suit, a carefully selected tie and hat, and Mom in a smart black dress, cinched with a gold belt, shiny earrings, and a spritz of Chanel No.5 that lingered in the air as they headed out the door.

I did not ever understand him choosing other women over my mom. He broke the straw with Judy, an alcoholic, who unbelievably had five kids. My parents' good friend, also an attorney, actually called Mom one day to tell her of the affair as he was representing Judy in her divorce. He could have been disbarred for making the call but truly cared about my mom. I shall never forget watching Mom on our beige kitchen wall phone, her fingers clenched around the curly extension line to balance her, her face transformed with shock and hurt, nodding her head, and hanging up. She got in her convertible and said she had to run an errand, tears already in her eyes.

When she came back in an hour, she told me and swore me to secrecy as she needed time to think about what to do next.

Her good friend, El, came to stay with us. One night my stepdad said he had to "work late." Mom and El said they were going to go to Judy's to see if my stepdad were there. I was in the ninth grade and mortified at the boldness of their plan, but they did it.

They knocked on her door, and she answered in an alluring robe, and there sat my stepdad—so busted!—in some kind of "Hugh Hefner" smoking jacket on her couch. Mom filed for divorce the next day and my stepdad moved out the following weekend.

Mom never missed a day of her mom duties either time. But I could see the forever hurt she carried from her husbands having affairs. Everyone, in my opinion, loses something with an affair. My mom, I think, lost her sense of being a beautiful woman and did not put on her high heels and fashionable dresses much after that. I think she was done with the life of cocktail parties and small talk. She went back to her farm roots.

She would always be to me and everyone in her life, a gorgeous, generous, vivacious, and loving person. But I know her heart was pierced from those vows being broken. Affairs are dead end streets for the heart.

As Vann and I sat on our big porch one Sunday morning, facing our Kansas golden prairie, we chatted about the fact that truly we were still living in too big of a house. Our move to South Carolina was our first attempt to downsize, right size, and create a new energy. But we had wandered back to Kansas to our home that had not yet sold.

We decided to go for a drive as we both always enjoy seeing the countryside change with each season, the cattle grazing gently on the grasses, and as was often the case, we wound up in Lawrence.

Lawrence has never lost its cool factor for this KU graduate, and we have both always enjoyed walking Mass St., the college energy, the local restaurants, The Merc, and Clinton Lake.

For the second time in two years, we saw an "open house" sign, talked to the realtor, and two months later, we are now closing on a cozy cottage in Lawrence, one thousand square feet of sunlight, a patio for the cats, a view to Clinton Lake, and I believe we have finally got this right!

Four thousand square feet to one thousand square feet required a month of donating, gifting, a sale of art and furniture, and we are ready to "right-size." Only this time, I know that everyone I love and the prairie that sustains me are still right here with me. Lawrence! Welcome to our new home!

First frost... Though it is "fall back" morning, my cats still think it is "wake up and let's do something" morning. We are all up at 7:00 a.m./new 6:00 a.m., and there is a crystal coating of frost on the neighbor's roof this morning for the first time this fall. In the sunlight, it glimmers like glitter from a hobby store randomly sprinkled along the eaves. My flowers have been transformed and look as if someone dried them to press into a memory book, their petals now half their color on their darkening stems. We drift into the season of quiet.

When I was a kid, November signaled much activity at our house. Mom had a list of kid jobs for my brother and me that included pulling the last things out of the garden and rolling up the hoses into green snakes to be stored in the basement. Mom always gave me the pleasant job of putting a new coat of paint on our handmade address sign. My grandpa made it with his wood router and Mom glued the handmade wooden numbers on it. Every fall and spring, it got a new coat of paint and hung on two hooks next to our front door.

Mom's holiday baking began in early November and was our favorite part of the new season. Almost every day when we slammed through the front screen door, we were enthralled with the scent of date nut bars, chocolate chip cookies, snickerdoodles, and cowboy cookies loaded with M&M's, oatmeal, and raisins. One of my favorites was her Swedish cookie, laden with butter, a thumbprint in the middle carefully filled with apricot preserves. She always packed tins of cookies in the metal "Currier and Ives" containers lined with wax paper, and they were delivered by us to friends and family over the holidays. I could hardly contain my excitement of ringing someone's doorbell and seeing their happiness when we handed them the tin of goodies. Sometimes, we would be invited in for coffee and hot chocolate and a sample of Mom's sweet creations.

It was time to go to the basement, get out our boxes marked "winter clothes," and put our summer clothes away until next spring. My sweaters smelled faintly fragrant from the moth balls Mom tucked around them. One Christmas, Grandma made us blue wool mittens lined with red soft flannel. They were always my favorite pair as they were made from a sweater that had been in a fire. The mittens always smelled like a Colorado campfire and the red flannel was so warm on crisp fall mornings.

Fall back. Slow down. It is time to gather round the kitchen table with a treat, a cup of something hot and chat about the day.

❁ ❁ ❁

Downtown... I remember going to my first dance in the eighth grade at Capper Junior High. I was wearing my FIRST pair of real stockings and dancing to Petula Clark's "Downtown." I hear that song and always think of the eighth-grade dance.

As kids, we referred to downtown Topeka as "going to town," and though it was less than ten miles from our home, it was always an adventure. Downtown Topeka was a vibrant place where we shopped for most of our store-bought clothes as malls had not yet been invented. Some of my back-to school clothes were happily purchased at Pelletier's Department Store with its super neat tube system for taking your money to some mystery place upstairs and returning your change. My stepdad would usually stop into Ray Beer's for a new tie or just to chat. We would take our film to Wolfe's Camera Shop and wait with excitement the whole week it took to be developed. Sometimes we would visit the State Capitol Building filled with massive murals painted by John Steuart Curry. As kids, we always scooted by the painting of John

Brown called Tragic Prelude. It gave us the creeps!

There were special occasions celebrated downtown at the Hotel Jayhawk with its iconic neon Jayhawk on top and the elegant Hotel Kansan where my grandparents celebrated their fiftieth anniversary. The downtown restaurants were equally magnificent, the Senate Cafeteria, Maynard's with their delicious pies and rolls, and my favorite, The Chocolate Shop. It was located near Pelletier's, and my grandma would occasionally take me there. I wore my good clothes and put on my white church gloves. It was downstairs and the owner kept all of the money in a cigar box.

Downtown was also the theater district. There were no mega theaters and going to a movie was a treat and a delight. The Grand Theater, The Jayhawk Theater, The Orpheum Theater and The Dickinson Theater all beckoned with their velvet seats, brightly lit snack bars, and most of them had young men with flashlights and snappy uniforms to guide you to a seat. The movies always began with a black and white newsreel we endured, the bonus cartoon, followed by the feature film.

Mom would drop my brother and me off with our movie money and sometimes one dollar to buy popcorn, a drink and candy. My brother and I occasionally opted for the giant dill pickles, and they puckered up our mouths for an hour.

My stepdad was a lawyer and worked in the majestic bank building at 6th and Kansas Avenue. It was an art deco building, and I remember, even as a kid, marveling at the beautiful details like the numbers on the clock and elevator.

Our school field trips always included a visit to the Kansas Museum. I thought it was the most gorgeous building I had ever seen, and I never tired of walking up the marble steps and wandering the floors of history. My favorite exhibit was the Native American teepee. I wanted to go in there and sit with them around the "light bulb fire" that was always burning.

Downtown was a place we could always go. I am still humming that song!

❀ ❀ ❀

New neighbors... Yesterday, our new neighbors moved in. They are a couple with two kids, no pet sightings yet. I watched their moving truck belch out boxes and furniture, and by 5:00 p.m., the lights were back on in the house like welcoming candles in the windows. The house had been sitting empty since August, and with each passing day, I swear it looked sadder. No kids shooting hoops into the late fall twilight and doing cannonballs into the pool, no one picking the random weed growing through the landscaped rocks, no mail truck stopping to leave a bundle of this and that in the mailbox. I left them a welcome card and a small box of cookies. Moving is very stressful and a most acceptable time to eat a whole box of cookies.

I have thought all week about how two years ago, we were packed and moving to South Carolina. It was a time of saying goodbyes, hugs, tears, seeing our home become empty rooms, and the cats wearing long whiskers as their stuff, too, was being boxed up. I am glad we moved to South Carolina as sometimes, you have to do something very outside your own comfort zone to find your true place. I will never forget turning left off of our street and knowing in my tummy that this was not meant to be. In the five months we were gone, Vann and I both learned that relationships are what make a place home.

The coolest town... Just got back from Lawrence—our soon-to-be new home! It is always like coming out of another dimension, the Twilight Zone in the best way possible, a time warp of college memories mingled with the present. My feet know every step on Mass Street, and I still marvel at some of the same stores that exist, like Sunflower Surplus, Mark's Jewelers, Louise's Bar and Weaver's Department Store. A walk-through Weaver's Department Store is a time warp in itself with its creaky, golden wood floors, '60s-like display cases, and preppy clothes from another era. No visit is complete without a stroll through The Raven Bookstore, like the one in You've Got Mail, the best local bookstore, complete with their cat who greets everyone. I cannot wait until we move into our new, tiny cottage!

When I was at KU, I might have spent too much time wandering around downtown and other haunts such as The Wheel, The Hodgepodge, and the Mad Hatter. My roommate, Leslie, and I thought it a worthy endeavor to frequent the Mad Hatter on Thursday night after doing our homework. Thursday was ladies' night which began at 10:00 p.m. I have to laugh—that is now past my bedtime.

Late night studying at Corbin Hall was rewarded with a 1:00 a.m. feeding at Joe's Bakery. Even before I pushed the door open, the smell of hot donut grease, sugar and spices would ignite my taste buds. I could not escape Joe's without eating at least two or three donuts. It was a ritual, a rite of passage.

Then there was THE season—KU basketball! Leslie and I would walk to Allen Fieldhouse and never fail to be awed by the majestic barn with tradition pouring out of every corner.

I love the local stores and restaurants. I love to sit at a window table with Vann and watch people sporting their favorite KU tee shirts, all the variety of shoes from old school Nike's to towering wedges, the parade of dogs from pedigree to pound puppies, and the always constant "honk for hemp" man who has replaced the "tan man," who had a tan no matter what the time of year and could be seen riding his bicycle around town and Wescoe beach on campus when I was attending KU.

My roomie and I had a great time at KU. We lived one semester at Ellsworth Hall, and on Friday afternoons, we hung a bottle of Boone's Farm Strawberry Hill wine out of our dorm window so it would be properly chilled for cocktail hour after class. More often than not, we rode our bikes back from class to see a string and the neck of the bottle blowing in the Kansas wind, a pale pink streak of sweet wine stained onto the side of the dorm. Oh well, we were back on our bikes and headed to Mass Street where there was always something to do and people to see.

I wish Joe's were still open. I would walk in there and eat two donuts right now. Rock Chalk. I believe we have found our forever home.

❁ ❁ ❁

Music to my ears... My high school friend posted a picture of Mary Travers and, of course, I started singing Peter, Paul and Mary songs. They were the first songs that I remember truly listening to the lyrics and hearing them make powerful statements through their music. They captured my generation's unrest for the upheavals of the '60s and '70s, the war, and the innocence that was slipping away.

My earliest musical memory is hearing Mom sing opera along with Mario Lanza records in our living room on Parkview Street. Even as a little kid, I thought Mom's voice sounded so beautiful when she sang. Someone in my family was always singing and we would put on our rendition of Oklahoma and South Pacific complete with costumes. I also liked to sing "Somewhere Over the Rainbow" from The Wizard of Oz and "Let's Get Together" from The Parent Trip, pretending I was Hayley Mills and had a twin.

As a kid, our stereo was a prized possession and my parents always had music playing—Frank Sinatra, Herb Alpert and the Tijuana Brass and Sergio Mendes and Brasil '66. In the car, Mom sometimes let us listen to KEWI, a Topeka rock n' roll station. We sang to the Beach Boys, the Beatles, the Mamas and The Papas, and Peter, Paul and Mary.

When I was in junior high, I had a small record player and started saving my money to buy 45s and if I were lucky, maybe a whole album. There was no instant gratification with music back then. You had to wait for the next record to come out, and I loved going to the record store and gently flipping through the different records and studying the album covers. One of the first albums I bought was the Beatles Sgt. Pepper's Lonely Hearts Club Band. My friend and I sequestered ourselves in our basement, put a sign on the door that said, "Do Not Disturb," and listened to that album over and over in teenage rapture.

Music and smells must light up the same part of our brain. I remember a 9th grade party in John Van's attic, the Left Banke playing "Just Walk Away Renee" in the background. I remember hearing David Bowie's "Changes" as I was fired from a job and riding home from the airport in a taxi. I remember hearing James Taylor's "Sweet Baby James" the first time Vann and I drove to the beach in San Diego.

I like how you hear a song and then can't get it out of your head for a week. Usually it is something like the "I Wish I Were An Oscar Mayer Wiener," but oh well, music is good for the soul.

Good sleeping weather… The 10:00 p.m. weatherman said the night would be "good sleeping weather." He was right. I have heard this quaint term for as long as I can remember. As I lay in bed early this morning, I thought about how perfectly it describes the delicious temperature in the fifties, windows flung open in almost mid-November.

When we lived in the San Diego desert, "good sleeping weather" was not a term often heard or felt. Many summer nights, the daytime heat of 110 degrees simmered into the low nineties at night and the constant drone of the air conditioner did not make for perfect sleeping weather. The sheets felt as if they had been starched and ironed.

On visits to Vann's family in Florida in the summer, the "90/90" as they call it, 90 degrees and 90% humidity, made the AC grind and the sheets feel as if they needed to stay in the dryer another ten minutes. The air was as thick as a bowl of grits.

There are perfect sleeping places, and Kansas is one of them. I will take a warm fall night and a breeze stirred with wildflower smells, pouring into our bedroom like sleeping tonic. Even the cats sleep in the chairs under the window as if they, too, know that this is a special night to savor.

It is snowing in Denver, but here, it is just good sleeping weather.

The last leaf... Standing at the kitchen sink this morning, I drift my gaze to the Autumn Blaze maple with one leaf still hanging on. The bluebird lands and the last red leaf falls off. The leaf lays on the ground and then is joined by the others on the north wind headed south where leaves, too, must migrate for the winter. I will see you in the spring, all shiny and green again.

The two deer on the skirt of our prairie see me at the window and raise their gentle heads. They both seem to nod to me as if to say "good morning" in deer talk. They walk as if wearing ballet slippers on their heart hooves.

The cats do their cat yoga stretches, grab some kitty kibble, and then somehow, they know this is not an outside day so they find sun puddles and there they will stay.

I remind myself not to miss these little gifts of life happening around me. I am glad I saw the last red leaf blow south.

In your smile... A perfect afternoon spent with my beautiful niece, Jordan, chatting away over yummy food in Aggieville, the college groove of Manhattan. I have seen her grow from a baby into a woman with goals, the love of her life, George, a constantly pleasant disposition and much loved by family and friends. I look at her and see pieces of me, maybe it is our smile, pieces of my brother, her eyes with a shine in them, pieces of her mom with her athletic body, and most delightfully, she looks exactly like my mom and has from day one. I look at Mom's pictures and Jordan's pictures and a generation of genetics look like they skipped one generation and settled nicely into Jordan.

One of my greatest joys is having nieces and a nephew. I do not have children, but I believe that nieces and nephews are the "fun" kids you get to have, with conversations about anything, advice you can lavish on without being bossy, love that is boundless and always at the ready, and a relationship that has been built over two decades of "Aunt Ann dates." Thank you, Jordan, for sharing part of this day with me. I am all the better for having you in my life and, of course, Mikey, Reagan, and Miranda, too. But today was a special Aunt Ann date with Jordan.

❁ ❁ ❁

Birdbrain... One of the hobbies my cats and I share is bird watching. We are fortunate to live in Kansas where we have so many migrating birds, seasonal birds, and those dear birds who endure the cold winter months with us. The cats and I do not care what kind of birds they are—we just like watching.

I put an apple in the front yard this morning to see who might enjoy it. I was guessing crows and I was right. When I got home from tennis, the cats and I watched as four crows had an apple meeting. Crows are so smart, studying the apple, circling it, discussing it, and finally by some crow communication, one of them is nominated to go check it out. So, Mr. Big Crow hopped over to it and back several times, assessing the danger and the apple's potential. "Yes," he crowed, "it is an apple. Something yummy for us!" They proceeded with a thirty-minute apple buffet. Lots of crow crowing, beak pecking until there was not much more than the core left. At last, one of the bigger crows stuck his beak in the core and flew off with it.

I like our gorgeous red-headed woodpecker, too. He comes to the feeder and does woodpecker crunches while he eats. His hat is so glorious with its crimson feathers, and he looks like he has a tweed suit of black and grey wool.

The cardinals probably win the beauty contest. The male is resplendent in his red coat and the girl cardinal wears her Coco Chanel gorgeous, gray-green cashmere feathers.

The blue jays are like the noisy cousins that come to visit, break the points off your crayons, and then get back in the car laughing all the way. They are comical birds and seem to have a sense of humor.

My favorite bird is the red-tailed hawk. I call them mile-marker hawks as we see them "posted" about every mile on I-70. They look like meatloaves with wings as they are usually fat from good hunting in the corn and wheat fields. They are still and then suddenly lift to show their white underwings and gorgeous red fantail.

I would like to be a bird for a day. Maybe a turkey vulture with wings so big I could catch the warm lift of a Kansas south wind thermal. Birds are little gifts for us, a feast for the eyes.

Hammocks are the invitation for a "staycation." They are a place to throw a worn, soft patchwork quilt, to keep a book tucked at the ready to read, and always a place to take a lazy afternoon nap with warm breezes and smells of summer swirling around. More often than not, I am joined by one of the cats who precariously walks out to edges of the webbing before settling down against my leg for a kitty nap.

We had a hammock when I was a kid, a plain piece of tan canvas with ropes stretched between two sycamores, a fine place to relax. In the Bahamas, I discovered one of my favorite hammocks after a morning of diving and a lunch of fresh fish and fruit. There were hammocks strung throughout the palm trees, and quietly, everybody seemed to find one and take a lazy nap.

I have seen hammocks hanging like spider webs on the edge of El Capitan in Yosemite National Park. I cannot fathom how the climbers secure their little sleeping hammocks to the face of the sheer granite, nor would I catch a wink of sleep in one of them. Still, they are fascinating to see.

I will take my prairie hammock. In the spring, I will lie there and see the first prairie wildflowers pop open, the robins land and sip from the bird bath, the cats nestle against me for warmth, and we shall again be in hammock weather.

✿ ✿ ✿

I look at the clock, 2:18 a.m. I snuggle back into our turquoise sheets and the white cotton blanket. I want to get up and get one more blanket, but Jazzy is stuck against me like a ten-pound heating pad. As a kid, I would feel Mom quietly come in my room and drape another warm blanket over me with a light touch on my shoulder and one more kiss good night. Things mothers seem to know to do.

In the north wind, I dream myself to Thanksgiving years ago. The weekend before Thanksgiving was a cooking marathon at Mom's and Grandma's, with family recipes spread out like a game of poker cards on the kitchen counters. Mom and Grandma always wrote the name of the person who made the dish on the recipe card like "Great Aunt Vivian's Million Dollar Best Fudge," and often there would be a short word or two about where they had it or how it tasted (yummy). The weekend before Thanksgiving was cookie and pie baking weekend, and Grandma was the Pie Queen. She saved the scraps of pie dough for my brother and me, sprinkled them generously with salt, nutmeg, churned butter, and cinnamon, and we ate them hot out of the oven, downed with cold milk so we could quickly eat another one.

Three more days of school and the teachers were as eager for vacation as we were, though as a kid, I never thought about them being happy about the kid-free break, too. The three days were filled with movies on the stage at Crestview, all of our little behinds lined up in rows watching movies on outer space, the creatures of the ocean, and on rare occasion, maybe a Disney movie. The stage was polished like fine furniture, and I loved the smell of pine, the dusty curtains, and thirty kids. We made our Thanksgiving cards for our parents by placing our hands on a piece of construction paper and drawing the turkey shape. Add on the beak and feet and the feather fingers were colored in with our Crayola crayons. Hallmark could not compete with a handmade turkey card so proudly carried home to Mom and displayed for weeks on the refrigerator.

On Thanksgiving morning, I would hear Mom up at 4:00 a.m. putting the giant bird in the oven. Under my warm blankets, I was transfixed by the sense of home, the smell of turkey roasting, and Folger's coffee drifting down the hallway to my bedroom. I was up early to be with Mom, to get a cup of milk coffee, and eat cookies

139

or whatever might be laid out for the day. It was a magical day of smells, tastes, family, our cousins stopping by, naps, and leftovers stored on the hood of our Chevy in the garage. We never worried about food poisoning back then, and at 4:00 p.m. we all seemed ready for more leftovers, turkey sandwiches, cold dressing and, of course, more pie and cookies. There was thankfully nothing open and nowhere to go except our living room to enjoy each other, and by 8:00 p.m., sated with food and family, I was ready for bed. I said my prayers knowing that I had three more days of Thanksgiving vacation. The north wind comes to remind me, it is the season for gathering round, for sharing, and for slowing down.

Around the table… My dear husband, Vann, and my honorary sisters, Marilyn, Jeannine, Jeanne, Nancy, and I gathered around Marilyn's table last night to gaily commence the holiday season with Friendsgiving. While paper plates and buffets have their place, Marilyn takes such beautiful care with her table that we felt like we were being treated like royalty. I have always thought someone who actually owns chargers knows what they are doing, and that is Marilyn. The fireplace was adorned with gorgeous twinkle lights and a fire sent a warm hug into the living room.

The food was a feast for the eyes and the tummy and served on gleaming china, with even a dessert fork at the top of the plate. To go with the scrumptious food, a prayer of gratitude by each of us, filled to the brim of what makes us thankful. For all of us, it is this gathering. We have come from such different places and melded into a family of friends, sharing a meal, bringing each other up to date on kids, and pets—what families do. I told Jeanne that the dining room at Marilyn's is so elegant that I feel like I should behave!

'Tis the season to gather around with family and friends, express gratitude, and dream of cold days with a blanket, book, hot cocoa, and cats piled on me like small fleece blankets. The shadows of winter put the sun to bed early as we approach December. I will remember the start to this quiet season with my husband, my friends and their precious pups gathered round Marilyn's table. Gratitude for our Friendsgiving!

Ready for school with my
Big Chief tablet and farm lunch box

Ponytails, Barbies and parties
with my best first friend, Deb (right)

Chapter Ten

WINTER HOME

Seasons tumble over each other and I am letting this day pass slowly like the Kansas River current seeking its winter home.

The sweater… One Christmas, Mom gave me one of the most beautiful sweaters I had ever owned. It was the palest yellow and made of mohair with little artful designs woven into its bunny-soft yarn. It had mohair-covered buttons, and every fall, I got so excited when the TV weather guy would pronounce it "sweater weather." I would head to the basement and find my boxes marked "Ann's Winter Clothes" and unwrap my yellow sweater. Mom was smiling as she heard my footsteps hurriedly going up the wooden basement stairs with my treasure. Even though it would be a late fall day, still too warm for a sweater, she would nod and say, "Guess it's sweater weather."

Back to my bedroom, I got out my white Peter Pan collar blouse and the wool skirt my grandma made me to match the sweater. She said she found fabric that had all the colors of fall heaped into it. It was the softest wool in a pale yellow, orange, red, and cocoa brown plaid. When I had my special outfit on, it seemed to make me feel more grown-up, and I could not resist touching the soft wool and especially the mohair.

Ann Anderson

I ate with extreme care at breakfast and lunch and did not chase at recess. One of my teachers always stopped and said, "My, what a beautiful sweater."

Walking home, I was ready to put on my play clothes and go back to being a tomboy. But just for that day, I had on my beautiful, yellow mohair sweater, relishing the joy of being a girl and savoring the first days of sweater weather.

Tonight, Vann and I will celebrate our early Thanksgiving surrounded by Miranda, Mikey, Jordan, and Reagan. It is our second Thanksgiving without my brother, and we will offer a prayer for him in Heaven.

When my nieces and nephew were six or seven, gathering them together was as easy as going to their house and loading them in the car. No drivers' licenses and they were all available and eager to go to a movie, dinner, or just hang out. Now the planning is complicated with college and jobs, so it feels extra special to have them around the table for an evening. Our "Thanksgiving" will be a seafood buffet, but the evening is still an event of giving thanks for the wonderfulness of having nieces and a nephew. They remind me of the beauty of family to share stories, to have traditions (as Mikey likes to say) and to peek into their futures and the dreams they share with us.

I look in the mirror and think "Hey, wasn't I just six?" Some days that is still the age I feel, excited about life and upcoming events. I am glad we shared so much time together when they were little, when they were teenagers, and now as young adults smiling back at me. I do not take this evening for granted—they are not six anymore. The times to all be gathered around are to be savored.

The scent, laughter, and sweet voices of my nieces and nephew still hang in the air. There was no beginning and no ending to our evening, having delightful conversations, making hot chocolate from the hot chocolate bar (Did you know you can put Reese's peanut butter chips, marshmallows, whipped cream, and cherries in the bottom of your cup?) and blowing kisses as I saw their red taillights turn the corner. My heart is swollen with love for them, for my husband who quietly enjoys their company and asks good questions about their college life and plans, and now we are ready for bed. Our Thanksgiving night stretches out ahead of us, me with my sweetie, a steady warm Kansas fall rain, and three cats eager to find a place near us, waiting for the fireplace to flicker on.

Geese on wing… After a day of being stuffed with stuffing and sitting by the fire, we all found it easy to nod off to dreamland. In the night, I heard the little pecks of sleet against the window and had to look. Like antique glass, our windows were glazed over with nature's paint. I quickly grabbed another blanket and snuggled back into bed, lifting my sleeping buddy, Jazzy, who nestled in against my leg.

This morning I tippy-toed outside and heard the fresh crunch of frozen grass beneath my shoes as I filled up the bird feeders. Then, as if Mother Nature rewarded me, a flock of over 200 geese flew overhead, making their beautiful primal sounds. I could hear the flap breeze of their majestic wings, and I swear one of them looked down and winked at me. I am so glad I went outside and did not miss the geese. They were making V's in cursive writing, and their beauty still lingers with me.

Now warmly back inside, I sift through the happy Thanksgiving pictures everyone has posted like a quick visit to each home. The scent of spiced pumpkin pie and red cranberries almost seems to float off the page. This is slow Friday for me. To take in the holiday, to touch the cards we received, to hug my hands around a mug of coffee and watch the little birds eat the seeds laid before them for their Thanksgiving. The sound of the geese soothes my mind. My heart flies with them on their southern journey, and I land on a warm beach in turquoise water somewhere.

Our garage band… On this icy day of staying put, I thought fondly about days like this when I was a kid. Mom seemed to always have an instant plan for some fun, and many times, it was our garage band. We did not have a name, but we had many lively sessions in our living room with our cousins or whoever was around and brave enough to join in.

My older cousin would usually play the piano, and my brother and I were relegated to the bongo drums and wooden sticks. We always made pouty faces until Mom announced with some bit of flair that every band needed a "percussion" section. Since that word sounded so important, my brother and I decided that bongos and sticks were acceptable instruments to play. I often wondered why we had a set of bongos. I have no idea where they came from, but they sat on our piano my whole childhood.

The prized instrument was the ukulele that only my cousin knew how to play. I was permitted to tune it to the "my dog has fleas" sound but then had to hand it back as it was not a "toy" as my mom would remind me.

Our aunt's friend who lived in Hawaii in the '40s and '50s brought it as a gift when I was three years old. It sat on our piano for almost thirty years, and after my mom died, I inherited the pineapple-shaped, beautiful instrument.

My ukulele bucket list is to learn to play the exquisite rendition of "Somewhere Over the Rainbow" and "What a Wonderful World" by the famous and, sadly, now gone, Iz Kamakawiwo'ole from Hawaii.

For now, I am content to take the ukulele out, play a few chords, and hear in my heart the many songs played happily in our home so many years ago.

Winter's morning long ago… With nature's own Christmas decorations hanging like ice tinsel everywhere this morning, I lingered under my covers and thought about the times Grandma brought me breakfast in bed. This was a winter-only event when it was just me staying at my grandparents' house. To have Grandma all to myself was like hanging out with Glinda, the good witch from OZ, as everything was happy and warm and I seemed surrounded by a pink bubble.

I slept in the spare bedroom with its goose down mattress and crisp white sheets. I do not think colorful sheets existed back then (Grandma would not have approved) and her sheets were always white and soft. The quilts, handmade by my grandma, were mounded on top of me. Grandpa went to the basement and loaded shiny blocks of coal into the furnace before bed, and sometimes in the night if it were extra cold.

On very cold days, Grandma carried in a worn wooden tray covered with a flour sack dishtowel, which she made look elegant. I sat up, rubbed my eyes, and she would say, "Good morning, sunshine." She set the feast on a pillow on my lap. It was usually her pancakes, as thin as paper and stacked four inches high, each layer hiding a teaspoon of butter that the day before had been fresh cow's milk, cane syrup running happily over the edges like a golden waterfall to the plate. If the chickens were in the mood, she would add a fresh egg sunny-side-up with a yoke that was the color of daisy centers. A glass of orange juice and a cup of milk coffee (three tablespoons of coffee, milk and sugar) rounded out my breakfast in bed. She kissed my forehead and back downstairs she went, leaving me to feel like a princess eating breakfast in bed. Grandma was the last of the pioneer women in Kansas who knew how to work hard, never complained, always put others first, watched over family like a Rhode Island Red hen, and cooked a feast in thirty minutes. She always had time for me, to teach me how to roll out dough so it was not tough, to make a cross-stitched apron, to write cursive letters, and most of all, she taught me how little things are what weave a perfect life together.

After I had dined, I carefully set the tray on the chest of drawers next to my bed, got dressed, brushed my teeth, and carried the tray down the sixteen steps to Grandma's kitchen. I hugged her so tightly and told her I loved her so much. My face pressed against her house dress that smelled of nutmeg, her arms taking me in like angel wings.

It is beginning to look a lot like Christmas... In a flurry of holiday eagerness, we carried the red and green boxes up from the storeroom and Christmas poured out like spilled eggnog here and there in our home. Queenie deemed the little tree "hers" and curled up under it. It is joyful to unwrap each ornament that has nestled for a year in its holiday tissue paper.

My oldest ornaments are from Mom's trees, little cloth angels she wrote my name on, two elves that represented my brother and me, and my favorite, a star she made of aluminum foil wrapped over cardboard to top our tree.

I also carefully unwrapped my mom's Gurley choir collection from the early '50s. When she displayed them each year, she set them on a piece of Styrofoam she sprayed with glitter and fake snow out of a can. They are actually candles, but we never thought to light them as they were so cherished. I wish I could ask her when and why she first got them. But I still have them—the boy and girl choir in their red skirts and bows, a little fawn, the Santa and a pine tree laden in winter snow for them to sing around. When I was little, I peered into them and wanted to go live in that enchanting village on the Styrofoam base.

One year in Brownies, Mom was our leader and my troop made Christmas trees with Styrofoam balls, hundreds of tooth-picks stuck in them, stacked and the whole thing sprayed with glitter and snow from the can (which was very popular in the '50s). The project was meant to resemble a Christmas tree and as eight-year-olds, we thought it was the most beautiful creation we had ever made. It must have taken most of the fall to make, and some-one is probably still cleaning up glitter in our old basement.

My snowmen collection huddles on a bench as if the Snowman Convention convenes once a year. There is something about a snowman that always makes me smile.

On our pantry door, our collection of my nieces' and nephew's Christmas cards and pictures brightens the kitchen. From their little years in Christmas sweaters to their grown-up years, their smiles stay constant and happy.

Vann has a Santa Pig, a stuffed animal pig regaled in a stock-ing cap and scarf which snorts out "Jingle Bells." This is Vann's yearly treasure to display and put batteries in its piggy behind.

On these dark winter evenings, it will be so nice to turn on the lights and look at the ornaments I have kept all my life.

And presents round the tree... I have been in and out of a few stores lately, and it is always fun to see what offerings there are for Christmas. I already hear from my tennis kiddos what they want, ranging from Frozen stuff for the girls to Star Wars anything for the boys.

As a kid, I remember all of the packages under our tree spread out like a feast for the eyes and mind. Mom had a Santa's Work-shop set up in the basement with a large wooden table for wrap-ping presents. The Workshop was strictly off limits for us from Thanksgiving on. We never thought to break her rules. There she would gaily wrap and ribbon our packages and use saved old Christmas cards cut into shapes for the name tags. Mom was the original recycler and generously added glitter, spruce and random adornments that seem to make our packages simply shine.

My brother and I both loved board games. We started with Candy Land, Chutes and Ladders and graduated to Monopoly, Clue, and Life. I still have our Monopoly and Clue games that are slightly worn but in perfect condition, complete with the tiny race car, dice, play money, and the Clue pieces of the rope, candlestick, and knife (in the parlor by Colonel Mustard). We played those games endlessly and carefully put away all the pieces as they were treasured toys.

My brother got an erector set one year for Christmas, and for months he was busy building Ferris wheels, robots and other metal creatures. I think he was inspired to become an architect because of that toy.

Some of our relatives gave us clothes which everybody knows is not something kids want for a Christmas present. We murmured our thanks and tossed the socks or giant sweaters in a pile for later.

The Avon lady always brought me a little bag filled with the one-inch lipstick samples. I thought they were simply darling gifts, I proudly displayed them on my desk, and I was permitted to wear them occasionally.

I was a teenager when I gave Mom a very special present. We were at JC Penney's, and she admired a black coat so much that she tried it on. It cost $60.00, and I vowed I would get it for her. I tormented everyone for odd jobs to earn about $40.00 and in a final fit of generosity, my stepdad gave me the last $20.00 and took me to Penney's to buy Mom's coat. The salesclerk wrapped it in a big box, and I was so excited to give her the coat she wanted. She wore it for many years, and it was a reminder it is better to give than to receive.

I float back to those Christmas days with the tree laden down with mystery gift cards in its branches and the presents spreading out from under its boughs. The holiday scent of cedar and nutmeg, stockings bulging with oranges and small toys, our hearts filling with anticipation. At midnight, we were all in the pews at church with our candles in our hands and singing of the true season.

Sun/moon… Saturday mornings are for sleeping in, restoring the body and brain from the week before. On Saturdays, even as a kid, I was up and dressed by 7:00 a.m. Staying in my pajamas and robe made me think I was not feeling well. Sweatpants are the exception!

Vann says I have the "getting-up-early" curse of my farm family heritage. My grandparents were always up at 4:30 or 5:00 a.m. with chores of milking the black and white cows, feeding animals, making breakfast, and by 8:00 a.m., they had put in a full day's work. If I got up early at my grandparents' farm, I went with Grandpa to the cold barn and sat on a three-legged little stool he had built for me to watch the cows being milked. He tried many times over the years to teach me how, but I did not inherit the milking-the-cow gene.

Grandma usually had biscuits rolled out and in the oven by 6:00 a.m. While they were still hot to the touch, she would top each one with a piece of sunny butter that melted like yellow sweet frosting. Out the door we went to feed her beloved chickens. The chicken coop was warm and dark, and I liked to hear the chickens cooing and clucking their greetings to her. Grandma was a cat and chicken whisperer. The farm cats lived in the barn and were wild, but they would come when Grandma poured them a big bowl of warm cow's milk along with a plate of leftover eggs and biscuits.

Most mornings, Grandpa would take a work break and drive their '57 Dodge to 29th and California. Back in the '50s, it was a corner with Falley's grocery store, a gas station, and a small ice cream store. There was nothing on the other corners. The gas station was the morning meeting place for the local farmers, and they sat around a potbelly stove drinking coffee and talking farm prices and weather.

At home, Mom, too, was up by 5:00 a.m., paper read, dishes done and usually at least one project underway by 7:00 a.m. I guess the early bird does catch the worm or at least gets more done.

This morning, Jazzy and I are nose-to-nose at 6:30 a.m., and she whispers, "Let's get up, Mama." And so, we did. The depth of darkness was lifting to the east, and a broken slice of moon still hung in the western sky. The sun was rubbing its eyes and doing its best to rise in the east but did not want to leave its blanket of pink and gray soft clouds.

I watched three shiny black crows pecking at the sunflower seeds spread out on the edge of the prairie and wondered, "Do birds ever want to sleep in?" I guess not. Jazzy always seems to think that her mission is accomplished with me up and has already curled back in the granny chair for an early morning snooze. It is me alone in the house awake. I can hear the house breathing slowly. I turn on the lights of the Christmas tree, and they shine as if the sun has been caught in our living room.

With a cup of coffee in hand, I have "coffee" with all my Facebook pals as I scroll down and see what is happening in everyone's life. It is the "most wonderful time of the year;" as the song goes and from the posts, it would seem also the busiest. Holiday gatherings, family pictures, pets, and cartoons stare back at me.

I watch the sun heave itself up in the east. I will pour you a cup of coffee if you want to come over.

Toys in my attic... Too little sleep last night and too many errands today. As I wrap presents and write Christmas cards, my mind wanders back to the toys I got at Christmas. I was a tomboy but did have a few dolls that I really liked. I had a Betsy Wetsy that my fellow baby boomerettes will remember drank pretend milk which produced a pretend wetsy. Hmm—oh well, she was very popular. I begged for a Chatty Cathy, but Mom declined my requests and probably just as well.

I still have Mom's doll from when she was a child. It is made of some type of clay, dressed in my baby clothes, and very fragile. I am not sure how the doll survived being played with by my mom and then by me, but she now has a place of honor on my shelf with her 85-year-old unblinking eyes, still dressed in my baby clothes and my first pair of shoes.

I also have the very old doll that Grandma gave me. She has real hair, clothes my grandma made for her, including "nylon" stockings, and a small cradle built by my Grandpa for her to lie in.

My all-time favorite doll is my Pollyanna doll. Mom gave her to me for Christmas when I was eight years old after the Pollyanna movie with Hayley Mills came out. I was in LOVE with Hayley Mills, saw every one of her movies, joined her fan club and, as my friend, Debbie, can sadly attest to, I even used a British accent poorly after seeing The Parent Trap. Anyway, Pollyanna came with a red-checked dress and high-top shoes. In a fit of sewing inspiration, Mom made my Pollyanna doll a pep club outfit with a wool skirt, white blouse, vest, and red knee socks. Amazingly, a pair of my baby shoes fit her, and that is the outfit she has worn for over fifty years.

I also loved my stuffed animals, especially my cats and teddy bears. They were heaped like down comforters on my bed and guarded me day and night. One of my best teddy bears was a polar bear, pure white and beautiful. One day I was playing "doctor" and gave him a tummy operation. To make sure he healed properly, I carefully applied mercurochrome and cried for two days when Mom informed me that the iridescent red liquid would not come off my white bear. Ahhh, we live and learn.

My friend Debbie had a Barbie doll and all of us kids were mildly interested in her as we had never seen body parts like that and the black and white swimsuit she wore so dashingly. I think Debbie also had the Barbie Queen of the Prom board game, the Barbie Dream House and the Barbie Ultimate Closet.

Somewhere between childhood, dolls, stuffed animals, and sports, I found a balance. I am glad I still have my dolls to connect me with those halcyon days of my youth.

In 1960, one very cold, snowy afternoon, Mom picked up my brother and me from Crestview in our Chevy. This was an unusual event as we always walked or rode our Schwinn bikes to and from school. But Mom told us that morning that she had a big surprise for us! Well, you can imagine I couldn't sit still and was unable to pay attention during Mrs. Beatty's third grade teachings of multiplication and counting to ten in Spanish. At 3:30 p.m., my brother and I rushed to our warm, waiting car and Mom handed us both a pair of new red mittens—store-bought—not knitted. Most of our mittens, when we were kids, were made by a variety of our relatives and usually had enough room at the end of the fingers to hide a small animal, so we thought the store-bought mittens were our surprise.

But no, Mom mysteriously drove us to the then-empty lot by C&W Market on 21st Street. There were already cars parked and people assembling. Our excitement was reaching fever-pitch although we could not imagine what would be at our grocery store that earned us new red mittens.

We stood outside for maybe ten chilly minutes and then heard a flap, flap, flap low rumbling sound. Suddenly, from the west appeared a helicopter. We about passed out with excitement as we had never seen one up close, it was so majestic and graceful in the sky.

Slowly it landed in the lot and who should appear but Santa Claus! Yes, Santa Claus stepped out of the helicopter and gave every one of us a small toy and red and white candy canes. He asked each of us what we wanted while giving us pats on the head.

As I stood there in the thrill of the holiday, I reached for Mom's hand. She always wore beautiful black leather gloves, and I squeezed her hand and said, "Thank you, Mommy." We watched Santa get back in his helicopter sleigh, and with much wind and wonderment, the helicopter ascended into the thin blue, winter Kansas sky.

We drove home, weary from the adrenaline we had pumped all day, licking our sweet candy canes and so happy our mom had shared this very special Christmas treat.

❊ ❊ ❊

My little brother… I turned on my computer this morning, and as if by magic, a photo of my brother was the first to float onto my screen. It was recently given to me by my ex-stepsister when she was cleaning out my ex-stepdad's things. In a box were ten Polaroids of our family and the keepsake of my brother's high school picture still in its 1972 frame.

His birthday would be tomorrow. We would be gathering at his favorite Mexican restaurant with a few presents wrapped brightly in birthday paper and, as a joke between him and me, I always gave him one wrapped beautifully in Christmas paper. Like most December birthday kids, he dreaded getting presents wrapped in holiday wrapping. Mom always made a big to-do about any holiday, and I think she gave extra attention to Mike's birthday, so it was not the least bit like Christmas.

Mike was born curious about the world and never stopped zooming even after he began chemotherapy for his cancer. As a kid, he was always building something—a box trap with a string to catch an unsuspecting wild critter, ramps in our basement for his pine derby race car, and once, he built an elaborate "stop and go" sign. Mom got a call from Mrs. Wray who lived on the corner of Burnett Road and 21st Street. Mike, probably age seven, had walked there and was standing in the middle of 21st Street signaling the cars to "stop and go" with his homemade sign.

He was a gentle boy, quiet and thoughtful. Grandma taught him how to cook, and he could whip up a delicious pot of potato soup or chicken and noodles.

He struggled all through school until he got to Kansas State University where he found his true calling as an architect. Like the boxes that he built as a child, he began to build larger things and was happy with his profession his whole life.

Cancer took him from us at age fifty-nine. His best accomplishment was giving the world my nieces and nephew. We will all think of him this week, of how he knew the layers of limestone in Kansas, of his ability to put together anything, and of the love we all shared with him on his short time on this Earth.

Spilling gladness… On this day of my brother Mike's birthday, my spirit was a little flat, sad for missing my only sibling, sad for his kids away at college and readying for another holiday without their dad.

As this season is filled with miracles, mine came this afternoon from my little tennis kiddos. One after another, they came running in the front door of the Jayhawk Tennis Center, hands full of cards for "Coach Ann," a Frozen popcorn tin with a giant pink bow on top, a handmade sack and ornament, a card with Christmas pictures and the big block letters of a five-year-old proudly writing his name, and a box of candy with three feet of ribbon wrapped, wrapped, and wrapped around it. They spilled the gladness of this season into my heart. They reminded me of all that is so alive in my life. They reassured me that although we miss those who are no longer here, we take refuge and find joy in those who share this life's journey with us no matter how young they might be. For three hours, we ran, we laughed, we wore Santa hats, we pinky high fived, and at the end, their little hands clutched the brightly colored candy canes I had given them. I sit with their treasures around me tonight. Little presents, big heart.

Fall holds onto us. A pale breeze brushes my cheek and leaves pink and gray dusts of color on me. I sniff the air and smell the dry golden Aspen leaves of the high Rockies quaking with the fall chill. On the south breeze, I smell chicory coffee and beignets as if the air has drifted over Cafe du Monde on route to these prairies. The air is too light for winter, the breeze too warm for the week before Christmas, and it makes me all drowsy like a worn hammock strung up between two oak trees.

I am feeling the Gulf sweetness, seeing the graceful shadows of the crows as they land to sip from the birdbath. There is a scent of dried lavender mixed with the nutmeg and cinnamon of Christmas. Seasons tumble over into each other, and I am letting this day pass slowly like the Kansas River current seeking its winter home.

Believe… Santa Claus was The Man, the cool guy at the North Pole with a sleigh and eight tiny reindeer. As a kid, just the mere mention of his name at any time of year could instantly correct my bad behavior.

When I was eight and my brother was six, our doorbell rang on Christmas Eve morning. Mom told me to go see who was there, an unusual request as she or my stepdad usually handled people at the door. I opened the door to see a young man in a starched uniform with his name stitched over his pocket and a Western Union patch on his shirt. He handed me two telegrams and to my utter surprise and excitement, they were addressed one to my brother and one to me. I hurriedly signed for them and shouted to everybody, "We got telegrams!" Well, telegrams were something I had only seen in movies. To actually hold the crisp light tan envelope in my hand was like Ralphie getting his Little Annie Decoder Pin.

Mom had us sit at the kitchen table, and we both opened our telegrams. Mine said:

Dear Ann: You have been a very good girl this year, and I will be bringing your presents and your Pollyanna doll to you tonight. So go to bed early. Love, Santa

Santa Claus KNEW I wanted a Pollyanna doll! My brother and I sat in stunned Christmas silence as we absorbed the fact that

Santa was coming in just a few hours and that he actually thought we had been good that year.

The rest of the day floated by, and I made sure I did everything Mom wanted as to not jinx the "being good" deal with Santa. I went to bed at 8:00 p.m. that night as if going to bed could get Santa down our chimney sooner. We left him milk and four cookies on the Christmas plate Mom used every year.

In the morning, as promised, there were gifts from Santa and my beloved Pollyanna doll with a big tag, "To Ann, Love Santa."

That was the only time in my life I received a telegram. I truly believed in Santa Claus until I was about ten and then, as usually happens, one of my older cousins clued me in. I still believe in the spirit of Santa, in the magic that can be created by all of us in this season, and in that very special telegram my mom and Santa sent so many years ago.

I have been thinking about pleasant Christmas memories this morning. One Christmas when I was probably six, we had a true Kansas blizzard. We were at my grandparents' farm and stayed there for three days until the roads were plowed open. For us kids, it was a huge gift as we built a yard full of snowmen, had sweets and hot chocolate lavished upon us by Grandma, sat in Grandpa's warm shed where he taught us how to carve and most of all, had a grand time. There is something wonderful about temporary isolation.

I felt myself smiling about the memory of my first Christmas with Vann. We had been dating for six months and he had placed a small ring-sized box with my name on it under his Christmas tree. (Well, that is what I was hoping for.) When I opened it, I discovered a gorgeous aquamarine necklace and matching earrings. He said they were "cut out of the ocean." Oh well, I would have to wait two more years before getting the real ring box.

I remember our home in Borrego Springs, California, in the San Diego desert. We had a big pink, wooden coyote wrapped in lights for a tree. In the desert, it was warm enough for a Christmas day swim.

When Vann's folks were alive, we spent many Christmas holidays with them in Florida. How strange it was to see flowers in bloom and be outside in our tee shirts. We would go to St. Augustine with his folks, his brothers, Andy and Jerry, and his sisters-in-law, Vickie and Sandy, looking for sand dollars on the beach and eating key lime pie.

The first Christmas after Mom died, I went to Colorado and skied. It made Christmas seem like a normal day. Every year has a Christmas memory to remember.

I will take my home in Kansas today. Cozy with the fireplace, our cats, Vann pouring eggnog for my nieces and nephew and making new Christmas memories.

Thank you, Santa… I awoke to see a white Christmas, the outside painted beautifully with fog so dense, white, and heavy it looks as if we have a light Christmas snow. I am savoring my first cup of coffee, and with a touch of my finger on my keyboard, I am suddenly with everybody, seeing kids opening their wished-for presents, families gathered near, and that magic of Christmas that comes together on this day.

I am sending prayers to all of those who have lost a loved one this time of year, to those who are ill, and most especially to those who will spend this Christmas in a foreign country defending our ability to have a safe Christmas.

The malls, for just a moment are closed, the streets quiet in the fog, the multitudes of laughter "and good tidings to all" float on the foggy Christmas air.

Tomorrow morning, my nieces and nephew will arrive for a post-Christmas breakfast celebration, and I will be eager to hear all that is new in their lives. The present of being together makes us rich.

But for today, a Merry Christmas, almost a white Christmas, and a full Christmas moon tonight to shine down upon all of us.

Celebrations… Now that the red/green sparkle of Christmas is fading and decorations are being put away, it is time to prepare for the end of this year. I stopped by the store to get some balloons for my tennis kiddos and thought, "Who the heck is having all of these New Year's Eve parties with all of the decorations they of-fer?"

Vann and I will not be headed out to a big bash, nor will we be putting up the disco ball. Our idea of a New Year's Eve celebration is being safely at home with a good meal, the kitties, and bedtime before midnight. I will probably wake up when I hear the fireworks and look out to see them, and then back to bed.

As a kid, New Year's Eve held a certain excitement as if something truly magical would happen when we jumped into a new year. Mom hosted kid-friendly New Year's Eve celebrations, and usually my cousins would stay over. We would all sleep on the living room floor with layers of quilts spread out and all the pillows we could round up. Dinner was pizza, chips and dips, and we drank as many "Shirley Temples" (ginger ale, grenadine and lots of maraschino cherries) as we wanted that evening. Just staying up until 12:00 midnight was enough to make us swoon with happiness. If we were lucky, my older cousin would regale us with some spooky ghost stories or we would watch TV. There was usually a package of Black Cat fireworks that one of us had saved, and we shot them off in the cold December air. Mom might finish us off with a warm out-of-the-oven German chocolate cake, and we would sleep in the next morning.

When I became a teenager, I discovered the angst of New Year's Eve. Like in the movies, there was the expectation that at midnight, you had to be getting the perfect kiss from Prince Charming. That expectation persisted with me until my thirties when I decided it was not very realistic. One New Year's Eve, two of my girlfriends and I went to a party at the Holiday Inn for other unfortunate singles. At 11:50 p.m., we got on the elevator to go to another party and the elevator got stuck, so we spent New Year's Eve in the Holiday Inn elevator. It was not the romantic vision we all had for the evening.

Over the years, I have decided the best place to be to finish out the year is home. It is a nice day to reflect on the highs, the lows, and the in-betweens of the year and look with promise and excitement to the new year shining ahead. I hope you all get your New Year's Eve kiss!

✿ ✿ ✿

With this ring... Twenty-one years ago, today, 11:00 a.m. Pacific Standard Time, Vann and I stood with fifty of our closest friends and family on the bluffs at Torrey Pines State Park in San Diego.

We were married surrounded by nature and the sounds of the Pacific Ocean gently touching the shore that day.

In twenty-one years, we have both come to fully understand our wedding vows "in sickness and in health, for richer, for poorer," and all the good times and challenging times that weave together a twenty-one-year marriage. Through it all, we have been each other's best friend, cheerleader, listener, and shoulder to lean on.

I remember worrying about my hair that day. Getting married on a Sunday morning meant I was my own hair stylist and, in the end, decided that my hot rollers and I could do the best job. Phyllis was my matron of honor and was our original matchmaker. Paul was Vann's best man. As Mom was no longer with us, we placed a bouquet of long stemmed red roses on the bench by my brother and we all offered a prayer up to her.

The Torrey pines rustled gently throughout the ceremony as if whispering in delight at a wedding in their midst. When the "I do's" had been said, one of our guests spied two whales breaching out on the edge of the waves as if they, too, were applauding in approval.

The celebration moved to Epazote's, a Southwest restaurant overlooking the Pacific Ocean in Del Mar. Our wedding cake was a croquembouche, a traditional French wedding cake, with sugar spun around it like delicate vines.

Our honeymoon was a week of being surrounded by friends and family from around the country. Every day was a visit, going to the beach and the anticipation of our new life together as husband and wife.

One of my friends sent me a Time magazine when I was forty. It said that the likelihood of getting married after forty was the same as getting hit by lightning. Well, that may be, but I had to wait for Vann. Every year, January 1st is the beautiful reminder of the start of our life together. Happy Anniversary!

Hangover... Is anybody else feeling the January "What's next?" Now that the holidays are over and almost everybody has taken their decorations down, everything looks positively beige and gray. The kids will head back to school tomorrow, and maybe it feels like winter has officially started.

I am trying to re-capture that kid joy of winter. In our hall closet, we had our winterwear at the ready, always hoping for a big snowfall. We had Flexible Flyer 41J wooden sleds with the steel runners patiently hanging in our garage. My grandpa showed us how we could make them go faster by waxing the runners with soap bars. At the first big snowfall, we all loaded in the car to go to Quinton Heights. Back then, there was no school building taking up half of the hill, and it seemed like on a good snow day, most of Topeka was there joyfully taking a run and landing properly on one's sled for the exhilarating ride down the hill. We thought nothing of trudging back up the hill as many times as our parents would let us.

Back home, we peeled off layers of wet wool snow pants, socks, boots, and mittens to hang dry in the bathroom while we drank hot chocolate and shared our best runs. One time I even rented skis from Litwin's and skied down Quinton Heights.

Snowball fights were frowned upon at Crestview recess, but they were too tempting not to enjoy. Most of the teachers looked the other way. If the snow were deep enough, we would build a snow wall and have a proper snowball fight from our own forts.

It used to be cold enough to skate on the small pond at Gage Park. I had a pair of skates that had two runners on each one, and I could go straight pretty well. The pond's surface was rough from the Kansas north wind, but we all imagined ourselves in the skating finals of the Olympics trying a few jumps and turns.

When you are a kid, you are oblivious to cold, and each day holds the promise of what is next. I think I am going to put up some pink lights and maybe a small disco ball. Time to shake the holiday hangover and get back in the spirit of winter.

Happy birthday, dear Kansas. You were the thirty-fourth child born into this great Nation and like most middle children, you have often been ignored. Not pretty enough, not glamorous, not boastful, but those of us that truly know you and love you, know better.

If I close my eyes, I can hear your ancient waters wash over the great prairies. I can see your sea creatures greater than anything that now swims in the oceans. You have hidden them as treasures throughout the state for us to find from time to time.

Now you own the last of the great tall grass prairies. No other child can claim that. They are the amber waves of grain that run your width, from Oklahoma to Nebraska, and are a healing power for all of us that stop and listen to the bluestem stir in the south Kansas wind. Your sunsets light up with pinks and purples every night.

Your muddy, wide Kansas River is a vein of beauty meandering along the flat plains. You have ponds and creeks and lakes where we spend our spring and summer days.

Many dismiss you and talk about having to "drive across Kansas." But I know your simple beauty and your ability to restore my soul with your quiet wonders.

When I was a kid, I made you a birthday card every year. One year, my artistic abilities were especially motivated, and I made a paper plate sunflower with yellow construction petals, coffee grounds for your dark brown face and green pipe cleaners glued onto the back. I was positively dazzled by my creation and walked home holding the card with both hands. Mom pronounced it gorgeous and promptly adhered it to our Frigidaire where all notable art was displayed.

Kansas, you are home. You are that comfortable pair of slippers that always takes my cares away. You are restful to my soul. Happy Birthday, Kansas.

Mikey and Vianei—happily ever after

Chapter Eleven

MORNING AIR

As if winter whirled away, the door is open; the cats creep along under the shelter of the eves and sniff this morning air.

Amost perfect spring day… Vann and I headed west on I-70 armed with large sweet coffees on this late, crisp spring morning and our destination, Hays, America (as some call it) to visit my nephew, Mikey. It is a three-hour trip, but I never mind the distance knowing he is the gift at the other end.

The prairie was magical today. With all the rain, there were surprise rivulets of tall grass brooks running randomly along ancient wagon ruts. By next week, they will be only a memory.

The herds of cattle dotted the emerald green land, and there were little dots of new calves standing next to their mommas.

The ponds were gorged with water, and many of them had claimed small trees and grasses as temporary hostages to their overflowing edges. The sky was heavy with the remnants of last night's storm and the fat, gray puffed clouds lounged along the prairie's edge, as if the clouds, too, wanted to stay and look at the beautiful green of this place.

I know each exit, each rise in the tall grass prairie, past the grasshopper legs slowly pumping oil at Russell, seeing the first snow gates as a reminder that western Kansas gets the real weather (there was actually snow in Colby) and finally, Exit 159.

We met Mikey at his favorite place, Gella's Diner, and it is always as if we had just had breakfast with him the other day and back together. Family chatter as sweet as honey, big smiles, the best hugs, and hearing his steady plans for his future. And today, we met his new girlfriend, Vianei. She is the girl for Mikey – I can just tell by the way they sit touching shoulders and praise each other's accomplishments. I think Mikey has found Mrs. Right!

I know this boy. I know him as he is a small piece of me and everything perfect in this generation of our tribe. I have seen him through all trials in his life and stare in pride and amazement at his achievements and gentle heart.

We have grown together, and wherever I am, I carry him in my deepest feelings of love. He is the "World's Best Nephew"—a title that I bestowed upon him long ago and that he has always lived up to. It was a most perfect spring day in Hays, America.

May Poles and May Baskets… May 1st and I am thinking of long-ago traditions we had as kids. At school, we celebrated with May Poles. I have sadly forgotten their true origin as I no doubt was not paying attention to the teacher. Instead, I was enthralled with the idea of decorating the tetherball poles on the playground with yards and yards of brightly colored crepe paper ribbons. The janitor would obligingly attach the streamers at the top, and then we were joyfully allowed to run in opposite directions until the poles were festively wrapped in a myriad of colors. My class window faced the playground, and I felt my eyes drifting all day to the magificent makeover we had created.

After school I ran home to Mom, who was waiting with construction paper, scissors, and beautiful materials for us to make May baskets. I colored some flowers on the paper, rolled it into a cone, and Mom stapled the paper handle across the top. We filled the baskets with lilacs and sweets and I wrote Happy May Day on the side. It was a secret delight hanging the basket on the door latch, ringing the doorbell, then hiding and watching my friends' happiness at discovering a May basket. It was one of the first random acts of kindness I learned.

✿ ✿ ✿

Our last Mother's Day... Can it be that thirty-five years ago we were celebrating your last Mother's Day? It is a crease in my brain and heart forever as it was such a special day and one that you rallied to enjoy for yourself and us. I remember you wore a pink mod wig as it seemed to lighten the occasion of knowing it was one of the "lasts." You wanted Kentucky Fried Chicken with the works and said that you'd worry later about gaining some pounds. We put pinwheels all across the backyard, and the breeze made them spin gaily all day long.

When I think of you, I always connect with a quote from my favorite book, To Kill a Mockingbird. "There just didn't seem to be anyone or anything Atticus couldn't explain." For all my life, that is how I have felt about you. Your talents were endless, yet I never saw you wish for attention nor recognition. You were the "Atticus" in my life.

When I was four and had eye surgery, the doctor had me wear a black eye patch for two weeks. I was so self-conscious about it and voila—you were suddenly throwing a pirate party and made all the kids pirate patches just like mine.

You were a liberated woman before there was even that term. Homeroom mother, Brownie leader, PTA President, Sidewalk Chairman, and Vice President of Kansas Day. I will never forget going to Kansas Day the year you were in charge, and you were at the head table. You gave a speech and threw me a quick wink. I thought, "My mom is the coolest mom in the world!"

You took me to so many meetings where I learned to talk to anybody and everybody, and you and I practiced doing a proper handshake and saying, "How do you do?"

You were always ready to head to the backyard with our mitts, bat, and a ball and teach me how to bunt and catch a fly ball, and you said, "Don't let a boy win just because you're a girl." You could hit a backhand down the line, whip up a four-course meal for un-expected guests in thirty minutes, bowl a 250 game while drinking frozen daiquiris with your bowling team, and then change the oil in our Chevy.

I still smell you. You are the scent of Juicy Fruit and Chanel No.5. I miss you. I have pieces of you in me, and I try to put them in your grandchildren though they never knew you. When I pass the Mother's Day cards this week, I will catch my breath with the memory of our last Mother's Day celebration so long ago, holding that day in my heart and knowing how much effort you put into making all of us feel "normal" for one last holiday. I still pick out a card for you that has just the right words and then gently tuck it back into the slot.

Breakfast in bed... Thankfully, the cats did not try to bring me breakfast in bed. They did manage to drag home a darling card from the three of them for Mother's Day.

When I was a kid, my brother and I planned our mom's Mother's Day breakfast in bed for weeks in advance. We would secretly give our grocery list to our stepdad, who was not a shopper, and hope that he brought home our desired ingredients. We always undertook "Julia Child type projects" undeterred by our lack of culinary skills.

Mom patiently waited in bed until 9:00 a.m. for us to serve her our culinary creations (she normally got up at 5:00 a.m.) After enjoying our feast, she entered her kitchen only to discover it had reached a level of DEFCON 3 clean-up! Our chocolate chip pancakes seem to ooze from between the burners, bacon grease ran down one wall, and orange juice spread out across the floor like a river approaching flood stage.

One year Mom switched tactics and started talking about her favorite breakfast. She announced one morning about a week before Mother's Day that she absolutely loved Rice Krispies with milk and fresh strawberries.

Geez, my brother and I looked at each other like we had discovered national secrets. So that Mother's Day and from then on, she was awarded her favorite breakfast at about 7:00 a.m., Rice Krispies with fresh strawberries.

One Mother's Day, many years later, she finally told us how she had solved her yearly kitchen clean-up dilemma and having to wait in bed until 9:00 a.m. Mom always seemed to have a way to solve a problem and everyone was the better for her solution. I guess that is one of the things that moms do best.

Sun catchers… The cats hang today like sun catchers in a window, turning toward the sunbeams. The cats are the sun's soulmates, tummies turned up to the warmth, shifting from side to side to get just the right light on them. My hammock is a dream catcher with me caught in its warm web today. I think about leaving it for some random errand, and then find I have been woven back into its deep comfort. The smell of the columbine hangs in the air like a ninth-grade girl's Ambush perfume. Lavender floats through the air, too, with clean scents of sea and sun.

Out across our prairie, the swallows edge and dip in the warm air. They have filled their bird condos with the first of this year's babies that have already fledged from their box to the big shade tree. Farther out, four turkey vultures lazily catch the Kansas thermals. From a distance, they are fetching, and I envy their flight and wing. And yet, there is no finer place than this hammock today. A Santa Fe blue pillow tucked under my head, a glass of iced tea and Pilgrim at Tinker Creek just within reach and that sense that this is the beginning of many lazy porch days.

Jazzy is transfixed by a roly poly bug until she loses interest and resumes her full sun stretch. We see the fat, comic bumblebees bump against the screen, and the robins are at the swimming hole for their first summer dip.

8:00 a.m. cloud… Somewhere over Hays, America this morning, a puff of cumulus cloud made itself appear. The dry, thin air of western Kansas is not an easy place to make oneself into a cloud, but it was the beginning. As it drifted east, it gathered some Gulf moisture blown up over the central Kansas prairie by Salina. Feeling more confident, it grew and added some little clouds to keep it company. By Abilene, the little Hays cloud had made a line of a cloudbank and thought—we can do this! It now stretches like jet contrails mashed together in the far western sky. Tonight, it will grow tall with giant tops and spin more moisture into its core.

When I lay my head down to sleep tonight, the little cotton ball cloud from Hays will be a thunderstorm. It will shower my blanket flowers and cosmos with fresh rain and leave drops hanging for the spider to drink in the morning.

Ann Anderson

Balloons float... May seems to come in like a lion and go out like a lion with a full month of events. We drove around town today and saw cars parked happily along the curbs, BBQ smoke and smells drifting up from the emerald green, just-cut lawns, and people spilling out of cars carrying bags full of graduation offerings.

At Lake Shawnee, there was not an empty picnic table to be found. People stood side by side and smiled into the camera lens to forever imprint this day into their memories. (Years of waking up, eating breakfast, going to school, studying, and being surrounded by friends and family who encouraged us to get it done.) I blink and think, I was just walking through the daisy chain graduation line at Topeka West, and then another blink, and I am walking down the Hill at KU to my graduation.

May seems like one of the happiest months with all the celebrations of new beginnings and what life holds in store for us. Another week and the official start of summer, Memorial Day. I am making myself a promise to savor this summer, to eat more chunks of fresh watermelon, to lie in my hammock every day and read dime store paperbacks with a cat or two tucked around me, to play lots of tennis with Vann, to see my nieces and nephew every chance I get before they graduate next year from college, and to taste all those things that summer serves up. I am floating balloons around me and making little pictures of all the beautiful events we celebrate in our lives.

Rain love... If you have never lived in the desert like we did, you might not truly appreciate rain. The San Diego desert averages three inches of rain a YEAR, if lucky, and it usually occurs in a one-day downpour. When we lived there, I literally bought CDs of thunderstorm music to play in my car and house, so I could at least hear the sound of rain. Growing up with Kansas rain, it is as much a part of me as the tall grasses and four seasons.

Rain slows us all down. We might fuss about it, but it is life-giving and soothing. There is nothing better than burrowing under a worn patchwork quilt, a book in hand and some cats to join me on a rainy afternoon. Listening to the gentle plop drop of the rain, sleep will soon overcome me.

Mom celebrated rainstorms with Coca-Colas, Rainy Day popcorn balls, and our webbed lawn chairs set out under our breezeway. We would sit there and watch the rain and have lazy chats about our hopes and dreams.

I am peaceful this morning, watching and listening to our rain.

I look like you... A friend told me the other night that I look so much like my mom. A lump was in my throat, and I said, "Thank you, but I just don't see it." When I got home, I stood in front of the mirror for the longest time trying to soak in your resemblance. You had shiny dark brown hair, dark brown eyes, full lips always sporting the latest dark red Avon lipstick shade, and a smile that seemed to rest on your face like you were born with it.

I have blonde hair, hazel eyes, fair skin, and, well, I want to see you looking back at me, but do not. Maybe the best thing is I feel the resemblance to you every day inside of me. I feel all of that joy you put out to the world, I feel the nurturing you gave to your family and friends, I feel the desire to run and jump and do sports, I feel your heart wrap inside me every day with your gentle words, your hugs, your fingertips wiping away a tear and your smile when I did things to amuse you. Maybe I have your laugh, your desire to make everyone feel a little better, to toss around some color and glitter, and to refuse to see the bad in people and the world. Maybe I have your tender hands that lift up a kitten and whisper to it and your fierce love of nature and the Kansas winds and prairie.

Maybe all that feels like you inside of me makes me look like you on the outside to everybody. There is nobody I would rather look like and be like in this world than you.

Rich.... I am rich. I have been lying in my hammock for an hour with two cats pressed against me, their motor purrs are reassuring sounds of peace. Every now and then, Jazzy will turn and press a sweet biscuit of cat paw love into me. Sigh. I am rich.

Yesterday I played tennis and taught tennis and then got the surprise of running into my nephew, Mikey, who was working out. A warm nephew hug, his smile so huge and true, knowing we are glued as family together forever. I am rich.

Today, Vann and I wandered through the rows at the farmers' market. We bought tomatoes red and firm and baby Yukon gold potatoes. Vann could not resist a small bag of oatmeal and dried cherry cookies. We sampled the hot kettle corn so tempting with its sugary salty crunch and discovered the lady with buckets of purple, yellow and lavender iris. I stooped down to breathe in their light spring scent.

We had a feast on the porch—roasted new potatoes, sliced tomatoes with sea salt and cracked pepper and fresh basil snipped from our herbs. We are rich.

To the west, the clear skies have darkened to thunderstorm blue, a color that I think should be a paint chip. It is marvelous to see against the new chartreuse and kelly-green leaves of the forest. I am rich to see such a beautiful sight.

I read a lovely post by my friend, Rita, about the simple life she sees outside her window. It made me realize that with each passing year, I more fully understand that being rich is having my husband, friends, family, my kitties, farm to table food, love, my faith, and the simple life of soaking up a day of small moments. I am rich.

Flyover state… I flew home from Denver across this Kansas prairie that is called a "flyover" state. From the dry, flat scrub land of eastern Colorado, we cross over into Kansas, her border still tugging at the Mountain Time zone for reasons I cannot fathom. Down below sprawls Goodland, Kansas, that edges into big, wide ranches dotted with cattle like brown and black Legos.

My eyes rest on the Great Plains so flat with shades of green, brown, rust, and yellow. The bright green rounds of irrigated western Kansas land fit neatly into the squares of the section lines.

I see Central Kansas and the gentle ground starting to swell with rivers running through it, brown murky water spilling over the banks from generous spring rain. The grain elevators are like tinker toys poking up to the sky, and by summer's end, they will bulge with the heartland's bounty of golden grains to feed a nation.

I look around the plane, and most people by now are dozing or intently watching something on a laptop. But I stay watching my flyover state now turning so green it looks like tempura paint has been poured everywhere, and then a child has finger painted in blue swirls of lakes, streams, rivers, and thin silver highways that hug the section lines so neatly.

The plane noses up, and wheels give that reassuring thump bump of a safe landing. At the gate, Vann is waiting with a hug, a surprise Starbuck's, luggage is claimed, and a welcome catchup on the ride home. The air is so sweet and scented. I am no longer Rocky Mountain mile high where I must take in two gulps for every one Kansas breath.

We sit on our porch. The neighbors are having a small pool party, the happy splashing of kids cannon balling in, the adults dipping toes in the water and sipping the first summery drinks. Summer sounds make me drowsy, and the south wind feathers across me. The cats are stretched and only an ear occasionally flicks when they hear a bird. They are too content to even move.

I am home to this place that so many know only through jet contrails streaking overhead in the late afternoon blue sky.

Pieces of you… Today was wash-my-driveway day. I love getting the hose on jet blast and cleaning out the crevices and cracks, seeing the dirt of winter wash away. I think of you cleaning our driveway and then proudly announcing, "You could eat off our driveway," and yes, that was true. Somehow, a little DNA of you is in me, and I, too, like that perfectly clean driveway.

As I was finishing, Vann shouted out the open window, "Good job, Irene!" It made me smile to hear him say that as he never got to meet you but knows of your legendary driveway cleaning. I have been finding you in me today for some reason. Playing tennis this morning, I heard you whisper, "Are you doing your best? Are you having fun?" Yes, Mom.

Then home to fix Vann a lunch somehow inspired by you. Cukes and onions in a vinegar and sugar water bath so fragrant that it could be a fine perfume, thick-sliced red tomatoes with snips of fresh basil, corn-on-the-cob with your ancient cob holders firmly pushed into each end, new red potatoes dusted with fresh sharp rosemary and thyme, and a bowl of watermelon chunks so ripe and juicy to finish off the porch feast.

Today is my dear friend's fifth year of surviving breast cancer, and maybe that is why you have been especially near me today. Your valiant and long battle with breast cancer was not to end properly at fifty-six, and, oh, how I so wish every day that you were here, and we were every year celebrating a birthday for you and another year of surviving. You spilled so many joyful memories into our lives as if you must have known you would be a short-timer angel on this sweet Earth and then leave us.

I remember the smothering summer night we had an impromptu water balloon fight outside. Finally, with everybody dripping and happy, we waved the surrender flag. We trudged into our house, and out of nowhere, you appeared and turned the hose on full blast in our dining room. We were stunned into place, and my cousins and I talked about it for days. What a cool mom!

Last night, I saw the first lightning bugs and thought of you. You filled up your short time with so much sparkle and then we had to let you go. I hold tightly to those pieces of you in me and think of you on this most special five-year anniversary day.

Dry line… After an evening of porch sitting, we watched the 10:00 p.m. news and saw that distinctive dry line out over Western Kansas. It looked as if a kindergartner had taken fat orange and red Crayola crayons and drawn a jagged line across the width of our state. I smiled, knowing that slice of a red-orange line would promise a late-night rainstorm for us. With cushions pulled inside, we tucked into bed with the warm rain smell already perfuming the air. I heard the storm start with my window open to catch its beautiful beginning. At first, the sound of raindrops plopped and then the red line brought the steady downpour that only a Midwest storm can accomplish. I slipped from the bed, put on my ancient KU hoodie, and found a place in the middle of the porch to take in the late-night treat. I am alone in the night. I am surrounded by the darkness of night and the neighborhood sound asleep.

I was delirious with the pleasure of sitting in the dark, the rain and nature all about me, the air washed so clean and fragrant, lightning like the Northern Lights making a curtain call across the western skies. Soon, the storm pulled the dream dust back over me and I nestled back into bed. Jazzy jumped up to fill up the space in my bent legs, and we were both fast asleep to the last drops of the dry line rain.

This morning, the sun warmth slanted through our shades and I blinked. Did I dream the rain? I turned on the TV and saw the dry line now melted into Monet pools of light green floating out to the Ozarks.

Float like a butterfly, sting like a bee.
Meeting the great Muhammad Ali

Float like a butterfly… I was at a friend's pool party and one of my friends said, "Great picture of you and Muhammad Ali." I was just astonished because I did not remember that this picture existed. A friend had posted it on Facebook to acknowledge Ali's passing.

I will never forget driving down Topeka Blvd. with my American Cancer Society colleagues, Sheryl and Tonnie. As we pulled up to the light at 17th and Topeka Blvd., a huge black limo rolled up next to us. We were crazy, happy young girls so we, of course, lowered our windows and started shouting stuff like "Who's in there?", "Are you famous?", "Roll down your window." And slowly, the back, rear window came down, and there peered out the amazing and real-life Muhammad Ali. His driver signaled us over, and for the next thirty minutes, we were chatting with him, and he was inviting us to a boxing event that night in Junction City. We should have gone, but I think the three of us were too stunned to be standing at 17th and Topeka Blvd. with "float like a butterfly, sting like a bee" Ali. He was so gracious, seemed to enjoy talking with us, and then we obviously posed for an amazing snapshot of happiness. I have never forgotten that chance encounter and always think of it when I drive by that spot.

We went back to the office and told everybody, and no one believed us. Now here we are many years later. It is a gift to again see our smiling faces gathered around that boxer, humanitarian, and gentleman who was nice enough to roll down his limo window.

❀ ❀ ❀

And the winner is!... A true short story. From the time I was five or six, Mom and I watched the Miss America pageant. We always cheered first, of course, for Miss Kansas. Mom even took me to Pratt one time as a surprise to see the Miss Kansas pageant. Though I was a devout tomboy, I guess there was enough girly girl in me to want to look like the participants.

For several years, I decked myself out like I was in the pageant on TV. Mom obligingly applauded with each of my entrances in my evening gown (my church dress), my swim wear (my tank suit) and, at a commercial, she came up with some clever question for me to answer. My talent consisted of playing the piano, turning a cartwheel, or singing a song.

Anyway, every year Mom and I parked on the couch in front of our big console TV with a bowl of popcorn and Cokes for THE event. There was the dazzling array of evening gowns heavy with glitter and pearls, the ever racy, before political correctness, swimsuit challenge, the yikes—question and answer session—and always the big dance productions and talent segment. And then—voila! Miss America would be crowned, and all the girls around her looking happy as can be. Even as a kid, I was thinking, "They are good actors."

I think it was 1964 when Mom and I watched Vonda Kay Van Dyke win the pageant. For some reason, she just stood out to us, and I always remembered her name. So, here comes the true story part.

Vann and I were living in Del Mar, California. Vann's college roommate, Sonny and his wife lived in Orange County, and Vann invited them down to meet us for Sunday dinner at The Fish Market in Del Mar. In walks Sonny, and he introduces his wife—Vonda Kay Van Dyke! Yes, my jaw dropped open and I was speechless. Then probably like hundreds of others I said, "My mom and I watched you win Miss America!"

About thirty minutes later, a young couple sat down at the oyster bar a few seats across from us. It was a slow evening and we nodded hellos to them. Then we struck up a conversation which led to introductions. Vonda Kay introduced herself, and the young woman said in a halting voice, "My name is Vonda Kay, and my mom named me after you."

I will tell you, the six of us just sat there in complete silence soaking in the utter astronomical odds of these two sitting at the same oyster bar in Del Mar, California. After the shock kind of wore off, the two Vonda Kays chatted non-stop and exchanged addresses and phone numbers. Our friend, Vonda Kay sent the young Vonda Kay several signed pictures and one of her albums.

It was a once in a lifetime chance meeting. Every time I see the Miss America pageant is on, I remember watching it with Mom and, years later, the magic of two Vonda Kays meeting each other. Ain't life amazing!

❁ ❁ ❁

While we were doing the dishes, I thought about how lovely it is to dine with friends and family and share a good meal. Restaurants are fun and easy, but there is something so nourishing to the heart and mind in making food and sharing it.

When I was a kid, there were few restaurants, and it was a very special occasion to go to one. Every morning I drink my smoothie and think back to Mom cooking eggs over easy, sausage, pancakes and bacon for my stepdad. Sometimes my brother and I would have the big breakfast, but usually we just had our regular bowl of Rice Krispies with about three tablespoons of sugar and whole milk. What a simple time that was when no one was counting calories, "low fat" and "sugar free" had not been invented, and about the only processed foods were macaroni and cheese and Chef Boyardee.

Mom was one of the best cooks, and we had somewhat of a food routine. We always had fried chicken on Sunday, chili on Monday, tacos on Tuesday, and when we got to Friday, for some reason as we were not Catholic, we almost always had fish sticks and Tater Tots. My brother and I thought that was about the best meal Mom could make, which was actually just dumping it all on a baking pan. But oh well, we liked it with lots of ketchup and tartar sauce.

In our childhood, we consumed thousands of sandwiches from liverwurst to bologna to my favorite, big chunks of bright yellow-orange Velveeta plopped onto white Wonder Bread and nestled in a pillow of Miracle Whip. To accompany the meal was some type of chip and our all-time favorite, Hawaiian Punch. I would have consumed Hawaiian Punch every day if Mom had allowed it. My brother and I had frequent discussions that when we grew up and had jobs, we would drink Hawaiian Punch with every meal.

I miss the days of not worrying about what you are eating, but a meal was just a time to gather around our Formica table, hold hands for a blessing, and hope that Mom might pour us some Hawaiian Punch.

Kansas rain… As if winter whirled away, the door is open; the cats creep along under the shelter of the eves and sniff this morning air. It is a morning to turn over and nest into the blanket, but the lure of a quiet rain pulls me from the warmth of my bed.

The grass is still pale green as if it has been spray-painted and needs one more coat. But it is not winter beige and it gladdens my heart to see the color.

My hammock stand seems to smile a crooked metal smile at me as if to say, "Come on out, let's give it a try."

Mid-century basement… When we were kids, we rarely ran out of things to do. But occasionally, one of us might say, "I am bored." Mom had a saying or quote for just about everything and she would reply, "If you're curious, you're never bored." Then she would give us a long list of things we could do like cleaning our rooms, reading the World Books, and practicing our numbers. Most of the time, we said we would go clean the basement which was just a way to head down to the basement.

We had the perfect 1950s basement, unfinished with a concrete floor and walls with steel poles standing like bare metal trees every twelve feet. Our basement provided us an endless opportunity for year-round fun.

On one wall, I meticulously drew a tennis net complete with posts and a menacing looking opponent standing on the other side. I was content for hours to hit against this guy until his chalk form would fade away from my blasts.

My brother and I also had a ping pong table, and it was always game on.

We had a small tool bench, and occasionally we were moved to create some craft. One year we got a thing that cut wine bottles in half, and we had a beautiful, if not rough, set of new glasses. We urged our parents to drink as much wine as possible to complete our set of green, thick glasses.

Our sidewalk chalk was in an empty Folger's coffee can, and we were free to create as many pieces of fine basement wall art as we wanted. We could play school, writing out sentences creating math problems-all on our basement wall.

We had our roller skates in the basement, too, and could snap them on our feet and skate fast, catch the poles and whip around like roller derby. We pictured ourselves as roller derby champions and made up scary sounding names for each other.

After playing all afternoon in the basement, we would trudge up the sixteen stairs, no longer bored, but happily weary and our minds still caught in whatever game we had created. Mom would have on her "Mona Lisa smile" knowing that she had worn the boredom out of us. We were rewarded with Hawaiian Punch and maybe a Hostess Cupcake. Mom was right. If you're curious, you're never bored. (Having a basement helps too.)

To everything, turn, turn, turn... (Ecclesiastes 3:1-8) ... I am awake this morning too early, but more and more, my farm ancestors seem to be invading my body and I think there are cows to milk in the dark at 5:00 a.m. The cats open one eye as if to meow, "Just curl up and go back to sleep."

As a kid, I loved to wake up early. My alarm clock would be the oh-so familiar tin pop of Mom opening a new can of Folger's coffee and the perk-perk sound of her GE percolator. She kept the coffee with a small silver scoop in her Tupperware container. I did not drink coffee except milk coffee but I liked to open the container and smell the rich brown crystals, and I liked it when Mom asked me to measure the coffee into the percolator.

Ann Anderson

The smells were so warm, inviting me to slip out from under the covers and join Mom in the kitchen. Miss Kitty, our Siamese cat, would have already been up, eaten and curled back in front of the heat register for an early morning nap. On a very cold day, we could wear pants under our skirts to school and recess would be indoors in the multi-purpose room. My brother and I would run the five blocks home in a cold, north wind at lunch and be rewarded with watching High Noon Cartoons and eating a Swanson's chicken pot pie, so hot that steam erupted like a tiny chicken volcano when our forks dug into the comfort food.

This week has been a swirl of emotions. From the death of two friends early in the week to a tennis training day with my fellow coaches and then, lunch with my beautiful nieces, Jordan and Reagan. We watched a video at lunch on their phone and laughed so hard that the people around us were smiling, too. Their youth was a tonic in the midst of the sadness of this week.

My soul was pulled down and, by week's end, restored with God's love.

"To every thing there is a season, and a time to every purpose under heaven.

A time to be born, and a time to die; a time to plant, and a time to pluck up that which is planted.

A time to kill, and a time to heal; a time to break down, and a time to build up.

A time to weep, and a time to laugh; a time to mourn, and a time to dance."

Life's big moments... In between learning our backhands tonight with the tennis kiddos, we also lost a baby tooth—a first in my years of teaching. It was exciting for everybody! We admired the loose tooth at the beginning of class with wonder. One of the boys suggested we tie a string around it, I could hit a ball attached to the string, and it would come out. This was met with much enthusiasm from everybody but me and the owner of the loose tooth. Cooler heads prevailed, and the tooth was bravely wiggled out. The tooth owner was then rewarded with extra smelly stickers from the Tennis Tooth Fairy.

It has been years since I have been witness to losing a baby tooth, and it will have me smiling all evening. So special to share in one of life's little big passages and to see a child, her tooth held proudly in a paper towel, growing up one baby tooth at a time.

Music to my ears.... As a baby, I had a musical toy hanging over my crib that played "Twinkle, Twinkle, Little Star." When I was four, Mom installed a magical device on my light switch that played "Lullaby and Goodnight." She would twist the knob, and I was instantly transported to dreamland. Some of my nicest toys were little music boxes. I would never tire of carefully turning the handles and hearing the nostalgic sound of their songs like long ago carousels.

As I grew older, music came to me through KEWI radio, and I owned a turquoise transistor radio that was never out of reach. I would shoot up its gleaming silver antenna and capture the crackling sounds of music. It was a necessity for spending long days at Crestview Pool or hanging out in the backyard.

I owned a small record player with the little inserts for 45s and had some 78s of Annie Oakley, Davey Crockett, and eventually, teenage records. It was so exciting to buy a 45 and rush home to share it with friends. Maybe I am wrong, but it seemed like music was more of a shared event when I was a teenager. We would sit around the record player and soak in the new songs from The Monkees, The Beatles, and The Rolling Stones.

When I was at KU, I remember sitting for hours in my dorm room with my roommate Leslie and listening to Neil Young. We refused to allow anyone in, so we could truly savor the songs. (What dorks!) We listened to Gordon Lightfoot and saw his concert on my twenty-second birthday at KU. We even tracked down his phone number and called him in Canada. Mom about passed out when she got that long-distance phone bill of $30.00. Oh well, it was worth it.

There were music sessions on soft spring afternoons after class with my friend, Susie, on her upstairs, flat roof at her house near campus. In beanbag chairs, we listened to Sweet Baby James Taylor singing "Fire and Rain" and it was like an instant vacation to the beach. KU students meandering by would look up and hum along. Music was ever present during those college years.

When I got my first car, I immediately took some of my work money and had an 8-track tape player installed in it. Could life get any better? I started my 8-track collection of chunky tapes—Cream, James Taylor, Crosby Stills Nash and Young, Bob Marley & The Wailers, ABBA and the Beatles. But by far and away, it was The Eagles "Hotel California" that was my go-to song. To this day, it is still my favorite song, and it transports me to those mystical days of listening to my new records.

It is good to have a song in your heart.

Snow falling softly on our cedars... I am taking in the quiet cover of snow on the prairie. We fed the wild turkeys a mound of ground corn which they promptly discovered in the front yard. I was astonished to open the blinds and see ten of them there. They are huge with feathers knit like a crazy quilt of soft brown velvet and tied with golden threads. They knew the cats and I were watching, and I swear Big Boy turkey winked at us as if to say, "Thanks for this snow snack."

Last night, I heard laughter and yelling and looked out to see the neighbor kids on their sleds zooming down the short hill by our house. Their laughter was infectious, and I stood there absorbing their joy. Like my friend Patty wrote about snow angels, watching kids and snow is just "Winter tonic."

I remember as a kid the anticipation in hearing that a big snowfall was coming. Usually our first hope was for a day without school, but then it was on to dreaming about our sleds, snowball fights, hot cocoa, and the task of building snowmen. Though we tucked our pants into our rubber galoshes with buckles, our feet would usually be small blocks of ice by the time we were done playing outside.

Snow slows the world, makes us take notice of its beauty, and I remind myself not to worry about shoveling the drive, but to watch the kids playing in the snow magic. The neighbors' dogs relish the snow like they have been given a giant dog playground. They run and roll and seem to feel that same childlike thrill of a snow day.

The Eskimos have fifty words for snow. Today, I just have one. Pretty.

The marshmallow test... Years ago, someone created the marshmallow test of putting kids with one marshmallow in front of them. The key was to wait patiently and if you did not eat the yummy puff, you would get a second one. I think I could have waited, and I might have talked somebody out of theirs, but I was thinking about it today as I went to the one-hour eyeglass store.

As kids growing up, we never ever expected anything immediately. One hour was a TV show, not the time it took to get pictures printed or new glasses made. When I was lucky enough to get new glasses, I would wait excitedly the two weeks it took to get them back from some mystery lab. Then the call would come and Mom and I would go to pick them up!

Before we had computers, my parents had magazine subscriptions to Life, Time and, for my brother, Boy's Life. It was always exciting to open our mailbox and see a magazine rolled up and ready to be enjoyed page by page. It would make the circle of our family, and then Mom usually passed it on to a neighbor.

After taking pictures on vacation or at Christmas, we dropped off the roll of film at Wolfe's Camera Shop. We waited with anticipation, thinking about seeing the memories that would spill out from the envelope. The pictures were ready in a week or so.

Somewhere, someone, somehow decided that one hour was how long we could be expected to wait for something and thus, the end of deferred gratification. One-hour photo, one-hour dry cleaning, one-hour glasses. Like Miranda Lambert's song "Automatic," we have all come to expect things in the snap of a finger. "Where is my second marshmallow? I can't wait!"

The eyeglass lady told me my glasses would be ready at 5:00 p.m. today. But you know what? I am picking them up tomorrow. I think I will wait and see what happens. Maybe I will get a second marshmallow for my show of patience!

Soup's on… After a healthy run to The Merc, Vann and I created two perfect soups, twelve-veggie soup and potato/corn chowder. We just finished lapping up two bowls like kitties licking cream and pronounced ourselves ready for the Food Channel.

When I was a kid, Mom was famous for her "dishpan" vegetable soup. It was a staple at our house, and she made it almost weekly, year-round. She literally had a big, white porcelain dishpan that covered two burners and made probably four gallons of soup. We loved it and ate it, but sometimes Mom would complain and say, "You kids don't like my soup." Ha! We would politely in-form her that we had eaten four bowls for three days in a row and maybe she should use a regular sized pan. Mom was a great scratch chef and the dishpan was employed for chili, spaghetti and all sorts of soups. My favorite soup was potato. It was so rich that our spoons stood up in it, thick with potatoes, onions, celery, carrots and usually a chunk of Velveeta cheese lobbed onto the top for that culinary flair! For the most part, there was not much processed food except cereal and mac n' cheese in a box when we were kids. Slowly, in the late 1950s, processed food started to creep onto the shelves, and Mom was appalled by the idea of not cooking everything from scratch, including her famous German chocolate cake.

I remember when Mom brought home the first giant can of Chun King Chow Mein, that was sprouts, water chestnuts and some other mystery vegetables cooked beyond recognition, with a can of "Chinese" crispy noodles taped to the top. We would beg Mom to fix it for us as it seemed so sophisticated. She occasional-ly obliged us, and we poured it over white Minute Rice. It probably had no nutritional value, but it seemed like we were eating some-thing most exotic.

When Spanish Rice-A-Roni appeared, we had to have that, too. We always admired the little red rubber flavor ball that some-how melted into the whole concoction. Add some ground beef and ole!

Sunday nights were always spent at my step-grandparents' home on Louise Street in Topeka. They had a small, neat house and Grandma C. had a huge garden of beautiful flowers in the backyard with a stone path. Her gardening skills did not extend into the kitchen, however. Every Sunday night, we ate Campbell's tomato soup. We ate it in front of their TV while watching Lassie. For dessert, Grandma C. served us spice muffins which were kept in her red glass cake pan on top of the refrigerator. They were drier than the Sahara sand. We politely asked for milk, and if we were lucky, she mixed in some Nestle's chocolate powder. Our cousins were usually there, too, and the grown-ups sat around the table visiting, forgetting about us as we secretly watched Bonanza (not approved TV watching because of guns and such.) Even as a kid, I thought it was so strange that the Cartwrights all lived in that big house and nobody had a wife. But oh well, that was Sunday night. Comfort food really has not changed much. A dish pan of spaghetti, chili or soup on a cold winter's night is truly fine dining! Soup's on!

✿ ✿ ✿

My first museum… Vann and I went for a country drive on this beautiful, sunny Sunday. The fields were still covered in a crumb coating of white snow frosting. Our trip sometimes takes us by my grandparents' old house on California Avenue. It seems virtually frozen in time with its expansive front yard, the two oak trees now grown so tall that they dwarf the two-story farmhouse. The majestic red barn is now gone from its hilltop base, but all the memories we made there still float over it like a ghost in a happy time.

The first "museum" of my childhood was my grandparents' home. While the first and second floors had the usual assortment of living spaces, the basement and attic were places to explore and get lost in for a day.

The basement was dry and smelled of Grandpa's tools, oils, and wood. It was a pleasant, pungent smell. Grandpa had a small workshop down there, and we were freely allowed to hammer to our hearts' content with any remnant pieces of the wood that Grandpa kept for us. It was worth the occasional smashed thumb to create a box or a cross, which we carefully painted and presented to our mom. She had quite an unusual assortment of homemade wood gifts.

The basement also held the coal storage area where we were not allowed to go. A large truck routinely came in the winter and sent giant jewels of jet black, shiny coal down the basement's side window. Grandpa would, without fail, keep the shards of coal stoked into the furnace which nicely heated their large farmhouse.

My favorite basement room, however, was the root cellar. It was a small room with raw wooden shelves on three sides. On the shelves, the glistening jars of wild plum preserves, red tomatoes, bright yellow apricots swimming in sugar syrup, dark red beets, green beans, strawberry rhubarb jam, and jars of pickles looked like a fruit and vegetable candy store. The pale light coming through the small, frosted window illuminated the jars. Grandma grew her vegetables and fruits and then spent many days canning the delectable produce to be enjoyed later in the cold of winter. It was a feast to open a jar of apricot preserves and instantly be transported to summer or to open a jar of dill pickles and smell the delicate scent of dill and other spices. I liked to hear that Pop! when Grandma was canning and she would say, "Now we know they're sealed."

There was also the attic to explore. It was accessed by a treacherous staircase that pulled down from the ceiling in the up-stairs hallway. The staircase was almost vertical, and my head would pop up at floor level and take in the dry, warm, musty smell of the attic, everything frozen in time. The unfinished wood floor held boxes of pictures, check stubs from the 1930s which were never discarded, some antique furniture, and a rocking chair that I would rock in, looking out across the neighbor's field to their black and white cows at the pond. It was a special world best to roam by myself. I never tired of paging through the old books or trying on vintage hats or clothes that had been sent to retirement in the attic. Sometimes, I would make a mound of blankets and take a fine winter's afternoon nap with the south winter sun warming the quiet attic. I would hear my Grandma calling up, "Who wants some fresh apricot preserves on hot bread?" Sitting across from Grandma at their kitchen table, we each spread the orange sum-mer fruit on thick slices of warm bread just out of her oven.

Gage Park… This afternoon I was running errands and thought, "Wouldn't it be nice to get a coffee and drive through Gage Park?" I have been in parks all over the world, but I think Gage Park is just about the sweetest, friendliest, and best park there is. I lived on Parkview Street until I was five years old, so Gage Park was in our backyard. We often walked there and went to the Gage Park Zoo. My all-time favorite part of the zoo was Monkey Island. I nev-er tired of watching the monkeys and thought they had the coolest hotel on their oasis island. I was sad when Monkey Island closed, and I wished they had kept it as a memorial to all the monkey fam-ilies who lived there.

My least favorite part was the rhino building. I did not think it was a very good exhibit, and even as a kid, I plotted to free the rhinos so they could roam outside. I also did not like the reptile building as I was not keen on snakes and lizards.

My favorite part of Gage Park was always the swimming pool, as big as a lake and always a welcome chill on hot Kansas summer days. Mom sometimes packed a picnic hamper with sandwiches, chips, water, and towels, and we spent the day at "the beach." It seemed as big as Lake Shawnee to us and we could hardly believe our good fortune in living just two blocks away from something so spectacular. The bathhouse was quaint and a good place to store our clothes and to change after a day at the pool. Walking home, we sometimes stopped to get snow cones. At night, we could hear the low rumble of the lions saying their good nights as we drifted off to sleep, happily tired from a day spent at "our" pool.

We are lucky to have Gage Park. Though it has changed much since I was a kid in the 1950s, it is still magnificent with its $1.00 train ride, the antique carousel, the beautiful rose gardens, the tulip pond, the wishing well, and the zoo. I do wish the two concrete lions that were guarding the entrance were still there.

Tennis Fairy Tale, Part I… I grew up in an airplane bungalow, post-World War II home on Parkview Street in Topeka. Our house looked like everybody else's except that beyond our front window, we had a view of the beckoning green and clay courts of Hughes Tennis Center. Every afternoon, I climbed on to our couch and perched my elbows to watch the lovely sport of tennis and the beautiful people playing it.

I begged Mom to let me go play, but she said, "When you are four years old, you may cross the street by yourself and play tennis."

Mom's best friend, Marge, built a grass court in her country home backyard. The two of them often hosted neighborhood tennis tournaments. Most of the time it was a muddy mess, but even so, we spent countless hours at our 'Wimbledon,' lobbing balls and rallying with each other.

When I turned four, Mom presented me with one of her wooden racquets, the grip neatly sawed off shorter and wrapped with tape, and said I could now cross the street. The excitement in me zoomed as I crossed the street to this magical dream park. Sometimes, Mom gave me fifty cents, and I sat savoring my Bomb Pop while watching the players' every move. Dressed in sparkling tennis whites, they played so competively and fluidly, yet always shaking hands at the end of a spirited match.There seemed to be a certain etiquette in their behavior. They stashed the racquets in

Ann Anderson

little wooden square presses and tucked them away in their bags and walked jauntily off those courts. I knew then that I wanted to be a tennis player.

From that day on, I was playing tennis. I started by hitting on the backboard, and soon some of the older kids, amused by my determination, agreed to hit tennis balls with me. Crestview Park, tennis tournaments, buying my first real racquet, a Wilson T2000, and teaching little ones in San Diego have all been part of my adventure with tennis, There has never been a time in my life that I have not played tennis. It is a part of me. It is who I am. It has given me my good health, much happiness, and some of my best friends.

Tennis Fairy Tale, Part II... I worked at Wood Valley Racquet Club when it first opened in 1974, and I had the chance to meet tennis legend, Bjorn Borg. He remains one of my all-time favorite players. In 2005, Vann and I moved back to Topeka and I had the good fortune to be hired again at Wood Valley. Daryl, the Wood Valley Director of Tennis, encouraged me to get a tennis pro certification and I did. I studied harder for my tennis test than for any class at KU.

For twelve years, I had the privilege of teaching at Wood Valley, surrounded by great staff and many friends. When we moved to Lawrence, it was time for a new tennis adventure. I walked into the just-opened Jayhawk Tennis Center and gave them my resume. Kyle, the General Manager, interviewed me and offered me a job. In some cosmic tennis life cycle, I am teaching at the Jayhawk Tennis Center, and I see my beloved Jayhawk on the wall every time I walk in. I am back teaching the little kiddos, and I never tire of hearing them say, "I did it, Coach Ann!" I am again surrounded by caring staff and new tennis friends. I also started a senior class for people who are over fifty. I adore my "young at heart" students.

Now it is time for Rock Chalk tennis at KU. I am still that kid, four years old, crossing the street with a racquet in my hand.

Legacy... At the graduation weekend, I see two empty chairs. What might have been and never to know. At our wedding, the empty chair with a dozen red roses marking your spot and the minister acknowledging your presence and absence.

Now, many years later, our family celebrates another first— your first grandchild, Mikey, to graduate from college. You would have worn something fashionable and your favorite high heels. You would have been on your feet clapping and whooping it up when they read Mikey's name. You would have baked a German chocolate cake, and you would have covered him in Avon red lip-stick kisses.

Next to you, my brother should have been sitting. He would be wiping a tear as he heard his son's name being called, seeing him walk proudly across the stage and flipping the tassel to the other side. I would have given my brother and my mom a little high five for all our accomplishments and for having such a great family.

I sit in the gold mist of the two people who were not there, and yet they are always there in me. Mom's legacy of positivity, laugh-ter, and "do your best" and my brother's legacy of lifelong learning, seeing the glass always filling up (not just half full) and believing anything can be fixed with duct tape.

I feel the firsts and lasts without them and all the in-betweens. Because of that, I feel the power to celebrate this precious life every moment.

Titles… I do not have letters after my name, no M.D., Ph.D., or even a Jr. I have come to love the four titles before my name. The first one I got was "Aunt," as in Aunt Ann, as in getting nieces and a nephew! Along my path, I have become an honorary aunt to about ten more kids, and I love hearing that title, "Aunt Ann." For me, it is a blend of second mom, friend, family, person you can call in all sorts of jams with no judgment, someone who will take you on an adventure at the spur of the moment and love you every day of your life. I always wanted to be an aunt. Aunt Ann.

The next title I got in 1995 was "Mrs." as in Mrs. Anderson. I know some women like to keep their maiden names, and while I treasure my so-Italian maiden name, Vigola, I loved becoming "Mrs. Anderson." While it is more fun to say Ann and Vann, Mrs. means that I belong with somebody, that there is a special some-one who worries when I drive out of the driveway until I drive safely back in, who knows I do not like the seeds in the middle of yellow squash and who can make me smile when I am feeling just a bit blue.

"Cat Mom" is two words, but all my life I have had cats and although I never had kids, I know what it is like to love little beings. I know what it is like to laugh at their playtime, to tuck them into a blanket at night and also to know the dagger of sadness when it is time to hold them one last time and see them to their Rainbow Bridge.

My last title is "Coach." "Coach Ann." It sounds a little like Aunt Ann to me because as a coach, I am kind of there for the same reasons—to encourage, to support, to inspire, to create some fun, and maybe just for that hour, to make some kids forget about their cares. I love to hear the little kiddos shout to me, "Coach Ann, I did it!"

It is great to have titles stuck to the end of one's name. But for me, I love having four titles at the beginning of my name. Mrs. Aunt Ann Cat Mom Coach Ann Rene Vigola Anderson.

I did it!... My ten-year pin from the Professional Tennis Registry arrived in the mail today. I held the pin and thought back to ten years ago and the many hours I studied to take my tennis certification test in Kansas City. I have often told Vann that if I had studied that much at KU, I would have graduated with honors.

As I walked onto that court for the two-day test, I looked around at the nine other hopefuls – all in their early twenties. I thought of Mom's advice to me, "Ask yourself at least once a month, 'What the hell was I thinking?'" Ha! What the hell was I thinking? But I had studied, I was ready, and I just kept pumping myself up that I could do this at age fifty-five. Just keep smiling. Just do your best. Just have fun.

By the end of Saturday, I walked off the court with the others and took a pass on going out for drinks. I went back to the hotel and studied until I could not learn anymore tennis. I drank three chocolate milks and ate two grilled cheese sandwiches from room service and went to bed.

Another day on the court, teaching a pretend lesson, and the two-hour written test. At 4:00 p.m., I walked out of there and felt so many emotions. I felt pride that I had stuck with it and gave it my very best, exhaustion in my head, heart and body, and the hope that I would receive a certificate announcing that I was an "official tennis pro." That day came ten years ago, and it has been the best job I have ever had.

What I have learned from all these years of teaching is that if you are not teaching 'fun,' nobody will want to come back – no matter what age.

Now, ten years later, I am so lucky to be at the Jayhawk Tennis Center. I am fortunate that I have found a tennis home with the little kids and the seniors. Their attention span and mine seem to match up perfectly. Their imagination span and mine seem to zoom together.

I have learned that teaching is not about what is in your pay-check—that is just a bonus. Teaching offers so many other gifts, like having a little boy hand you a monster truck picture he colored "just for you." It is about hearing kids go from saying, "I can't do that – it's too hard" to shouting, "I did it!" Those are the payments of the heart I get for teaching. Lucky me, I get to teach fun.

Spirit hawk... For Mother's Day, I gave myself a gift of some quiet time at Clinton Lake. I found a picnic table, and as I would do as a kid, I stretched out on it with my head happily resting on crossed arms for a pillow. For over an hour, I soaked up the sweet peace of nature and just being me. As I lay there, my spirit bird, the red-tailed hawk, swung a circle over me. I could see her golden eyes casting down as if to say, "Come fly with me." I lifted my heart up into hers and we became one. We rode the hot thermals that rise off the warming slopes of the Wakarusa River hills, and I felt her strong wings beat into me. We studied the fields, some burned by fire and still sooty black and others sprouted so green that it was a shock to the eyes. We saw the delicate first wildflowers of summer already on the stem, pink cosmos, white dogwoods and wild yellow mustards.

We landed on a wide, sycamore branch that hung out precariously over the water, but we were steady on our perch. Below, a tiny field mouse stilled and lifted its pink nose to scent on us. But hawk and I were not about the business of hunting, only about our boundless togetherness in flight. We turned our heads, and if hawks can smile, we did, and the mouse ran for the cover of the leaves.

Ann Anderson

I feel hawk lift higher over the lake and look down to see the watery white caps cut irregular waves blown from the strong Kansas south wind. We are not a water bird but watch some geese bob happily and lazily on the rough surface. Maybe they will find some sweet greens for their babies tucked away on shore.

As if hawk knew that I must be a person again, she set me back on Earth. I feel my wings become arms and gravity settles me safely back to the picnic table. My spirit hawk circles above three times as if to boast that she is free and off to places I can only dream of. I will see her again as she sits on the signs along I-70. She will turn her regal head with golden eyes, and she will wink at me.

The rope swing held by the big oak and
the bigger love of my grandparents

Chapter Twelve

CANE POLES

When the cool of the evening was slipping to us, Grandpa would appear with four cane poles and say, "Let's go catch us some dinner."

G old friend... A Rock Chalk welcome visit from my KU roomie and bestie for over fifty adventuresome years. Leslie and I were love and trouble at first sight. I am afraid to admit that I was usually instigating ideas and Leslie had the talent to implement them. I also always had a suggestion for things we might do other than go to class, but my future university professor was usually the one to herd us both to class.

We sat in our dorm room and did crafts, made snacks with appliances that were not allowed, hung Boone's Farm Strawberry Hill wine out of our window on cold days for that elegant glass of chilled sweetness on a Friday afternoon, and made frequent pilgrimages to her Prairie Village home or to my mom's home. We were nonstop decorating our dorm room with the latest tie-dye sheets, wind chimes, India print quilts, incense and all the décor of the 1970s. The sounds of Brewer and Shipley, Gordon Lightfoot, Crosby Stills Nash and Young, and James Taylor were the background sound of our college life. When we had extra money, we were down at the Mass St. Deli and riding everywhere on our bikes.

We are forever linked by our KU college life. We float easily from those days to the present days and to our future. Today, we are back in Lawrence, two coeds owning Mass St., laughing, trying on KU stuff, and instantly back together. Thank you, Leslie, for forty-six years of true friendship. Rock on, rock chalk!

Big dog deal... I like the way the Topeka & Shawnee County Public Library lady recently described their national award for Best Library: A big dog deal. That sounds like something Grandma would have said and it just made me smile.

I thought of my first library card. Mom frequently took us to the library to look through the picture books and read to us. It was always an exciting place to go with the big windows, comfortable chairs, a childrens' section generous with kids' books and people of all ages quietly reading.

When I was six, Mom deemed that I was responsible enough to get my own library card. She made a big production out of it as she could do with the smallest of life's occasions. We had dinner at Bobo's Drive-In and while that would usually have been all I could stand of enjoyment, I fairly sailed through my Spanish burger and slice of apple pie with constant urgings to Mom of "Let's get to the library!"

My head was barely above the counter, but I had rehearsed saying, "I would like a library card, please." Oh, the thrill of those words coming out of my mouth. Minutes later, the library lady emerged and handed me a crisp, small card with their logo, a number, and most importantly, my name in big block letters. I was dazzled by holding it. It was truly the first thing I had owned that made me feel like a real person and something with my name on it that had not been written by Mom.

I kept it on my desk in my room—ever at the ready for our trips to the library. I would search the aisles, the smell of warm, dried paper so pleasant, the low whispers of respectful people using their library voices, and I would select an armful of books to be devoured over the two-week loan time

At the checkout, I carefully filled in the information on the little card in the book pocket and off we went with our treasures, all acquired with the library card. I lived in kid fear of not returning them on time as I think Mom said something about a "huge fine."

But that never occurred, nor did I ever spill anything on any of the beautiful books. They took me to countries, to different lives, to new adventures, to happiness and sadness. I have never been without a library card since.

In high school, I became familiar with the card catalogue and stood like other scholars in front of the open, wooden drawers to identify just the right book. I wrote down the Dewey Decimal number and made my way through the stacks. With my head turned sideways, I searched the rows of books until finding the matching number. And voila! Book magic!

The library has, of course, evolved over the many years. It has rooms for meetings, art exhibits, a cafe, and the kids' reading room. It still holds familiar, inviting smells and sounds.

It is a big dog deal to go to the library and discover a new friend in a book.

I took refuge on the porch, as night was just mixing into day colors.

Daddy's little girl… I saw a young woman at the store this morning buying a Father's Day card. She had an easy-to-read tattoo on her forearm that said, "Daddy's Little Girl." I wanted to tap her on the shoulder and ask her what that felt like.

If I would point to a sadness in my life, it would be when my bio dad left us. I was four and my brother was two. My dad had an affair, a divorce, a few visits, and then he was missing in action for the rest of my life. My brother told people that he had died in a forest fire, which I guess made it sound better to him. But I was older and wiser and knew from an early age that he did not care about us.

Early on, our Saturday visits by my bio dad consisted of sitting on the bar stools at Gage Tavern on 21st Street, watching his buddies and him play pool and drink beer. As a six-year-old, I decided to tell Mom we had a nice time and no details. But our trips to the Gage Tavern were short-lived and his visits became a drive-by on Christmas Eve to hand us five dollars at the door.

The last time I saw my bio dad, I was sixteen and had my driver's license. It was Father's Day, and I drove to his house in

Lawrence. I had called him, and he acted like we had spent every day together and cordially invited me to come by.

I knocked, and he yelled, "Come on in." For the hour I stayed, he never got out of his La-Z Boy and continued drinking beer and watching some sporting event on TV. I am not sure what I was expecting. Maybe being sixteen, I thought he might suddenly become interested in my brother and me and at least ask, "Well, what are you two up to these days?" But I was not to be "daddy's little girl."

When I was in my twenties, I wrote him a letter telling him that I was graduating from KU and that my brother, Mike, was going to K-State to be an architect. I did not expect an answer, nor did I get one. I would be with my bio dad one more time in 1981 at his funeral. It was as if someone I barely knew had died, but my brother wanted to go. At the funeral, my brother sat sobbing and mourning the loss of a childhood image he could never capture.

I learned that you can find good men, and I have surrounded myself throughout my life with wise, kind men who are good fathers. Vann is, of course, the most gentle, intelligent and loving man I have known, and he is a wonderful father to his three kids and our three cats.

Happy Father's Day to everyone who is a dad, and Happy Father's Day to those strong, caring men who make me feel special every day of the year.

☼ ☼ ☼

Dream catcher... Sleep eluded me last night with visions of tomorrow's Father's Day celebration, Vann's birthday, and the first official day of summer. As night was just mixing in the day colors, I took refuge on the porch to quiet my thoughts.

I blinked twice, and out on my prairie, I saw a circle of teepees being readied for the move to their summer home. The teepees hit the bluestem grass and flowers without a sound. The acorn color of the men's arms that worked expertly to roll and tie them into neat teepee bundles. The few final ones still stood pointing to the morning Kansas sky. The women were stirring out the last embers of a breakfast fire, and I thought I could smell corn and venison lightly on the south breeze. The Kaw boys raced and darted like swallows then ran up the cottonwood tree like squirrels. I could not hear laughter, but their heads tilted back with the joy of a cool, early summer morning on the plains with no adult responsibilities.

The girls sat apart, braiding their hair into shiny black ribbons tied off with bits of cords and beads. A few of them glanced to the boys, but then they were back to their circle of girls.

The painted ponies stamped their heart hooves as if they knew they would be making a trip today. Their heads all bowed down, nibbling on the bountiful new grasses, lifting them occasionally to nuzzle each other.

At daybreak the camp was packed up. I blinked again and saw the last of the Kaw tribe heading northwest, perhaps on their way to a cooler summer camp. A thin whisp of smoke lifted from the remnants of the campfire and blew into a trailing cloud south.

When I blinked again, three red glass beads from a moccasin lay at my feet.

You before me… Today, a letter came from my cousin Johnny. I have read it three times to soak in its contents. He wrote about my mom, his "favorite aunt," and told of some marvelous remembrances, like Mom baking a birthday cake for him on his fourth birthday, the two of them decorating the Christmas tree at my grandparents' farm, and the two of them playing together when he was young. She would lie down on her back, feet sticking straight up and balance him on top of her feet, giving him an exhilarating 'airplane ride.'

My cousins, Linda, Stevie, Johnny and Nancy, lived on a beautiful farm west of Alma. It was a home-base to us for many summer visits. The ancient limestone farmhouse seemed like a castle with its majestic walls, wrought iron fencing, a school house where we played, and the farm full of cattle, cats and dogs, chickens, and a strawberry patch that was always full of big, bright red strawberries. We blasted out the farmhouse door after breakfast to Mill Creek and swam in its cool, big pools every day. After a snack of homemade cinnamon rolls, we were off to the barn to climb in the big hay mounds. We were never out of things to do. If we were on our best behavior, Uncle John would load us all in the back of his pickup truck and make the short drive to the Volland Store for a treat.

Mom would sit at their round oak table and visit with Uncle John and Aunt Ione. Usually, when we came in from playing, there was a big bowl of steaming chicken and noodles on the table waiting for us. Our cousins, Stevie and Linda were our constant companions, and Nancy and Johnny were "OLD" in our estimation as they were already in high school.

As a kid, I just thought of my mom and my brother and did not really stop to think about how the relationships fit together... It was just family.

Reading Johnny's letter made me smile and think that Mom was not just "my mom," but also a favorite aunt, a daughter, a wife and other relationships before there was a "me." I was born when Mom was twenty-seven, but she was an aunt long before she became my mom.

One time my cousin, Linda, was telling about something at Grandma and Grandpa's and I said, "You mean MY grandma and grandpa?" She just laughed, and I thought "Well, of course, I just wasn't born yet." My brother and I were the youngest of the "litter" as my grandma often said.

For most of our young lives, we had our grandparents all to ourselves and never thought or realized that a bunch of our older cousins had been frequent visitors, had slept in "our" spare bedroom, had helped Grandma pick off tomato worms and ate her foot-high angel food cakes or listened to Grandpa's railroad watch and shared his orange circus candies. By the time we showed up, the place belonged to my brother and me.

I smiled, picturing my mom enjoying her role as an aunt to her nieces and nephews. My cousins were all older than me, and I was the flower girl in my oldest cousin's wedding. My brother and I were just the little kids and thought the world revolved around us!

Thank you, cousin Johnny, for the lovely letter. It was like reaching back and having a visit with my mom.

Bugs and such... I saw the first bright yellow, hard-shelled, tobacco-spitting, scratchy legged grasshopper this morning. I was in a Zen moment of looking at my blanket flowers and out he pounced on my arm. I shouted something appropriate and off he took to the high grasses. With so many swallows in our back prairie, we are rarely bugged as the swallows swallow so many bugs.

When I was a kid, it seemed like we had bugs around every summer day. On warm nights, our front door would be open, and the screen door would be a landing strip for June bugs. They were like fat cockroaches with wings.

There was always a passel of grasshoppers from golden yellow ones to bright little green ones. Grandma had much to say about them—all not good—when she found them eating her garden. Her revenge was gathering up a can of them and going to the pond. The bluegill and sun fish found them quite yummy I'm sure.

Then there was the most dreaded stink bug, a nasty looking green bug that bit my brother once. For a week, his chin was a raw-looking, oozy thing that Mom found impossible to keep a Band-Aid on.

A good catch with our cane poles at the farm pond

The lightning bug signals the true beginning of summer nights with their "come and try to catch me" blink-blink in the dark. (I am sorry I made so many of the poor things into rings when we were kids.) Cicadas are nice. They signal the official end of summer and make a lovely rattle buzz buzz buzzzzz sound in the evening.

At the hardware store, I saw a sign for a remedy to get rid of bagworms. Oh my. Maybe one of the worst bugs. Unfortunately, Mom deemed that I was the "bagworm remover" in our family. Mom had no fear of anything and would unceremoniously snap them off with her long fingernails. I resorted to heavy work gloves, pliers, and other tools so that my fingers never touched the beasts. They hung like bad Christmas ornaments from our cedar bushes, and with dread, I pinched them off and into a one-pound Folger's coffee can just right for holding such creatures.

Two of the scariest bugs when you are a kid are the sneaky brown recluse spider and the mysterious black widow spider. Like all '50s ranch houses, our garage was unfinished and had the perfect dark corners for spiders to set up home. I was forever checking the corners for the brown recluse and the black widow and reporting my findings back to my mom.

Today I have a fondness for the honey bee and 'bee yard etiquette': Don't be afraid. Don't be an idiot. Don't swat. If you feel angry, whistle. Act like you know what you're doing, even if you don't. Above all, send the bees love. Every little thing wants to be loved. (Sue Monk Kidd, 2003)

Grandma's toys… I was a lucky mid-century kid. We had just enough and maybe the last generation when "consumption" was not yet considered a hobby. We had Little Golden Books that we treasured and read over and over, my beloved doll house that my mom made one Christmas out of orange crates, our rag-tag assortment of hand-me-down baseball mitts, tennis racquets, all sorts of balls, and lots of crayons and paper.

When we visited our grandparents' farm, the farm itself was a giant adventure. Exploring the barn, making hay forts, discovering a cache of newborn kittens, timidly petting the fresh calves, and wandering down to the pond to skip rocks was better than any of our toys from home.

Grandma did have one stash of toys for us to carefully use. It was a set of John Deere green and yellow die cast farm machinery: a tractor, a tiny plow for it to pull, and a small wheat truck. The toys were carefully stored in their foyer closet and with permission, we could take them out to the garden and play under the shady oak tree. We would load up the wheat truck with acorns, make roads with sticks for the farmer to drive the tractor on, and hours drifted by like the warm Kansas white clouds overhead.

When we were done playing, Grandma wiped off the green and yellow toys with a damp towel and safely stored them back in the closet. I do not know what happened to those toys after she died, but I think of them from time to time on a hot summer day. We never tired of regaling her with our story of what the farmer did that day. We were rewarded with just-out-of-the-oven cinnamon rolls and milk from her pitcher that always sat on the kitchen table. She would plop a chunk of daisy yellow butter on our roll and it would melt as we finished telling the farmer's adventure of the day.

In the evening, we gathered around together in Grandma's yellow motel chairs under the two giant oak trees. She read poems to us from her books. We often did not understand the meaning of the words, but it was magical to lean against her strong side, her housedress always perfumed from brushing against the Jim Dandy roses. We fought to keep our eyes open as the night pulled the sun into the west.

The Eleventh Commandment... With all due respect, I have created a summer "eleventh" commandment. "Thou shalt not covet thy neighbor's swimming pool." Oh Lordy, help me, but I have sinned and broken that commandment maybe every day since they opened the pool in late April. It sits tauntingly less than one hundred yards from my porch; its glistening turquoise water laps at me, beckoning to me like forbidden fruit that I cannot reach nor have.

When the cover is pulled over its shimmering surface, I still want it, knowing what is underneath and then, the torment of hearing the cover slowly being pulled back, revealing my longing. Oh pool, you are so beautiful. I want to slip on my swimsuit and dive beneath your sparkling blue water, feeling the chill of your coolness on these hot summer nights.

To add to my misery, the neighbors have upgraded you with pool toys, a basketball goal, and a fountain that beckons with each drip, drip. They have floating pool lounge chairs with cup holders that no doubt hold sweet umbrella drinks that I do not have. Ahhhh, it is too much to bear. And yet, I am glad you are there as just seeing you makes me think happily of endless days spent at Crestview Pool. Admission twenty-five cents. My Schwinn bike would obligingly take me there, a basket could be rented for ten cents for my valuables, a worn beach towel would be spread out and the turquoise transistor radio would be permanently dialed to KEWI for the afternoon.

I will break this summer commandment every day until summer's end when you are closed for the season. It is hard to live next door to a swimming pool. Marco? Polo!...

Mind wanderings to mid-century kid and spending the Fourth of July at my grandparents' farm. A paper sack filled with cutoffs, underwear, tee shirts, and toothbrush was all we needed. Simple. My grandma usually purchased a yard of darling red gingham material and some big, shiny blue buttons from Pelletier's. She held a newspaper up to me to make the pattern and then cut out the material. After a bit of sewing and inserting a strip of stretchy elastic, I had a new outfit for the Fourth of July.

If it were hot, we would swing out by the big rock under the shade tree. The patch of earth under our swing was always worn down to dirt from pushing off. If it were rainy, there would be a puddle under the swing that we would have to avoid or go bare-foot, letting our feet touch lightly in the water.

The big rock was a fine sitting place for Grandma. She sat there with a dishpan of green beans to snap and sort for dinner or it might have been a basket of bright yellow corn out of the field. She shucked down the silky strands and green wrappings and out popped the fresh ear of corn. Sometimes, she made me a corn hair doll with the silken corn threads trailing down her corn back.

Grandma also brought us lemonade made with her glass lemon squeezer and molasses cookies with soft, buttercream whipped icing.

When the cool of the evening was slipping to us, Grandpa would appear with four cane poles and say, "Let's go catch us some dinner." He tucked them over his shoulder, and, in his other hand, he had a much-worn tackle box that held everything from fishing lures to a hidden bag of candy.

We walked down the cattle trail to the pond and instantly felt cooled by its watery reflection. Grandpa obligingly baited our first hook with a fat Kansas earthworm, and my brother and I tossed in our lines with the expectation of catching the "big one."

I loved watching the red and white bobber. Whether I had a bite or not, it just always seemed like a lovely sight watching the bobber floating and drifting on the pond. A shimmery dragonfly landed on the pale line and rested. Then the moment of sheer excitement!—that quick tug on the line and the bobber going just slightly under water. Grandpa would quietly guide us by saying "Be patient" and then "Set the hook." If we were lucky, we caught a proper blue gill and Grandpa put the fish on the little stringer line. We thrilled at seeing the line fill up with six or seven fish. After an hour or two, we carefully rolled up our lines on our cane poles, tucking the hook back into its line, as Grandpa showed us how to do.

We proudly skipped and ran back to the house to present the dinner we had caught to Grandma. With hands washed and at the table, we said our prayer and then Grandma would heap our plates with fresh green beans, corn on the cob laying in a pool of churned, sunshine butter, and our just-caught fish fried in egg and corn meal. Grandma seemed to always have a bowl of cucumbers and onions to add to the feast and a plate of biscuits with wild plum jelly.

For dessert, we might have store-bought Neapolitan ice cream. I always traded my row of chocolate with my brother for his row of strawberry. Or Grandma might pull out of the oven a peach cobbler still bubbling with sugary peach lava juice, her cinnamon and nutmeg crust baked to a perfect golden color.

We cleared the dishes and out the back door we all headed to their white chairs Grandpa had made. There in the Kansas summer dusk, we slowly ate our cobbler, talking about the "big one" that got away.

Summer streetlight… Hot summer nights on Burnett Road were when the magic commenced in our neighborhood. We gulped down our dinner, asked to please be excused, and waved as the screen door smacked shut. There were about ten kids in our neighborhood, and there was always somebody ready for a game of basketball "HORSE," a game of pick-up baseball, or more often than not, we jumped on our Schwinn's and rode up and down the street, trying to ride with no hands. Some nights, we just sat under the streetlight at Burnett and 23rd Street and watched the thousands of bugs circle up high.

Decorating our bikes was a summer pastime. The best was putting playing cards on the spokes with clothesline pins, which made for a semi-motorcycle sound as we raced up and down the street. I was lucky to have long, plastic pink streamers coming out my handlebars and thought the whole image was so sophisticated.

Our neighbors had a real tennis court in their backyard, and we were welcome to use it. We lobbed the ball back and forth to each other, but spent more time digging the ball out of the bushes than playing.

One year, Debbie and her family got a slip-and-slide. That was endless evening fun, though now that I think about it, it is a wonder we survived running and throwing ourselves on the ground covered only by a sheet of wet plastic. Oh well, it was hours of entertainment.

If we had money and Mom's permission, we could ride our bikes to Tastee Freez on 21st Street and buy an ice cream cone. I loved getting the ones dipped in chocolate.

Ten o'clock seemed to be the understood summer curfew for our neighborhood and by 9:45 p.m., we were saying our good-byes and heading back to the lights of our home. Mom usually had a snack waiting for us—maybe German chocolate cake still warm from the oven or fudgesicles. Mom was into clean, but in the summer, a dip in the pool or a run through the sprinkler usually sufficed for a bath. We would put on our pajamas with that slightly summer-sweaty kid smell clinging to us and drop off to sleep, re-living the adventures of that evening.

When I became a teenager, summer nights were saved for seeing a special boyfriend. My first boyfriend, Mark, rode to my house on his Stingray bicycle and I hopped on the handlebars. I wanted those moments to last forever. A brush of a hand when you are thirteen is the stuff of romance novels. The first kiss, under a streetlight in 1966, stays forever in my mind. I was fourteen, and after Mark had kissed me, the night smelled like English Leather and sweet words. I remember sitting for a long time just soaking in the happy. I must have looked dizzy when I came in the door as Mom inquired if I were feeling OK. Oh yes, just my first kiss, and I am floating on air.

Many years have gone by since those mid-century summer evenings. But I can still hear our bikes making the rat-a-tat-tat down the street, and I can remember a first kiss of summer under the streetlight.

❁ ❁ ❁

For my Banndit... A shadowy cloud gathered over me this morning, and I wondered what it was. Then I knew it was the date of your leaving us six years ago. You always creep into my heart on this date.

We found each other quite by chance...or not...on a perfect May San Diego day in 1997. Vann was getting the car washed, and I was looking at the cat rescue place in the little shopping center. And there you were in a cage. When I walked up, you stood on your back legs and put your paws through the cage to me. The cat lady came outside and said, "Be careful. She might bite." Oh no, I knew you wouldn't bite. I asked to hold you and the lady said, "Yes, but be careful."

I reached for you, and into my arms you came, with your fur that smelled like sugar cookies and your pink nose pressed against my neck where it would stay every day for the next thirteen years. Your name was Rocket, and somebody had left you in a box by the rescue center door. Vann came to get me, and the next thing we knew, we were putting you in a carrier and you were going home with us. Your little raccoon markings did not look like a Rocket, and so on that first day, you became our Banndit who would steal our heart every day we had you.

You were maybe three months old, and I don't think anybody had ever held you. I nestled you into me, and your tiny purr started. You learned how to purr. At night, you would lie across my arm and knead little biscuits until I heard you sigh and go to sleep.

When you were two years old, we got you two kittens, Leche and Noche. Well, I guess the two kittens still wanted a momma kitty because you started nursing them. I took you to the vet when your tummy was pink and swelled up, and she said, "Banndit thinks she's had kittens." You nursed Leche and Noche another six weeks, and you all became a kitty family.

You and I were always soul mates as if a piece of my DNA and your DNA had been pressed together. You really did not like anybody else but somewhat tolerated Vann. When we clipped your nails, Vann would bravely hold you and I would clip away, with you putting out the scariest hisses ever. I would offer you a treat for your patience and all would be forgiven.

In July you became very ill all at once. The vet tried everything, but you had gotten the bad food. The last time I took you to the vet, they gave you fluids, and you looked at me like "Let's don't do this." The vet said you would tell me when you were ready to die.

On your last morning, I looked into your beautiful blue eyes and you said, "I'm ready." I wrapped you in your favorite pink fleece blanket and held you silently all that day. We both knew that thirteen years had come down to the last hours. You were ready for the journey, but oh, how I wanted just a little more time with you.

When the vet rang our doorbell, my heart shattered knowing it was time. I held you so softly, your nose resting where it always was against my neck, and you gave two strong breaths and then floated up from me.

Our grief for your loss knew no boundaries and was not to be consoled. We put your ashes in a blue velvet bag and put them in a beautiful box with your picture and your name on it. It sits in our bedroom, and I touch you lightly from time to time and remember that special day you reached your paws out to me.

Road trip... With the beginnings of back to school ads, my tennis kiddos have been announcing their summer vacations are coming. When we were kids, every summer, my grandparents, uncle, aunt, my mom and my brother and I would pile into two cars and head to Big Stone Lake. Big Stone Lake is a massive northern lake that straddles South Dakota and Minnesota. I never thought to ask as a kid how that became "our" lake, but that is where we went. It was over a mile wide and seemed like the ocean to Mike and me.

Our cars were loaded literally to the roofs with suitcases, rods and reels tied on the sides, and food. With a big snack bag, Mike and I rode, like royalty, in the back of the station wagon on top of the bedding. This was before the seatbelt laws, so we rode comfortably in the back, dozing on the bedding, and when we stopped, somebody opened the gate and we rolled out.

It was a long day's drive. Grandma always made a big lunch for us of cold fried chicken, biscuits, sliced tomatoes, and any fruit from her garden that was in season.

Our destination was a small fishing area on Big Stone Lake that had a convenience store/bait shop/coffee/arcade store, a small, low-slung motel with a neon light of a fish and individual lake cabins. We stayed in two cabins, my grandparents in one and the rest of us in the other.

It was a week of vacation perfection. Every morning, my grandma and Mom would fix breakfast as soon as we caught lake bass. The feast would include eggs and new potatoes my grandma brought. Almost everything we ate on the trip was carefully packed in coolers or bags for the week. Tomatoes, potatoes, fresh fruit, eggs from grandma's chickens, corn meal for the fish, and cucumbers and onions. Whatever else they needed, like milk, they would buy from the convenience store.

Mike and I got fifty cents a day from our mom for our vacation money. We usually spent it on the same thing, two games of pin ball for twenty cents and two Creamsicles for thirty cents. The Creamsicles called to us on the hot afternoons. Their smooth, creamy orange chill tasted wonderful, and we slowly savored them. Sometimes we bought a postcard for our friends back home and a Milky Way candy bar. We were rich.

Every day, my family rented two fishing boats which were filled with minnow buckets, rods and reels, tackle boxes and a basket of lunch and snacks. Most days I went with them although I was never much into fishing. I didn't like seeing the hook in the fish's mouth. Mom and others often wondered out loud if I were really a Hubert, but it was with a wink and a smile.

I just liked lying in the bow of the boat on a couple of life preservers and floating on the water all day with a hand or foot luxuriously dipped over the side into the water. When we stopped for lunch in a shady cove, Mike and I jumped in and swam in the chill of the deep lake.

Some days, I stayed on shore to be with Grandma. We borrowed some books from the convenience store, found a shady motel chair, and happily fiddled away the day. One time when we stayed on shore, we walked down to the dock to meet our boats coming in. Everybody was unloading, and with so many people on the ancient dock, it suddenly gave way, and we all went in. We were only in four feet deep water, but Mom was holding the minnow bucket up high. My uncle shouted, "Irene, what are you doing with the minnows?" She replied she didn't want to get them wet. We all had a good laugh about that at dinner.

At the end of the week, we loaded up the cars and the frozen fish that had been carefully iced and wrapped in newspaper for the trip home. Those trips float in my memory like my hand dipping in the cool lake water.

❁ ❁ ❁

Sky seasons... I stole from bed this morning as I knew the western skies were gathering a storm over Salina. A hot mug of tea with wild clover honey, a cushioned chair on the porch, and three sleepy cats stretched by me. The cats looked around to see if we were watching rabbits or a wild turkey, and then with a stretch of the paw and a lick of the pink tongue, they curled back to sleep.

I am deliriously wide-awake, steam from my hot tea floats up, the honey scent in the air mixes with the unmistakable smell of the thunderstorm.

Kansas sky. I have loved you all my life. You touch down to your prairie. Each season, you watercolor into another shape and shade. This morning you are dark navy while silver and gold strike through you to the Earth. I see the lightning blink and count the numbers to the thunder. Mom taught us to do this when we were kids, and it is automatic in me though I do not remember if it is "divide by five" or say "One-Mississippi, two-Mississippi…" But no matter. The thunder comes sometimes with a Fourth of July bang and sometimes like a rolling drum line of deep bass sounds.

The rain was beautiful. Steady, rich, and encompassing everything for a time. Now your sky is sunny summer. I know that sky too, as I have lounged under it on a blanket at my grandma's, watching and counting puffy white clouds float overhead. Grandma and I would guess where they were going.

I have felt your August sky with a mirage hot sun and the thinnest of blue coming through. Then your fall season fades into a cool gray and pink, and shadows the Autumn Blaze maples when they turn their orange and red colors. You try to outdo yourself with fall sunsets as if to challenge the trees to a coloring contest.

The winter skies melt into flat matte grays and snowy whites. We will watch you from inside, again our hands cupped around hot chocolate, and you reward us with snowflakes. I have lived under the Chicago skies that are seemingly endless shades of gray. I have lived in the California desert with dry, cloudless skies, longing for a Kansas thunderstorm to blot out the hot orb of the desert sun.

I love the Kansas sky seasons. You are the blue river that floats over my prairies and through me every day.

Remedies… Chatting with my gal pals last night about an event today at the hospital. It brought back a memory of Mom and her cure for my "crabby pants" as she called them. I rarely got them, but when I did, I was in a snit over some injustice or something I did not get. One summer, I desperately wanted to buy a troll doll. They cost $1.25—almost three weeks of allowance. Mom did not want to advance me my allowance and said, "Save up for it and I will take you when you have the money." Rats! So, I had crabby pants.

Mom's remedy for that "ailment" was to load me in the car and take me to the hospital. She occasionally volunteered there and when we walked in, I was immediately so humbled by seeing people in wheelchairs, with crutches, and many life-challenging issues. I quickly counted my blessings. Mom offered greetings to the staff and we headed back to the car. I meekly told her that I understood that I was a pretty lucky kid.

Grandma used to say to me, "You never know how someone starts or ends their day." That was her way of telling me to be grateful, and I still think about that when I see someone having a tough time of it. No, you don't know how life is for many people.

When I complained to Grandpa about something—usually a chore of weeding the strawberry patch—he would offer, "If you need a helping hand, look to the end of your own arm." Boy, when somebody tells you that, there is not much discussion.

In To Kill a Mockingbird, my favorite book and movie, Atticus tells Scout, "You never really understand a person until you consider things from his point of view… Until you climb inside of his skin and walk around in it." It is so easy to quickly judge a person.

I remember these gentle sayings and remedies from Mom and my grandparents. They were given to me in love and to help me understand all that I had as a child. They still work, and I say them to myself whenever I feel a case of crabby pants. You do not have to look very far to see your blessings.

✿ ✿ ✿

Reuniting… Tomorrow, the family tribe started so long ago by my grandma, her beautiful brothers and sisters and those before them, will gather for another afternoon of cementing that bond of family. I wander through those many years when Mom would announce "Our family reunion is tomorrow." She spent days preparing for the big event.

I always wore my good clothes, hair properly combed with even some Aqua Net sprayed into my fine, flyaway hair. Mom would bake a German chocolate cake, her date bars, a lemon pie with meringue so high that it dwarfed the pie, and I was always in charge of the relish tray. With great artistic flair, I filled celery sticks with pimento cheese and peanut butter and arranged bread and butter pickles, olives, and dill pickles that Mom had made in the summer.

We carefully loaded our Chevy with the offerings and headed to Maple Hill. My Great Uncle Frank and his family called Maple Hill "home," and it was a second home to all of us, too. We gathered in my cousins' spacious basement with tables laid end to end to carry the spread of food.

I always made a food inspection to make sure I found Grandma's cinnamon rolls, angel food cake, Great Aunt Vivian's Million Dollar Best Fudge, and Aunt Ione's chicken and noodles. There were yeast rolls that scented the air with warm bread smells, golden fried chicken, cobblers of every fruit, and a table of sides. Mashed potatoes standing in pools of hot butter, pan gravy, potato salad, Waldorf salad, my outstanding relish tray… it was like Thanksgiving. After our plates were loaded, Uncle Frank offered up a prayer. We all ate and talked and maybe went back for seconds and thirds.

The adults gathered around to look at old pictures, perhaps remembering the generation before them. My cousins, Stevie and Linda, and my brother and I were free to run to the grade school down the block and play on the teeter-totter and jungle gym.

By 5:00 p.m., we were packing up leftovers and hugging our way through cousins, great aunts and uncles, and my grandparents. By the time we were back on I-70, my brother and I were sound asleep, sated from food, playing with Linda and Stevie and dancing to rock and roll songs with our older cousins, Nancy, Johnny, Lana and Larry.

Those reunions were a happy family time when we were all together, great aunts, great uncles, grandparents and parents. And now, my generation gathers to eat the same foods, look at the old pictures, and make new memories.

Family tree… The casserole dishes have long been washed and put away. Still with me after the reunion, the scent of cucumbers and vinegar lingering in the air, the image of desserts weighing down one entire table, and familiar voices floating over the prairie.

Lying in my hammock last night, I was still trying to soak it all in, starting with the wall filled with Post-it Notes showing the descendants of our family—Benjamin Franklin and Ida Mae Short Mackie, my great grandparents, who started us all. Did they ever convene on a Saturday afternoon with their cousins and food and catch up?

I knew my great aunts and uncles, and I am grateful for that. Great Uncle Ted lived in Taos, New Mexico, and I only met him once. Great Uncle Ted and his wife ran a trading store/post office and maybe from him, I inherited my love of silver and turquoise. We must have been one of the few families who had Navajo rugs strewn about as if they were everyday occurrences in Kansas. I have one faded black and white photo of me in front of Great Uncle Ted's store. Since I was four years old, I have had a turquoise bracelet on my wrist.

Great Aunt Elizabeth lived in Silver Lake and was a gentle, kind soul. She was never well, it seemed to me, and she had a little dog who was her constant companion. She raised her grandkids, and I was in my thirties before I found out they were not her own kids. I think she had a hard life.

Great Aunt Gladys and her husband had an apple orchard in Yakima, Washington. It is funny, but I have no idea how she got there, and I never got to visit her. She came for a couple of Maple Hill reunions and, of course, brought apples and her gorgeous smile.

Great Uncle Frank was my favorite uncle with his kindness, his deep laughter, and his willingness to always teach us how to fix something. I liked their home as it always seemed peaceful and smelled like peach cobbler.

My favorite aunt was Great Aunt Vivian. She seemed to live an exotic life, married to a railroad guy. They lived in a brownstone flat on Walnut Street in Kansas City. She was my only relative who lived a city life, and we were regular visitors to her home. Her skin was so soft, and she smelled like violets. She always kept a supply of little wax bottles of flavored water (Nik-L-Nips) for us in her fridge. She had a delightful sense of humor, and I loved being with her.

Of course, my grandparents were the essence of my kid universe, and so much of who I am came from them. Grandma loved to write little stories and poems about her friends, her flowers, the seasons and had a sketch book filled with pencil drawings of animals and farm life. I did not inherit her gift of sewing, but I know I inherited her love of living on the prairie and writing stories.

Grandpa was a quiet man who taught us how to take care of the animals, was not afraid of hard work, and never spoke harshly to anyone. He always smelled of sweet pipe tobacco and the garden.

Benjamin Franklin Mackie and Ida Mae Short...What pieces of you are in me? Did you like to walk across this prairie and let the bluestem brush against the palm of your hand? Did you spread a homemade quilt out under the stars at night and watch lightning dance on the western edges? Did you take a piece of charcoal from the fire and sketch out a story or a picture? Oh, how I wish you could have been with us on Saturday at the reunion.

Grandpa Hubert... In the last remnants of family reunion thoughts, I realized that this week was my Grandpa Hubert's birthday. He was a steady male presence in my early life but often times, he was in the background. My family was dominated by strong prairie women, who could plow a garden, sew a new dress, cook dinner for twenty people, and fix a car by noon. I was raised in a "you can do anything" environment created by my grandma, my mom, and the other women in my life.

I enjoyed many quiet moments with my grandpa. He was born in Minnesota and made his way to Kansas through railroad jobs. Like most people of that generation, he made a living by farming, raising some cattle and whatever it took to make ends meet. He was a tall man, blonde hair turned gray and the bluest eyes that always had a sparkle in them. He and my grandma lived on a beautiful farm on California Avenue, just south of Topeka.

Except on a few holidays and sad occasions, I never saw him wear anything but his faded blue denim overalls, a blue work shirt, and his denim coat with pockets for a carpenter's pencil and small tools (sometimes he had a kitten in there).

Some days, I spent the morning with him. Holding his hand, rough from work but gentle around my little hand, we would walk to the barn and he would place me on a three-legged stool to watch the milking. I never tired of seeing him wink at me and squirt the barn cats with a mouthful of warm fresh milk. We would go to his shop where he might teach me how to hammer and cut with a small saw he kept for my brother and me. One time, he secretly helped me make a wren house that I painted with daisy flowers on the side. My grandma was delighted and properly exclaimed about my building prowess.

Grandpa's shop was a conglomeration of three railroad cars meshed together to make his work area and a garage. He had a small stove in there, and it was a fine place to work on a cold afternoon. It smelled like warm woods and Folger's coffee with cream and sugar. He tuned the radio to WIBW and we listened to farm reports and country music.

He was not one for idle chatter, and we both seemed to enjoy each other's company without the need to visit. He read history books constantly, and often I would receive a brief lesson on some historical event. I would nod appreciatively and try to remember the facts.

He never spoke harshly to anyone and never, to my knowledge, raised his voice at my grandma. They seemed to have a life rhythm that was perfectly in sync. After the noon meal was finished, Grandma and I would do the dishes and at exactly 1:00 p.m., As the World Turns would come on their TV. Grandpa would sit in his big Mission chair and Grandma and I would sit together on the couch. Grandpa would maybe light his pipe, but other than the strike of the match, it was understood that for the duration of "their" show there was no talking allowed. Grandma and Grandpa watched that soap every day they were home. When it was not on, they often discussed the lurid details of what was happening and who was doing what to whom. The only other TV show they truly enjoyed was Gunsmoke on Saturday evenings. On Sunday mornings, over plates of thin buttery pancakes, sausage and golden eggs, they discussed whether Miss Kitty and Marshal Matt Dillon would ever get together. That conversation was never interesting to me.

Grandpa kept a journal, something I never would have guessed he would do. His entries were about the weather, the farm, animals being born, and family get-togethers. I wonder how he decided to sit and write about all of that with his square carpenter pencil.

Grandma got breast cancer when she was eighty-one. She died in April 1970. My uncle moved my grandpa in with him near Willard, and Grandpa went from being a vibrant, strong man to a shell of a man. One time, my grandpa drove from Willard to the gas station/coffee shop near their old farm, where throughout

Ann Anderson

his life, he spent most mornings chatting with his buddies. When he got back to Willard, I asked him, "Grandpa, did you have a good time seeing your old friends?" He slowly replied, "Yes, but it wasn't the same without coming home to Grandma." Without any medical cause, on December 15, Grandpa died that same year as Grandma. I would have written on his death certificate: "cause of death—broken heart." He loved grandma so much.

I have the railroad pocket watch that Grandpa proudly carried every day of his life. He would let me hold it, and I could hear its gentle tick like the beat of his heart.

Snow day with my little brother

Chapter Thirteen

GARDEN ROWS

we walked the garden rows every day. Her seedlings were planted by February and tiny shoots emerged from old muffin tins placed in her south windows.

Surprise! It has been many years since I have had a surprise birthday party. Vann nonchalantly suggested we go for a drive by Clinton Lake to look for eagles the Sunday after my birthday. Twenty minutes later, he had driven to our dear friends' home and I saw the first adorable homemade signs that said "Happy Birthday, Coach Ann" and brightly colored arrows with stickers pointing the way to their door. I was overcome with the happiness of knowing this family. When we moved to Lawrence, Kyle, Brit, and their kids, Wyatt, Miles and Sadie, became like a second family of the heart to Vann and me. When we entered the house, the kids were tucked under the kitchen counter and all jumped out and yelled "Surprise!" It was a lovely surprise to have this blessing from them with chocolate chip cookies, candles to make a wish and small presents they had made. Wyatt had programmed his robot to belt out "Happy Birthday," and I was so happy looking around at each of them. I am grateful to God for giving us this heart family. It is a beautiful surprise.

A nod to R. Frost's Nothing Gold Can Stay... The Bradford pear trees are already shedding their whipped cream blossoms. They can hold the beauty of white blossoms for only a moment. The bluebirds are finding their little boxes, and soon the babies will look out from the holes with their cartoon yellow beaks. Then they fledge. Nature has a plan—nothing gold can stay.

When I was a child, I could hold onto that gold seemingly forever. Mom standing at the kitchen sink and turning to kiss my head as I flew out the door with my tennis racquet. Sitting in the breezeway with Mom and my brother during a Kansas thunderstorm, Rainy Day popcorn balls between us and icy 10-ounce Coca Colas in our hands. It was golden and time seemed to tick to more gold. I turn and I was just sitting there with them. Now they are gone.

Maybe that is why most of us do not like change. We want the gold to stay, we want everybody we love to stay and yet, nothing can. I picked up my Jazzy last night and nestled my face into her fur. Jazzy was rumbling with a happy purr inside and smelled like a warm sugar cookie. I did not want to let her go, but after a while, she wiggled free.

I watch Vann read the Wall Street Journal every day and listen to the quiet of our home. I want it to stay this way. This is gold.

My brushes with the law... Most of you think I am a "Miss Goody Two Shoes!" Well, I've had a few brushes with the law. I will start at age four when I stole the one and only thing I ever took from a store. It was a Milky Way candy bar—worth five cents back in the day—but still, I took it. Mom caught me snarfing it down and quite calmly said, "I hope the police don't come for you." Well, I was struck dumb with fear and spent about four hours hiding behind our TV set in the corner of our living room. Finally, I decided it was safe to make a break to my bedroom to hide under the covers. The faint sugary, fat, whipped filling of the candy bar still was pleasantly in my mouth, but I wasn't truly enjoying it.

Fast forward to age nineteen, and I am working as the hostess on Saturday night at the Flaming Steer that in 1972 was THE place to eat and drink in Topeka. I was closing with our manager, John, and we walked out the back door at 2:00 a.m. on Sunday morning. From around the corner came two guys in ski masks with guns. The one guy took John back into the restaurant and the other guy took me inside the wooden trash enclosure. I was scared to death but trying to be calm. He had a gun on me and asked if I had any money. I told him I had $2.00 which is all I truly had with me. And then—genius me—I told him I could write him a check. Geez. He laughed, and I said, "Oh my gosh, that was really stupid." I told him I was scared. I think it helped as he probably thought, "What a dumb kid."

They herded both of us back inside the restaurant where they stole $6,000.00 from the safe. The guy kept the gun on my neck and he was shaking. For about a week, the red scratch marks were plainly visible. After they got the money, they put us in the walk-in freezer which was set at ten degrees. We stood in there about twenty minutes, then bolted out and ran to the donut shop at 37th and Topeka Blvd. to call the police. I kept that job the rest of the summer but only worked during the day.

My next brush with the law was in the Kansas Governor's Office. I was the receptionist and a guy with a "Crocodile Dundee" machete stuck in his waistband came in and said he wanted to see the Governor. They had not covered "guys with machetes" in our staff training, so I asked in my most polite voice if he would like to be seated while I let the Governor's secretary know that he had a visitor. For some bizarre reason, I told the visitor that we had fresh muffins and would he like one. Maybe because he had been in prison, it had been a long time since someone had offered him a muffin and coffee. He surprisingly asked, "What kind of muffins?" and I said "Well, let's go look at them." As I stood up, I pushed the security button that was underneath my desk and desperately hoped that "Barney Fife," the one security guy the Capitol Building had at the time, would notice it.

The machete guy and I went in and surrealistically picked out muffins to eat. Suddenly, seven highway patrolmen arrived with guns drawn and took the guy away. I almost felt bad that he didn't get to eat his muffin.

Peonies… Forty-seven years ago, my grandma died from a valiant fight against breast cancer. She so wished to die at home, but on that final day, she was taken by ambulance down California Avenue to the hospital where she died.

Mom rode with her to the hospital and later told me that Grandma, using her last bit of strength, raised up on one elbow and said, "I'll never see my garden again." Grandma would have lived to be 100 if not for cancer, but she packed 100 years of life into her eighty-one years.

As a child, she was home base for my heart, a touchstone for energy, and my biggest fan. I always jumped at a chance to spend the day at the farm with her, and time passed like the slow water of Mission Creek on a hot Kansas day. We would fix a big breakfast of French toast drenched with homemade butter as yellow as daisies and golden cane syrup. Doing chores never seemed like work to me with Grandma as we were always tucked next to each other, a pleasant conversation going and a trip or two in for snacks of biscuits filled with apricot preserves or cold chicken legs and tomato sandwiches. Sometimes, she put an old flowered-print tablecloth on the big rock by the swing and we had a proper picnic. From the big rock, we could survey all of the farm, the majestic two-story red barn, my grandpa's railroad car shop, and the beloved garden.

Her seedlings were planted by February and tiny shoots emerged from old muffin tins placed in her south windows. By late April, they were nestled into the rich soil in her garden.

Grandma seemed to be a garden whisperer, talking to each plant, encouraging it, and picking off the random tomato worm. She was rewarded spring through fall with a bounty of lettuces, red and black raspberries, beets, onions, carrots, potatoes, and many tomatoes, that she canned into all sorts of exotic concoctions for the winter.

Grandma was also a cat whisperer. The farm, like most farms, had a menagerie of farm cats, too wild to hold, but they knew a good thing, a warm barn full of hay for their kittens, fresh milk squirted in their mouths by my grandpa, and cream and bread put out for them on winter days. No one could get near them, but when Grandma brought them cream and bread, they would magically appear and wrap themselves around her legs like fur snakes and then lap up the delicacies.

I never heard Grandma be cross with anyone, including my grandpa. She was always making something for an ill friend, a pot of vegetable soup or a casserole, and we would drop it by with flowers from her garden.

Grandma's kitchen was never empty of something delicious to eat and smell. There would be cinnamon rolls so laden with spices, raisins, and frosting that I wanted to eat the whole pan. Or she would have an angel food cake on its stand turned upside down on a 7 UP bottle, waiting to be righted and frosted with a drizzle and its hole filled up with fresh strawberries.

Grandma never wore make up, never had her hair done, used Corn Huskers lotion, but to me, she was a beautiful woman. Her hands knew too much hard work, but her touch was as soft as cotton when she held my hand.

Besides her garden, Grandma always had her flowers. Jim Dandy roses that were bright coral and lined her front path, iris in random rows of white, purple and lavender, gladiolas of deep orange, or "glads" as she called them, and lilac bushes that lined the backyard like a purple scented fence. Her favorite flower was the peony with its fluffy big head of pinks and whites that came for Mother's Day and stayed for Memorial Day. She would gather them like prizes and display them in her cut-glass vases throughout their house. They were the smell of my grandma.

Rescue pup... We have been to Idaho to visit Vann's daughter, Lori, and her wonderful husband, Greg, affectionately known as "Mrs. Socks and Socks." They built a log cabin with their own hands in the tall pine woods. To be there is to step away from civilization as there are only 700 people in the whole town, a small general store, one restaurant and cell phone service only if you stand under the one cell tower out on a hill. Our days are spent sitting and lazily chatting around their fire pit made of native stone, situated in the tall pine forest.

It is enchanting to be there in the quiet nature world of the pines and the river. On our visit, we met the newest member of their family, Shoes, their rescue pup. Shoes was found living with an old man in a trailer. The dog was six months old and had never been outside. Lori and Greg took him to their home when the man could no longer keep him and began the challenge of turning him into a happy dog. They did this with constant love and direction (and probably a lot of treats). He is a sweet dog and loves to chase the chipmunks and seemingly never wants to come inside except to lie on his bed by the fire. Outside in nature is his true calling. I love being with the three of them. Lori is like the daughter I never had and she calls me "Mom 2." Mr. and Mrs. Socks and Shoes. It's a happily ever after story.

School dances and proms... I stopped by the store to get balloons for my tennis kiddos this afternoon. The floral department ladies had boxes and boxes of beautiful corsages laid out on the counter. Roses on pink ribbon wrist bands, orchids with baby's breath on pins, and an assortment of corsages in all colors. I thought with a smile—school dance!

The rest of the afternoon, I thought about the good, the bad, and the ugly of my junior high and high school dances and proms. For the most part, it was a mixture of anxiety and feeling lonely as I rarely seemed to time a boyfriend right for the big dance. Mark was my boyfriend for several ninth-grade dances and was the first boy to send me a corsage to wear for the dance. The flower shop delivered it on a Saturday morning. It was a pale white orchid nestled in tissue. The flower guy said to be sure to keep it cool. Mom was unfortunately gone that day so I thought, "If he said to keep it cool, why not the freezer?" Yes, I was fifteen and dumbstruck with love. Several hours before the dance, I checked on my first corsage and was horrified beyond words that it was frozen and brown. In tears, I showed it to my stepdad who graciously went to Custenborder's Florist and brought back a similar corsage. We then went through the awkwardness of pinning it on my dress and voila!—ready for an evening with Mark.

I remember going to the winter Topeka West "Snowball" dance with Kyle. He sent me a wrist corsage, and this time, I wisely stored it in the refrigerator. I remember admiring it on my wrist all evening as we slow danced. We all gathered at the Pizza Hut on Gage for a post-dance dinner.

I did not have a date for the junior or senior proms. I wasn't that good at dating actually. I remember feeling lonely when prom was approaching and seeing some girls with the "perfect" boyfriend getting ready to have that very special evening. I went with my girlfriends to both proms. There is something that feels like the movie Sixteen Candles when you are sitting on the bleachers all dressed up, hoping somebody cool asks you to dance, trying to act like it is a wonderful evening.

Times have changed. I remember my nieces and nephew going to their high school dances and proms. They involved so much more preparation: hair appointments, tux rentals, before and after parties, and huge photo sessions with all the girls locking arms.

The school dance... A passage in becoming a teenager.

❀ ❀ ❀

Prairie night... The moon is eclipsed or perhaps these two weeks of Kansas wind have blown some stars and space over it temporarily. Tonight, the cats and I are silent watchers of the moon as it meanders across the sky and nestles itself like a Christmas star on top of the distant red cedars.

We heard the last robin give her goodnight call and two deer puff breaths down in the wild honeysuckle bushes. The cats know the deer are there as they lift their cotton candy pink noses to catch their scent in the air. I know the deer are there by the sound of the heart-print hooves moving across the prairie.

Today, I planted more native wildflowers that in the spring will reward me with a riot of colors and nourish the bees and the hummers fattening up for their migration to their southern homes. But that is a lifetime away. For now, I am content to think of the seedlings tucked in their earth beds, sprinkled with water and waiting to pop out with green shoots to the warming sun. I am lying in the hammock, chilly but too happy to break this moment. Too content to herd the cats inside. Too spellbound by the moon pushing its thin light down on us. The moon, the deer, the robin, the seeds, the cats, and I are woven into one quilt on this dark Kansas night.

I will wake up tomorrow and go down to look for the heart prints.

❀ ❀ ❀

All the postings yesterday for Siblings Day and I needed a day to think about my one sibling, Mike, now gone but always remembered. He was not into holidays, so he would have found Siblings Day to be a thing not to celebrate. Being the oldest, I would have talked him into doing something—especially if it meant my buying us lunch at his favorite On the Border.

I always (and still do) wanted an identical twin, but I got a brother instead. I was almost three when my mom brought home "the little bundle" as she called him, and I remember thinking, "There goes the neighborhood." But as he grew, I came to find out that having a younger sibling was quite handy and wonderful.

He was somebody to go exploring with at the Shunganunga Creek on a hot afternoon, riding our bikes across the narrow path, jumping off together, and letting them thud to the ground. We would spend the afternoon poking around in the muddy water looking for minnows, snakes, pretty rocks, or our favorite, tadpoles. Once we snuck a tadpole back to our house and kept it in a bucket hidden from Mom until it actually sprouted legs. We had no idea what to feed a tadpole, so it got a mixture of earthworms, apples and lettuce. Finally, we decided to sneak it back to the creek and let it become a proper frog.

If we had twenty-five cents, we headed to Crestview Pool and spent an afternoon with our friends daring each other to do belly flops and cannonballs off the high dive.

At night, we played tetherball until after dark and then with our rooms next to each other, we made secret Morse code knocks on our wall. Finally, we both drifted to sleep.

We had our sibling fights, but they never lasted long as we were on to the next adventure. By the time I was twelve years old and my brother was almost ten, he was bigger, so I could only use my wily wits to win our sibling battles. I guess he sort of became my big brother. He became my protector, and I could always depend on him to show up.

He gave me four of the best gifts I will ever receive—my nieces and nephew. They are pieces of him, the best pieces of his intellect, his great sense of humor, kindness, and constant need to learn something new. He made some wonderful kids to carry on. Happy Sibling Day, Mike. If you were here, we would be talking about layers of limestone, planning a trip to Colorado, or looking at the redbud trees casting their beauty on us. I am lucky you were my brother.

"My larder is full"… A perfect Wednesday, seeing our friend Vickie at the Topeka Civic Theater, playing tennis with Vann, getting my little yellow car washed, eating lunch on the porch with our cats lounging about in the sun, and I heard myself say "My larder is full." Grandma used to say this all the time, usually when she had finished the dishes or had spent the day working in her garden. She would fix a big glass of iced tea or a bowl of ice cream, find a shady spot and make that announcement. My brother and I always looked at each other as we had no idea what a "larder" was. We both thought it sounded like garter. Our other guess was that it was a body part, and we certainly did NOT want to ask our grandma where one's larder might be—especially if it were full. As I grew older, I learned what it meant by just soaking up her use of the expression.

Our family, like most, had various sayings that would be deployed when needed. Mom had one that I still use—joy pirate. She reserved this term for anybody who was cranky, grouchy, or wished to rain on her parade. Over the years, I have wisely learned to eliminate almost all joy pirates from my life.

When I was a kid and would lose something, I would ask Mom where it was. She loved to say, "Well, the last time I was wearing/using whatever, I left it..." That was her not-so-subtle hint that she had not been using it and I had best start looking. When we were in grade school, Mom made two boxes, one for my brother and one for me, with our names written in large letters, and ceremoniously placed them by the back door to the garage. Everything she found that was ours was tossed in the boxes. It became the first place we went to look for lost items. I also found it handy to just put stuff in there and hope I could find it more quickly.

Occasionally, our cat would jump on top of whatever was in the boxes, and we never tired of yelling, "Mom, we found the cat." We were obviously easy to amuse and thought that was hilarious to say.

Over the years, we were told "don't count your chickens before they are hatched," which we pondered and then hoped that we were getting chickens. We were told not to put all of our eggs in one basket and again, we figured we might be getting chickens. We were told to measure twice and cut once—advice to this day I don't really use and should.

Grandpa did not use sayings much, but he did say, "If you need a helping hand, look to the end of your own arm." That was the kind of advice that meant kick it into gear and get to work. My grandparents believed in shoulder to the grindstone.

But like Grandma would say when all was right with the world, "My larder is full." And that's how I feel today. Everything right with my world.

❀ ❀ ❀

Prairie. Home. Companion. An impossibly beautiful day. At daybreak, the pasture smoke and fog hangs like Spanish moss across our back trees. The sunrise is garishly orange from spring smoke as if hot Velveeta has been poured over it.

I lie in my hammock and see the swallows cut through the air, their shiny blue feathers mixing into the thin blue Kansas sky. They edge and dart as if they are a fast kite caught on mixing winds. One of them has claimed a bluebird box, but I do not mind. I know they will eat up lots of bugs, and the cats and I love to watch them swoop and soar. Our prairie grass blows like a young girl's hair while riding in the back of a pickup truck. I planted more giant sunflower seeds, dreaming of the feast they will make for the birds late next fall. Two crows hop near me chatting about waiting for me to go inside and "Let's dig up the seeds." I chat back to them and say, "Best to wait for a big feast next fall." I like the shiny black crows with their intelligent eyes and the back and forth cock of their heads.

The cats are just about useless on a day like today. They lie like fat floor mats on the "catio" stones. Dozens of mice could run by and perhaps one of the cats would open one eye. I agree with them. Today is for savoring, for daydreaming of the prairie coneflowers with their vibrant heads of crimson, yellow and orange, and thinking of the chives that scent the air with crisp, clean green smells. I wait for the tall dill to bloom with chartreuse green blossoms, reminding me of Mom's dill pickles, in the stoneware crock adorned with blue flowers on our back porch.

My favorite is the lavender that warms its flowers during the day to delight the night air, an ancient scent of the ocean dunes.

This land is my companion, and I am less when I am away from it. Like Tara was to Scarlett, this prairie is my home companion.

❀ ❀ ❀

Running away... This is the kind of day as a kid that would have made for a great "running away" day. I don't think any kid ever planned out an escape when it was cold, snowing, or raining.

When my brother and I were kids, we planned to run away at least once a year. My brother did it more frequently, timing it to avoid a test at school or to avoid going to a girl's birthday party.

I held to higher principles, and my running away usually was based upon my deciding that I had been wronged or not allowed to do something that I was "old enough" to do.

My brother made a hobo stick with a red bandana attached to the end. In the bandana, he managed to cram a sandwich and chips, which I guess he deemed the right amount of food for running away. He usually ran away to his friend's house down the street. After about three hours hanging around, his sandwich eaten, he returned home from his big adventure.

My running away was infinitely more complex, and ironically, Mom would get involved. She employed reverse psychology on me. I would, with great flair, announce that I was "Running Away!" She would say, "Well, I don't blame you. Let's pack what you'll need." Thus began the weird process of getting out my suitcase and Mom literally loading it up with clothes, toiletries, books and whatever else weighed a ton. After it was properly packed, she would tell me that they'd miss me and to have a good time.

Geez, at that point, I kind of had to follow through on my running away plans, and now I had a big heavy suitcase to drag along. But undaunted, I headed down the street with a quick look back to see if Mom were watching. Rats, she had already gone back in the house. Running away is not nearly as dramatic when no one is convincing you to stay.

I would sometimes ditch the suitcase at the neighbor's house and then decide where to better spend the afternoon. Usually, I headed to Crestview Recreation Center, which was a fine place to run away to with its craft room, basketball court, and other kids hanging out. If I had fifty cents, I would go to Tastee Freez on 21st Street and get some ice cream. After what seemed a decent amount of time for my family to grieve my leaving, I would reclaim my plaid suitcase and slip in the front door. Mom would always act like it was business as usual as I unpacked my twenty-pound suitcase.

Running away is a good thing to do and running home is even better.

The 59th Street Bridge Song with a nod. Feelin' groovy! A perfect Sunday, I drive by myself through the back ways of the Flint Hills. Almost got lost, but I have "west" in my genetic coding.

Ann Anderson

Down by Deep Creek, gravel roads, like small veins across this great grassland, and past beautiful farms and weathered barns that could come down in the next big south wind.

I stopped at the Konza prairie lookout. I was alone. Dark gray clouds were landing on the prairie and kissing it with the first rain-drops. The new fall colors blended into the still green grasses and it looked like ancient sand art.

Past the brown and white cows with their sweet faces nodding to me, past the mile markers and red-tailed hawks grown already fat from a good summer, to my final destination, my twin nieces in Manhattan. We sat at Radina's Bakehouse with hot chocolate and croissants as I listened to their lives spill out like brightly colored Lego blocks. I had on my one K-State shirt and pink K-State hat, happy to blend into their "wildcat world."

Reagan has found the love of her life, Brandon, and it was a delight to listen to her talk about him. Jordan's boyfriend, George, is from Hawaii. I drifted off listening to them. They used to talk only about soccer and whether to order chicken strips or chicken Alfredo. I love them. I am happy for both of them to have found companions in this life. Reagan said she wants to be a boss and get an important job. Jordan said she wants to work somewhere pretty where everybody has interesting clothes.

I hugged my twin nieces goodbye as the chill fall rain began. I drove back to Topeka, choosing this time the safety of I-70, as I know every foot of that friendly road from here to Denver. By the turn to Alma and Wamego, my tummy thought of the Friend-ship Cafe in Wamego with their fresh pastries, but I wanted to get home.

Finally home, opening the door, the cats lying against it, and hearing Vann inquire, "How was your day?" Well, just groovy! I love my twin nieces. They line my heart with enchantment.

✿ ✿ ✿

Postcards from the edge... I happily extracted a postcard from my mailbox today. It was from my lifelong friend, Debra, and showed a vintage picture of the cherry blossoms in Washington D.C. A postcard is a picture and worth a thousand words though you only have to write a few. It is a gift from the sender, a little me-mento of their travels, and the discovery that someone has been thinking about you.

224

I loved getting and sending postcards when I was a kid. My favorite scrapbook is jammed with postcards from friends and relatives, glued in place for enjoyment so many years later. Pictures of Disneyland, Mount Rushmore, Yellowstone, the giant sequoia trees, and my favorite, the postcards of palomino horses Mom sent me from Colorado.

I adored palomino horses and still do with their gorgeous golden coats and their to-die-for pale blonde manes. I wanted a palomino horse and was constantly begging Mom to get me one. But alas, I had to settle for postcards featuring the beautiful horses. Mom sent ones of palominos adorned with silver and turquoise on their saddles, and sometimes, she would write that they had ridden them. Oh, I just about passed out thinking about my stepdad and her riding those gorgeous horses in Colorado. I was probably a teenager before I realized she was just kidding, but oh well, I have lots of palomino postcards to still enjoy and smile at her tall tale.

Postcards were probably the first offerings we made as kids to let others know we were thinking of them. I remember carefully planning just the right words to write as there was not much space and I was a little intimidated by the black line with the words "Do not write below this line." I would carefully address the postcard, adhere a stamp and off it would go. It was a wonderful gift to send on our vacations, and Mom would let us get extra ones for our scrapbook. Long before "selfies," postcards were a way to remember the fun and beauty of a special vacation.

Postcards... Having a wonderful time. Wish you were here!

It's the shoes... As I was getting ready for tennis today, I stopped with a smile and looked at my shoe rack. Since retiring from the corporate world and becoming a tennis coach, my shoe collection has definitely made a major shift. For decades, my shoe collection featured stylish high heels in all colors. I was especially fond of the two-toned spectators. My favorite pair were turquoise and white. When I put them on, I swear my feet were smiling. I am not really sure how I walked, danced, and worked in three-inch heels, but I did so for many years.

As a kid, I owned probably four pairs of shoes. I had a yearly summer pair of Keds that Mom would buy me the week school got out. I would go out of my way to not get the beautiful white shoes dirty. I loved the small Keds' blue rubber tag on the back of the heel and would protect it from wearing off. I owned a pair of "thongs" as they were called then – "flip-flops" now. They were the go-to shoe for days at Crestview pool. I had a pair of "good" shoes for church. My favorite shoes I had as a kid were my Poll Parrot saddle shoes. They always looked amazing and Mom bought me a small shoe kit of white and black polish to keep them looking brand new.

We shopped at the shoe store at 21st and Fairlawn. Just walking in the door was heavenly, the smell of new leather and canvas overwhelming our senses. If we were lucky enough to get a new pair of shoes, the shoe guy would throw in a Poll Parrot clicker. I liked sitting in the comfy overstuffed chairs and having a professional shoe guy measure my foot. I would properly place my socked foot on top of the gleaming silver shoe size contraption and then step down. The shoe guy would make the adjustment for length and width and then voila!—out from the back he would come with three or four shoe boxes balanced in his arms.

Mom was big on squishing her thumb at the end of my toe to make sure it was the proper fit. She always adhered to the advice to buy a half size bigger so I could grow into them. But whatever, I was just beyond excited to be getting a new pair of saddle shoes. I would walk around the store to make sure they fit and stop spellbound at each floor mirror to admire their look.

I would still like a pair of saddle shoes and find it odd that they do not make them for all of us mid-century kids. At least now I have a shoe rack of spiffy tennis shoes in all colors next to my small collection of dress shoes.

Poll Parrot, Poll Parrot, they're the shoes you want to buy!

World Books and cookbooks… Vann and I took a lovely Sunday drive around Topeka to admire the early spring flowers and trees. We could not help but notice that it was the season for garage sales. They seem to spring up with the dandelions, and they were doing a great business today.

Back in the day, Mom would spontaneously announce on a Friday evening that we would be having a garage sale the next day. My brother and I knew there was cold hard cash to be had, so we were instantly in our rooms, rounding up unused toys and outgrown clothes, and our bounty belched into the garage. Mom would tidily arrange our offerings into neat piles with pieces of masking tape noting the price on each item. By 7:00 a.m. Saturday morning, our homemade sign was nailed to our faithful elm tree and we were "Open for Business."

We had a steady stream of customers, and Mom cleverly also made a "FREE" box. The free box was an assortment of things usually missing something but nevertheless the free box was an instant hit with all the neighborhood kids. Sometimes Mom would get a call from a parent politely asking Mom to ban their child from bringing home any more "free" stuff.

One time, we had a huge turnout and Mom felt inspired to head back to our basement and put out a new assortment of sale items. She carefully instructed my brother to run the sale for a while, and if he got into trouble, he was to holler for us.

Well, after fifteen minutes, we returned from the basement with our arms laden with more stuff. My brother was fairly hopping from one foot to another with a check in his hand, overcome with capitalist glee. He told Mom that a nice lady had bought all the books and cookbooks we had out. She had then asked if we had any more books for sale. "Of course," my brother replied. He went in the house and brought out Mom's heirloom Searchlight Cookbook, her best cookbook, and topped it all off by bringing out our ENTIRE set of treasured World Book encyclopedias. I thought Mom was going to cry, and I was steamed because the World Book encyclopedias were my complete source of knowledge for book reports and schoolwork. To add insult to injury, Mike proudly displayed the check and said he sold everything for $20.00!

To our surprise, Mom ran inside the house and called the phone number on the check. Fortunately, the lady was very nice about the mistake and offered to return the vintage cookbook and our World Books. An hour later, they were safely back on our shelves, and my brother was never again permitted to run the garage sale by himself.

I still have Mom's Searchlight Cookbook, and I think of it with a smile whenever we pass a garage sale on a fine spring day.

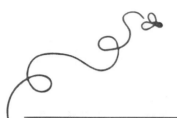

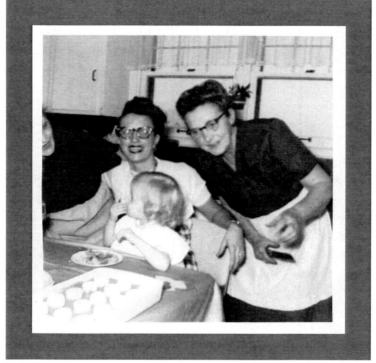

Canning day, an apron and the best year yet

Chapter Fourteen

BEST YEAR YET

By late afternoon, Grandma and I sit at her table. Grandpa comes in from the barn and says, "This looks like the best year yet."

The gift… As Father's Day approaches, it feels so different to me than Mother's Day. Mother's Day always tears off that Band-Aid over my heart. I loved my mom so much. My bio dad left us when I was four and my brother was two. In reality, he probably was not really ever there. He and Mom got married because they enjoyed playing softball, sports, and probably after the war in the late forties, they both figured, "Why not?" An affair would end their eight-year marriage. I only remember one Father's Day with him when I was about seven.

He picked us up one Saturday morning so we could spend the weekend together at Lake Perry. He had married his girlfriend, Glenda, and he had a big boat at the lake. My brother and I thought this could be the turning point—he liked us after all. I had asked Mom to buy a bottle of Aqua Velva cologne for him and I wrapped it in blue paper with a big bow. I was so excited and kept it hidden in my paper bag of clothes to present to him on Father's Day.

That Saturday was one disaster after another. Glenda clearly did not like us. I overheard her say to my bio dad, "This is the last time you will bring those kids here. They are ruining our weekend."

She just wanted to party and drive the boat around. I remember sitting in our little tent feeling so angry, not sad. I was glad my brother felt none of this as he was happily out fishing most of the time.

At about 5:00 p.m. that day, Glenda announced that she was quite ill and we had to go home. The tents were packed, hot dogs and s'mores left in the Coleman cooler, and we all loaded into the Ford station wagon. I remember riding back to Topeka and putting my hand in the paper bag that held the once magnificent Aqua Velva Father's Day gift. Its blue tissue paper still seemed soft, and I made the decision that it was not for my bio dad. He had already left for another life that did not include us.

The next morning, I gave it to my stepdad, who graciously accepted it although I don't think it was his favorite scent. Mom showered us with hugs, but nothing could soothe the sting of our bio dad not caring about us. That was one of the last times I would see him.

You are probably thinking this sounds sad. But sometimes people give you a chance to make a decision, and my bio dad did just that. He saved me a lot of additional pain by drawing the line in my sand heart.

I will always remember touching the gift wrapped in the blue tissue paper. I learned that day not to let my heart get stuck.

Rock Chalk! I was asked this week to help at the KU Tennis Camp. I tried to be cool and answer "yes" without jumping up and down.

Sunday started with greeting almost two hundred kids at the door at the Jayhawk Tennis Center with a couple of the KU tennis players. We all high-fived the kids, welcomed them, and tried to get them relaxed as they started this new adventure.

I knew how they felt because I am confident of my skills, and I know I can put out great energy, but I kept thinking, "Is this a dream? Am I really at KU Tennis Camp?"

We had a blast, and by Wednesday, everyone was tired, full of information and new skills. I learned so much from Coach Todd, and I will remember his quick encouragements of "Watch and learn," "Be coachable," and "Contribute."

As we stood in a big circle of goodbyes, Coach Todd began the awards ceremony. I heard him talk about the coach who brought the best energy, was always early, and made a positive contribution every day. Then I heard him announce, "Coach Ann is 'Coach of the Week'!!" I would have done cartwheels if I could have. I was so happy. After I left tennis camp, I bought a cupcake. I had to do something to celebrate! It was an award I will cherish forever. It was a reminder that you might not be the best player in the game, but you can work harder and bring your best attitude. I could hear Mom whispering, "Are you doing your best? Are you having fun?"

Kansas is hearing a screen door slam and a tray of lemonade being set down in the cut hay dusk.

Canning day... I hear my grandma stirring, putting on her housedress made of cotton so soft from wear that it feels like a bunny's ear. All her housedresses have simple buttons and pretty floral prints that seem to blend into her country life. She has aprons, sewn from leftover materials, with ties sometimes of a different print. The aprons have pockets on the front for whatever she might need during the day, and if I am lucky, she will tuck a few butterscotch pieces of hard candy in for me.

Today, I am helping her can. The fruits and vegetables are at their peak of summer ripeness. We have spent this week on the farm gathering cucumbers, wild plums, apricots, apples, raspberries, and all of the vegetables that only six months before were lying in seed packets on Grandma's kitchen table. Grandpa cut rows as straight as a ruler through the black earthworm ground. Grandma and I walked behind and dropped and patted the seeds into their beds. Grandma has boxes of Mason jars scrubbed to a shine waiting to be filled. I am her "sous chef," carefully cutting and seeding whatever she gives me. My heart swells every time she looks over at me and nods her approval. When she bends down to kiss the top of my head, I am sure she is an angel and God has just let her come down and dress up like a grandma for me.

We start with the cucumbers that are are sliced pickle-thick. They are stuffed upright in the jars awaiting the scalding brine, which Grandma carefully pours over them. The kitchen is a dizzy scent of fresh dill, pickling spices and vinegar.

We move on to the tomato sauce that next winter will be blended into soups and spaghetti. Then on to the corn, neatly trimmed off its ears and into the jars. The taste of summer is tricked into staying in the jars as Grandma works so quickly.

Grandma saves the fruits for last as she always says she wants the kitchen to smell like "cinnamon and spice and everything nice." That always makes me smile.

We stop for a lunch of cold fried chicken, some of our leftover veggies, and a chunk of whatever cake Grandma has made that week. As we are working so hard, Grandma pours me a cup of "kitty coffee" as she has named it. An inch of coffee with fresh cream poured on top and a teaspoon of sugar. Between the caffeine and sugar, I am ready to tackle the fruits with her. Her wild plums are a dazzling shade of dark magenta and purple. The golden orange apricots look so vibrant sitting next to the purple plums, and they literally sparkle in their new Mason jar homes. The last fruits to be put up are the apples. Grandma and I carefully cut them into chunks, and they go into their big pot with cinnamon, nutmeg, sugar, and vanilla. The mixture bubbles like hot lava and I want to taste it so badly. I know Grandma will dish me out a small bowl for being her helper when we are done.

By late afternoon, Grandma and I sit at her table. Grandpa comes in from the barn and says, "This looks like the best year yet." They smile as he says this every year. But every time we can together, I too think this is the best year yet. As Grandma and I sit there eating our warm applesauce, we hear the first of the lids pop, telling us they are sealing up for their trip to the root cellar.

We will sit out in the front yard after dinner in the white wooden chairs Grandpa made. We will count the neighbor's milk cows going in for their feed, exactly thirty-eight, but we still like to count. I lean against Grandma, trying to stay awake, but so happy for the day, and the smell of spices and herbs on her are a tonic for sleep. Up the stairs to the spare bedroom, a bath and pajamas on as I listen to Grandma tell Grandpa what a good day we had canning.

Eulogy… Almost three years ago, I was standing with our loved ones at my brother Mike's "Celebration of Life" in the quaint

Mission Cemetery at 29th and Urish Road (or the blue light cemetery which we called it when we were kids). There was never any discussion of where he wanted to be. It was always at the Mission Cemetery with its mature cedars' over-arching shade and the eclectic, non-conforming decorations. And the bonus: Mike said he would be right by Dillon's if he got hungry.

As I remember this anniversary, I am reminded to express thoughts not to be saved just for eulogies but to wrap my friends and family in heartfelt love that is sometimes saved for too late.

Life river…I am floating down this river, my life. When I was small, Mom was my boat captain and kept me safe. She taught me The Golden Rule. She taught me to choose happy and always try my best. I floated by many people and experiences and soaked them in.

Sometimes, they were hurtful: my bio dad who left us, the illness that would take my grandma, my mom, and my brother too young. I held onto my boat and kept it floating steady.

Some were beautiful experiences: jobs that let me be with caring, giving, amazing people, travel to cities all over the country, learning, and steering away from the bad.

My river took me north to Chicago and it was frozen. Too cold, too gray, and I drifted to the ocean. Turquoise, warm, sunlight went back into me. The neon colors of Los Angeles revived me and smoothed out the Pisces water girl.

My river flowed by Vann, and he would join me for life. A traveler who loved the journey and a heart that thumped with mine, eyes that filled with tears at my sadness and twinkled with happiness at my joy. Hand in hand.

The river is home. The river has my nieces and nephew who will always be just around the bend. My kitties keep a perch on the bow of my boat, purring through my life.

The river has brought me to such good people. The people of the south wind, my Kansas friends, who grow in me like the tall grass grows on the prairie. I share their lives and they soak into mine.

My dear friend, Kyle, sent me a text today expressing his gratitude for our friendship, for being a part of something great. On my river, I will share this kind of goodness with those who need a lifting up of their hearts. It is never too late to find love and happiness on the life river of our hearts.

I think of all the people who have helped me row my little boat and of all the people who have pushed it through shallow, troubled waters. I also think of all those people who have dipped their toes in the sweet water with me when life is at its best.

Tonight, I am on my river. It runs deep and pure.

"Kids, don't move! I'm going to go get Sam." Mom said this with such a command and sharpness in her voice that I was startled and scared. She never raised her voice to us. Sam was our Siamese kitty who just appeared one morning while Mom and I were reading the paper on our front steps. He plopped down by Mom's feet and began grooming as if he had always lived with us.

As Kansas kids, the shrieking, wailing sound of the tornado siren was something that we heeded, but we were never afraid. We dutifully went to the basement and leaned against the Maytag washer and dryer in the southwest corner.

But on this summer day in 1966, the skies were a "Wizard of Oz Emerald City" green, and Mom seemed nervous. She never brought Sam to the basement when the sirens went off as he usually found his own place in the closet.

My brother and I did not move as we were tucked under a heavy, oak table and Mom had uncharacteristically piled all of the basement quilts and pillows around us. My brother asked if we were going to "play fort."

The air in the basement was suffocating, claustrophobic, and stuffy. Mom went upstairs and returned with a surprised-looking Sam in her arms. He, too, seemed to sense something was not right as he took his place with us in this hastily built fort.

I remember being scared as I watched Mom's face. Her face was almost always relaxed with a smile that went into a laugh. But she sat with us, hunched over and clutching my turquoise transistor radio. I remember hearing the pouring rain and the sirens continuing their mournful warning. Why didn't they turn them off?

We did not speak, and I was again startled when Mom said, "Don't move, I'll be right back." She told me to watch Mike and Sam. I suddenly felt so small and did not want her to go upstairs.

She came back as pale as a marshmallow, and I asked, "What

did you see?" She did not reply but pulled us around her. Normally, the light scent of Chanel No. 5 would be pleasantly intoxicating to me, but at that moment it only added to my sense that something bad was happening.

After about twenty minutes, Mom told us we could come with her. We went upstairs and the rain had stopped. We looked out on a bright sunshiny day. I was so confused. She had us get in the car, and we drove to 25th and Gage where we saw the backside of the tornado, massive, menacing and eerily glowing white and gold with the west sun on it. At that point, it was chewing up Washburn University and heading to downtown Topeka.

Mom drove to 29th and Gage where the sadness and devastation began. All of the roads were blocked, and people were walking in a stupor of disbelief, many of them with bloody gashes and some holding a few belongings. Mom, no doubt, did not want us to witness this. We drove silently back to our home, which I worried had been taken away while we were gone.

I picked up Sam and held him against me to resettle my world. It was the summer of my fourteenth year. It was the June 8th tornado of 1966.

We watched the Space Station go by at 17,000 MPH last night. We waved to them. Did they see us and wave back and smile?

Summer 1964... Twelve years old and growing from kid to teenager. No matter what the trials of my life would be, I would take refuge in my grandma's tree swing. It was under a tree so big that it seemed to shade part of the garden and most of the yard. Its rope handles had been held by all the older grandchildren to the point of feeling like smooth velvet in my hands. The simple, wooden seat that Grandpa made was likewise worn into a pleasantly indented surface from the backsides of all of the cousins.

The swing was on a very long rope, so I could pump high into the sky and almost see the pond. Most summer days, it was pleasant just to sit on the swing and lightly push my Keds into the dusty, worn down earth under the swing.

Grandma would stop by and bring me a grape Nehi, my favor-

Ann Anderson

ite, or sometimes a dish of homemade ice cream topped with her wild plum or apricot preserves (summer in a jar).

I was twelve. In the evening, Grandma sat on the big limestone rock by the swing, shucking corn and snapping green beans. We sang, "This little light of mine, I'm going to let it shine."

Sitting outside early morning and thinking about my twin nieces. For as long as I can remember, I wanted to be a twin and still think about it. I guess God did the best by gifting me with twin nieces. I have been smitten in love with them since I first saw them lying side-by-side. They have always been side-by-side. They have always been each other's cheerleader, confidante, and best friend. When we went on our "Aunt Ann dates," they always chose to go together and always had the same two lists of what they wanted to do: museum, mall, movie, and Maggie Moo's (cotton candy ice cream). The twin list!

I watched them as soccer teammates when they were five years old with braids blowing back and colt legs running to when they were eighteen and in their first year of college. They chased up and down the field and always rushed over if one got hurt. They are two people who make each other all the better for the things they share. I admire how they have stretched to try new things on their own while always knowing they have a twin to come home to.

The summer after they had finished their Associates Degree at the community college, we met for lunch. They said they had something very important to tell me. They were uncharacteristically nervous and finally Reagan told me they had decided to attend Kansas State University. I guess they thought I would be upset after all the KU t-shirts I had given them over the years.

They made a good choice and, unbelievably, their college years are about to come to a close. I do not envy them that doubly-hard twin question: How to separate when you have been together your whole life? (If I were a twin, I am sure I would live next door to my twin.) They both have promising lives ahead with new careers, boyfriends, friends and maybe someday, families with great-nieces and nephews for me to spoil.

They forever have that most enviable twin connection.

"Be coachable," or as Mom would have said, "Don't be a know it all."

Smooth stones... Somewhere between where the heart and the mind link, you have been in my quiet thoughts this week. I have been thinking of the last days of hearing you talk. When I took you to the ER for the last time, you were in such pain and yet, so happy. You had just spent three days at the Lake of the Ozarks with your high school buddy, doing all the things you should not have been doing and yet, maybe knowing you had to experience them all one more time.

You told the ER doctor you had so much fun, eating steak, drinking rum and Coke and even trying to water ski. For once, I kept my big sister mouth shut as I was stunned that you had done all of this, and I also realized how important it was to you with not much time left. Why not? The ER doctor winked at me as if he too knew that this was your way to go out of this life.

The last time I would hear your voice was two days before you died on August 1st. On a Friday, you came out of the fog that had hidden your smile and, just for a day, your kids and I gathered around you soaking in your words, your grin, and those fleeting moments that God shared you with us. Jordan brought you a lei from Hawaii which you wore with your coral polo shirt while lying in the hospice bed. You almost tricked us into thinking you were just taking it easy for a day. You told me that you wanted Vann to take you to Camelot to be with King Arthur, a story you loved as a child. By 9:00 p.m. that night you began your passing from us. You would not get to open the card Reagan had made for you with two lottery tickets taped inside and a note that read, "Dad, call me when you wake up." You had started your journey to Camelot to be among the knights.

When you were little, I pretended you were my baby doll. You quickly outgrew me and became my protector, somebody to play tennis with on hot afternoons and somebody to ride bikes with to Crestview—fifty cents in our pockets and fifty cents more for a popsicle.

You gave me nieces and a nephew. You gave me away at my wedding. You made all of us laugh with your sweet sense of humor, you impressed us with your breadth of knowledge and your inquisitive mind, and we are all the better for having you for fifty-nine short years.

My heart is like a little stone with edges still jagged from your passing. Each year, time helps smooth some of the rough edges, making it like a river stone where the sadness can roll off.

I am memorizing this night. I am happy to sit and watch a cloud.

The Arkansas traveler… I have been back to the Natural State – Arkansas, twice in one week, once with friends to see the Chihuly glass exhibit at Crystal Bridges and then back again to wander with Vann. It was our first sojourn in our small TAB camper, setting the mind straight and the heart free. We walked quietly through the forest at Crystal Bridges so Vann could see the stunning Chihuly glass seemingly growing up from the cool, dark, forest floors and spilling from its ancient branches. Then we escaped to the quiet of the lake.

One of my friends has her navigator set to "interstates only." I thought if there were a setting that Vann would choose, it would be "gravel roads and roads that don't show up on the maps." He is the Life is Good tee shirt that says "Not all who wander are lost."

Our camper nestled in happily at Beaver Lake. One night we were treated to an Arkansas blow: fierce, pelting rain, straight line winds, and we feared we would all be tossed into the lake. By 10:00 p.m., all the power was out and it was as if an early nighttime eclipse had visited us. There was only a glint of a pale moon on the lake and a few hardy campers trying to encourage a campfire.

The following day, after exploring all the roads not found on maps, we took our chairs to the water's edge to wade about like egrets, eat snacks, and talk about the day's sightings. We saw a mama deer with triplets so tiny and leggy, covered in white polka dots. We saw two eagles, a boat fall off its trailer, and kids on their inner tubes.

We went to the Roaring River just on the Missouri side, and it was Kids' Fish Free Day. Kids were happily fishing and shouting as they reeled in the trout and then released them. I loved looking at the rainbow sides of the trout swimming in the clear water of the river.

We found a small town consisting of two sad-looking stores with hopeful signage and offering Arkansas antiques—whatever that meant. Inside one store, we met a happy Florida transplant who chatted with Vann about the business of Florida. She had her own little coffee station set up. She ground up the dark-roasted coffee beans, poured in her own homemade huckleberry syrup, and some cream. What an unexpected find!

I am like the salmon of the great rivers. At a certain point, I know it is time for me to go home. I marveled at the Ozark mountains laden with trees so thick they made a blanket of greens. At our campsite, a skyful of vultures were riding the hot thermals above us and cutting the air perfectly. But I am not a mountain girl. I am a prairie girl, and I yearn always to see the horizon and to smell the grass kissed down by the south wind.

Silver linings... When I was a child and thought some atrocity had befallen me, I would sometimes whine to Mom or Grandma about the injustice. With a smile on their faces, they would bend down to me and say, "Look for the silver linings in the clouds." It would be a few years before I understood silver linings.

I was sidelined at tennis today after having a skin cancer removed on my hand. That saying from long ago came whispering back to me. I sat and watched Vann play tennis for ninety minutes. At age eighty, he decided he was ready for some tennis lessons. Now it is something we share and enjoy together. At one point, he looked over at me, winked and then deftly put a drop shot over for a winner. Silver linings from the sidelines.

Then on to teaching the kiddos at the Jayhawk Tennis Center, seeing them spill in and eagerly hearing their latest "five-and six-year-old" news. My buddy, Wyatt, dug in his tennis bag and proudly handed me the sweetest card. It had stickers, which he carefully showed me, some of his first cursive writing, and my name, Coach Ann, proudly displayed. I bent down and gave him a hug that was not nearly big enough for what I was feeling in my heart. I am so grateful for knowing this boy, for his kindness, for getting a card from him and seeing his happiness at beginning to learn how nice it is to make others feel special.

I looked down at my bandage and silently thanked God for the silver linings that came from slowing down for just a bit. No dark clouds, just seeing their shiny, silver linings.

Senior Class… I have played tennis for over sixty years. I firm-ly embrace the quote by George Bernard Shaw that says, "We don't stop playing because we grow old; we grow old because we stop playing." I asked Kyle if I could start a "Senior Class" at the Jayhawk Tennis Center. Kyle said, "Of course!" and I beat the bushes for senior players who would like to be in a weekly drill. As the first class approached, I looked at the sign-up sheet and there were only four players. Well, it was at least enough to have one court.The day before the first class, I checked the sheet again and twenty-three players had signed up! I was elated. As we celebrat-ed our two years of the Senior Class, I felt grateful. The class has become a group of good friends staying young together.

On the first day of class, twenty-three strangers walked onto the courts. They were all apprehensive, and to break the ice, I asked, "Who was President when you bought your racquet?" Most of the racquets they were holding were dug out of their garages after being put away in the 1980s when they thought they were done with tennis. At the end of the first class, one of the players came up to me, thanked me and said, "Jimmy Carter. Jimmy Car-ter was President when I bought this racquet." Here's to the Se-nior Class at Jayhawk Tennis Center—Rock Chalk!

My mother's child… I sit outside tonight with cats curled about my feet like summer slippers. We are quiet and watch the water-color, hot day wash into a deep, navy blue evening with a cool, south breeze. The tips of the leaves stir as if touched by God's fingers.

I smile. I think of the countless summer nights on Burnett Road that I sat with Mom and Miss Kitty in just this way. From our webbed lawn chairs, Mom and I kissed the day goodbye and watched the sunset. Miss Kitty stretched out to catch the last heat off the warm concrete and her sweet, brown ears listened to our words. We talked of the day, of what the garden had given us (a beefsteak tomato that would sit on a BLT sandwich the next day), of a tennis game which Mom won, as usual, by lobbing my team until we smashed all the balls into the net laughing. We talked of our hopes and dreams, of the evening breeze, and of where the

240

planes were flying, blinking like stars and disappearing into the western rainbow night.

Sometimes, we would just sit and not talk. No matter, our hearts communicated the love and happiness of being together on those warm summer nights. Miss Kitty would jump into Mom's lap and they would both sigh with contentment. They were quite the pair. She was my kitty, but she chose Mom to be her special place.

Across the street, our neighbor's mom called for her boys to come in. More often than not, her boys were gathered with our other friends under the streetlight on 23rd and Burnett Road. It was a fine place for hanging out, leaning on the curved handle-bars of our Sting Ray bikes, or sitting on the curb and looking up at a zillion bugs dancing in the light.

I was happiest sitting with Mom, watching the moon wake up and the stars take their place in our night world. She point-ed out the Big Dipper and Little Dipper and her words were the sandman's dust sprinkled over me. With Miss Kitty nestled in her arms, we went back into our home and I crawled happily under my sheets, the attic fan whirring gently in the background. The cool air was pulled out of the night and washed over me.

Now, so many years gone by. I am on my own patio with my kitties and wonder where the blinking light of the plane overhead is going on this warm summer night.

Mom's last holiday... Labor Day weekend 1982. The Septem-ber blues float over me every year about this time as the heart remembers your last holiday. Though you had long been confined to your hospital bed in the living room, it would be the last time I heard your voice.

Sometime that weekend, the angels floated around your gold-en soul, ready to tuck you under their wings.

Your occasional words became different that weekend. You wandered back to a very happy place and talked to maybe the angels about fishing with your brothers, finding arrowheads on the old farm by Mission Creek, playing in the cornfields with your dog, Pete, and helping your mom make cherry pies. You did not talk to us, but I sat there and soaked in the sound of your voice, each word imprinting on my heart, each last memory being staked out for me to savor. By Labor Day evening, your eyes closed peacefully. For three weeks, you would stay with us but no more words, just the breathing between Earth and Heaven's journey.

Miss Kitty, my cat who loved you most, stayed by your side all that summer. She seemed to still hear you after you quit speaking and she lay quietly against your side.

Fall was always your favorite season. I knew it was your time with the maple leaves starting to turn, the first chill in the morning air, and the sumacs edging toward red.

I still see your face, Miss Kitty making little biscuits into you.

The Brownie pin… I was looking for my old watch this morning and came across my Brownie pin and the little patches for my troop, Number 118. It is good to hold those kinds of childhood things in our hands as they instantly transport us back to that simple time.

I was so excited when Mom said I could join the Brownie troop and then, of course, Mom and another mother volunteered to be the leaders. I was fairly dizzy with the awe of the pale brown uniform, a proper belt, and the embroidered patches attached to the sleeve. I had a dark brown Brownie beanie that resembled a Mickey Mouse hat without the ears. It had a little loop on the top. With matching Brownie socks and saddle shoes, it was the first uniform I would ever wear and the first time, other than church, that I belonged to a group.

Our little band of girls met each Monday, sometimes at Crestview Methodist Church across from our grade school and sometimes in my own basement. I could barely sit through school on Mondays waiting for our Brownie meeting to begin.

Mom had the official Brownie Leader Handbook, and I would sneak peek at it to see what we would be creating in the coming week. We always began with the Brownie pledge, and then we worked on earning our badges, volunteering, exploring nature, and having new Brownie adventures. I loved selling Girl Scout cookies! Sandwich, shortbread and my favorite, Thin Mints! Girl Scout cookies selling was the precursor to spring!

Sometimes Mom would create an activity about the season. We made fall displays by spray-painting hedge balls bright gold, we made Christmas cards with red construction paper, a sprig of spruce glued on, the whole thing drenched in spray-on snow and we made a Brownie birdhouse unsuitable for any bird. Of course, I always thought the results were simply dazzling.

We each brought a dime for the meeting. Even though Mom was the leader, she made that my responsibility, and I would open my little bank and tape a dime to my book that day. Sometimes we had treats, and I am sure the dime did not quite cover the cost, but it felt good to contribute to the cause.

By the time I was ready for Girl Scouts, I had discovered sports and piano lessons. I think Mom was tired of being both a Brownie leader and also my brother's Cub Scout Den Mother. Somewhere in growing up, I probably gave the uniform to a younger friend, but I have held onto my Brownie pin and the patches for my troop number, 118. They are sweet reminders of such a gentle time in the 1950s when a Brownie uniform, belonging to a little group, and having a dime were so important.

Up with the roosters... I guess I have the DNA of Grandma and Mom that sets my "get-up" to "Early." I spent many glorious mornings with Grandma and Grandpa who both routinely got up at 4:30 or 5:00 a.m. to begin their day. There was never any discussion of it being early as there was strong Folger's coffee with fresh cream ready at our places, pancakes so light they were more like crepes, warm cane syrup, and scrambled eggs from "free range" chickens before there was that term. Grandma's chickens were like her kitties, all had names, were fussed over by her, were let loose during the day to bug and grain hunt, and were carefully placed back in their big coop at night. They rewarded her each day with large eggs and yolks as golden as wheat. It was frequently my job to gather the eggs. Grandma handed me the worn basket and shooed me out the door. It was still dark. I was always quite sure a coyote might eat me, and they'd all be sorry they had sent to me to get the eggs. But the real reason for my fear was that the hens were not too cordial at 6:00 a.m. If Grandma went with me, they instantly lifted off of their precious eggs and clucked happy sounds to her. When I gathered the eggs, the chickens sat like fat hens firmly on their treasures and gave me a few pecks of "leave us alone!" But I had a task to do. With remnant beak marks on my hands, and having escaped the imagined coyote attacks, I made it back with our breakfast eggs. By 6:30 a.m. breakfast was eaten, Grandpa was in the red barn milking the cows, the barn cats were on their hind legs getting milk squirted in their waiting whiskery mouths, and Grandma and I had started in on a batch of cinnamon rolls.

If a written recipe ever existed in Grandma's kitchen, I never saw it. She would take out her worn pans, grease them up in Crisco, and begin the whirling process: scooping into her flour bin, dipping a coffee cup into the big sugar jar, shaking spices into the bowl, adding butter and eggs, and every time out came the perfect mound of dough. She worked it with her hands and then into a long rectangle with the wooden rolling pin. After dotting the dough with butter, spices, and raisins, she rolled it up, cutting and placing the generous slices into the 9"X13" pan. As her assistant, I was posted on the red step stool. I loved to see her hands, worn from hard work, capable of running a corn shucker or just as easily creating a piece of lace. The rolls would come out, and she would drown them in pale, creamy frosting that seemed to sink into every empty space.

She had a song she always sang to me when she baked. "Can you bake a cherry pie, Billy boy, Billy boy, can you bake a cherry pie, charming Billy? I can bake a cherry pie quick as a cat can wink its eye, he's a young boy and cannot leave his mother…" I still hum Grandma's version of that old nursery rhyme when I am in the kitchen and those smells drift back to me.

Grandpa came in from his morning chores by 8:00 a.m. and we enjoyed a hot roll and the two of them drank coffee. Grandma poured me "kittycream," as she called it and I thought I was quite grown up drinking coffee with them.

Fortified with sugar and caffeine, we spent our mornings weeding, hoeing in the garden, painting an outbuilding white, or whatever the farm needed that day. The farm was hard work, so I guess they had to get up early. Everyone ate well and we all were properly tired after a day of chores. It was a gentle life, full of purpose, good food, being together. I would love to walk in that early dawn again to the chicken coop, wary for the coyote, lifting the warm hen with her soft feathers, and feeling her little beak peck my hand.

Fall back… We sleep with the windows open on this early November night, and I am warmed by at least one kitty pressing against my back. I hear Vann at 5:00 a.m. (6:00 a.m. old time) turn on the heat for the first time this year. A click, a spark, and the smell of warm, ozone furnace floats through the house, a true signal that it is "sweater weather"! With one more hour, I fall back and snuggle in.

Prayers… Tom Sawyer said that his Aunt Polly told him he should pray more. He thus began to pray for fishhooks and such and said his prayers were not answered. I figure God must hear all prayers, little thought bubbles from the heart.

As a mid-century kid, the nightly routine was a bath, putting on my jammies and kneeling with Mom on the rug beside my bed. Hand-hooked by Grandma from colorful scraps of wool, the rug was a soft cushion beneath our knees. I liked to press my forehead against the sheets, especially if they had hung on the line and were smelling of lilacs. I said the same prayer every night which was "Now I lay me down to sleep, I pray the Lord my soul to keep; if I should die before I wake, I pray the Lord my soul to take." It was not my favorite prayer as I always kind of jumped over the "if I should die" part. I liked it when we followed it with showering special "God Blessings" on different people: my family, friends, teachers, pets, food. Sometimes too many for Mom who would gently say, "That's probably enough blessings for tonight." It was a routine that seemed to magically close my day and take me off to sweet dreams.

In church, we said the Lord's Prayer. As a kid, I mumbled it and it really held little meaning to me. I asked Mom more than once what did "give us our daily bread" mean. I was thinking we were going to get some Wonder Bread from somebody. I also thought "trespassing" was like the signs posted at farms on the way to Grandma's house. I have come to understand that prayer more fully along the years.

Our prayers are good for the person on the receiving end and ultimately, good for us, too. I wonder what if the whole world sat for one hour in prayer? I'm quite sure the world would shift.

Tonight, I will say my prayers again for all that surrounds me.

Sea lake... On these fall mornings, so pumpkin-spiced and perfect, the kitties and I take our places on the patio. I stretch out on two chairs and grab a not-yet-put-away beach towel as my throw. I read the Lawrence newspaper and smile when it announces that Lawrence will attempt to break the "zombie" record.

I feel like a passenger on a grand cruise ship, neatly covered with a blanket, sipping a hot dark coffee, reading a morning newspaper. This ship has even provided me with a sweet kitty who lightly jumps up, circles, and settles down on my lap.

The cats and I lazily watch the gulls and the geese traverse back and forth between Clinton Lake and Yankee Tank Lake. This morning, the turkey vultures make wide circles so high above us, that we forget their huge beaks and craggy necks. Vann always laughs and says, "No problem, as long as they're not circling over me!"

A cardinal lands briefly on our fence. He knows he looks dashing in his coat of crimson feathers, like a minature Jayhawk, sans the blue and yellow. The soaring gray and white gulls remind me of our years in California. Somehow the sea and prairie have merged together. Against the pale cover of fall's sky, the gulls appear to be woven of silk.

I feel Jazzy sigh, turn once and then she is fast asleep. The kitties settle on the "Lido deck" for a snooze. Muffy has tired of bird watching and climbs into her chair. Our Queenie has gone in to find her "cabin" and perhaps go through the food line before her morning rest. I am lazy too, in ever the best way. This deck chair on my little ship seems just right for a morning sail.

Ninety-three... A missed phone call yesterday afternoon from Camarillo, California. When I listened to the message, it was just garbled voices and kids in the background. I tried to call back as I realized the only person I know in Camarillo is Susie, the daughter of one of my dearest friends, Phyllis. I was out the door to teach tennis at KU and for the next hour, my heart was aching at the thought that Susie was calling to tell me that Phyllis had passed. Why had I not called her just to chat more often? I call her every couple of months, but when someone is ninety-three, that is too long between calls.

I drove home and thought of Phyllis. She is ninety-three and was born just two weeks before my mom. Having her in my world seems like God has given me a small piece of my mom to have in my life. Mom would have been her age, and Phyllis is a brilliant, caring, and fun friend.

She was my administrative assistant in Los Angeles for the American Cancer Society. Before I moved to LA., she sent me a very organized box of files and a sweet welcome note that said, "By the way, you can see the 'Hollywood' sign from your new office." We were instant and forever friends from that moment on, sharing many Southern California adventures.

Phyllis can claim matchmaker to my marriage with Vann, of which she is quite proud. When Vann was my consultant for the American Cancer Society and I had known him for about a year, Phyllis announced out of the blue to me that she thought Vann and I would get married. I just laughed and said, "What makes you say that?" She said she just saw something there and reflected that Vann and I both liked to organize things. Two years later, she would stand as my matron of honor on the hill at Torrey Pines State Beach in San Diego.

With fingers that felt too big, I dialed Phyllis' phone number, and my heart took flight when I heard her voice. It was as clear as ever, and we talked about our families and this and that. I told her that Susie or one of her great grandchildren must have dialed my number. I did not tell her that I really thought an angel had dialed my number as a reminder to stay in touch with my dear friend who is ninety-three. I must not take for granted the conversations we have yet to enjoy. Ninety-three... Phyllis died one year later. We enjoyed our monthly chats until her death.

Seasons... The cats and I were on the patio early, 7:00 a.m., with my steaming cup of Earl Grey tea with a generous teaspoon of Michigan cherry honey stirred in, and the Sunday newspaper ready to enjoy.

Jazzy is quick to find my lap even before I sit down, so the paper is happily tucked away for later. I inch the warm tea close enough to drink and soak in this cool fall day. I soon realize that my shorts and a hoodie are not quite in order, but we are all too comfortable and lazy to go change. Jazzy has begun her biscuit making. Queenie is curled up in the chair cushion like a possum, and Muffy is tucked under the table out of the breeze.

I hear Vivaldi's "Four Seasons" playing in my head. It has been a weekend of the summer season change to fall. A visit to the Lawrence Public Library, coffee and a scone at Alchemy Coffee and Bake House, looking for books at The Raven Bookstore, having lunch with my friend, Ronda, at WheatFields, and surprise coconut pie for Vann from Ladybird Diner and watching Late Night at the Phog on TV.

I pull Jazzy closer and she makes a little mew when I tell her, "I love you kitty Jazzy." I look at her cornflower blue eyes, and they are the color of the sky that hangs over Clinton Lake. There are gray puff clouds that are stacking up in the west for some rain this week. I think about making a pot of soup and a dense loaf of bread later, but we are stuck living into this day. Nature holds us so we may soak up the ebb of summer and the wave to fall.

I smile when I look at our five herb pots still producing green offerings. Most years, they would have long dried up by August and would have been washed and stored for the following spring. The wildflowers too, seem to relish this day with yet one more burst of color.

We turn and the old season is gone. Tennis camps, pool days, vacations, peaches dripping juice on our chins, and a boat ride across the big water of Lake Superior. I tuck myself into this new season. The cherry honey tastes like sweet fall.

I walked out of the Lawrence High School gym last night after a spirited five-set volleyball match. The Lions won. I looked around the gym and was transported back to Topeka West in those high school days when I fit in and then did not fit in. Maybe we all felt like that, but just kept going. I said to my friend who walked out with me, "It's good to be back in a high school." Somewhat to my surprise, he responded that he wouldn't want to go back to those days for anything.

My happiest days were in grade school, perhaps because my stepdad had not left us, I adored my school and teachers, and Mom was years away from getting cancer. It was our Polaroid picture of a perfect mid-century life. My grandparents were vibrant, and the family, my little city, and the world all beat together.

High school was suddenly lonely for me. I filled it with good grades, sports, writing and studying magazines to see how to dress. Maybe the high school years are still like that, but I like to think they are better and easier for kids now. I envied the kids who always seem to move together in a small herd from class to class. I learned to smile and radiate cheerfulness and as Debra calls it, be "stubbornly happy."

I listened to my friend say that he didn't care about high school and straight from my heart, I said, "I like my life now." As I drove home in the deepening pink light, I thought about how truly happy I am with my life. I am sixty-seven, I have a loving husband, nieces and nephew as my family, kitties to tuck around me, a church family, my dream tennis job at the Jayhawk Tennis Center, friends that are young and old, and never the worry of those high school days of "Do I fit in today?" Yes, Mom, I am doing my best. I am having fun.

We have such a gift of journey on this Earth. There is really no time not to fit in and as we are all made as God wished, we are all perfect in who we are, and we are all different as intended. In the light of that high school gym, I truly realized that my life has turned out just right on this beautiful prairie.

Mom and our beloved Miss Kitty on Burnett Road

Mom's Cranberry Salad —

2 c. cranberrys } cook 10 minutes
1 scant c. sugar }
1½ c water }
orange / cherry jello – 1 pkg.
one can (little) crushed pineapple –
one apple, nuts (pecans)

Mom's Date Cake

1 lb. Dates
1 cup nuts
1 cup sugar
1 egg
2 tablespoon butter
1½ cup flour
1 tablespoon soda
1 cup boiling water

Pour boiling water on chopped dates + soda. Let cool + add other ingredients. Bake at 350°F until tooth pick comes clean –

MID-CENTURY KID RECIPES

MOM'S RAINY DAY POPCORN BALLS

(Best enjoyed during a Kansas thunderstorm in the breezeway with 10 oz. Coca-Colas)

Ingredients:

12 cups popped popcorn
1 cup granulated sugar
½ cup Karo light syrup
¼ cup butter (not margarine)
½ tsp. salt
½ tsp. baking soda
1 tsp. pure vanilla extract

Directions:

1. Spray large roasting pan with cooking spray or melted butter; add popcorn and place in 300 degree oven until warm.
2. Combine sugar, corn syrup, butter and salt in a heavy 2-quart saucepan. Stirring constantly, bring to boil over medium heat. Continue stirring and boil 2 minutes.
3. Remove syrup mixture from heat; stir in vanilla and baking soda.
4. Pour syrup mixture over warm popcorn stirring to coat well. Cover hands generously with butter and work quickly into twelve 3-inch popcorn balls.
5. Cool and eat on the breezeway.

GRANDMA HUBERT'S SUMMER LEMON ICE PICK CAKE

(The centerpiece dessert for a hot Kansas evening with home-made vanilla ice cream)

Cake Ingredients:

1 pkg. lemon cake mix (Grandma used Duncan Hines)
½ cup cooking oil
4 eggs
1 cup water
1 pkg. lemon Jell-O

Topping Ingredients:
1/3 cup fresh lemon juice
2 cups of powdered sugar

Directions:

1. Pre-heat oven to 350 degrees.
2. In a large bowl, add ingredients to cake mix and beat until smooth.
3. Pour into a greased and floured 9"x13" inch cake pan.
4. Bake about 45 minutes or until toothpick comes clean.
5. When cake is done and just cooling, mix 1/3 cup fresh lemon juice and 2 cups powdered sugar.
6. Poke holes in warm cake with an ice pick.
7. Drizzle lemon glaze over the cake.
8. Let set 2 hours or enjoy immediately!

MOM'S GERMAN CHOCOLATE CAKE

(A treat on many occasions and her most requested cake for family reunions)

Cake Ingredients:

1 18.25-ounce package German chocolate cake mix
1 cup buttermilk
½ cup vegetable oil
3 large eggs
1 tsp. pure vanilla extract

Directions:

1. Preheat oven to 350 degrees. Mix the cake mix, buttermilk, oil, eggs and vanilla in a large mixing bowl on low speed for one minute until combined. Beat at medium speed for two minutes more.
2. Pour into two greased and floured 9-inch round pans. Bake for 30-35 minutes. Cool on a wire rack for 10 minutes and remove from pans.

COCONUT ALMOND FROSTING

Frosting Ingredients:

½ cup butter (not margarine)
1 cup sugar
1 cup evaporated milk
2 eggs, beaten
1 tablespoon pure vanilla extract
1 7 oz. package sweetened flaked coconut
1 cup sliced almonds

Directions:

1. Combine butter, sugar, evaporated milk and eggs in a saucepan.
2. Cook over medium heat, stirring constantly, for about 12 minutes or until thickened.
3. Add vanilla, coconut and almonds.
4. Cool to room temperature before frosting cake.

GREAT AUNT VIVIAN'S MILLION DOLLAR BEST FUDGE

(First Lady Mamie Eisenhower's recipe which my great aunt loved to make for family reunions.)

Ingredients:

4 ½ cups sugar
Pinch salt
2 tablespoons butter (not margarine)
1 (12 ounce) can evaporated milk
2 cups coarsely chopped pecans
1-pint (1 jar) marshmallow cream
12 ounces semisweet chocolate chips
12 ounces sweet chocolate chips

Directions:

1. In a heavy saucepan over medium heat, bring the sugar, salt, butter and evaporated milk to a boil. Boil for 6 minutes.
2. Meanwhile, place the pecans, marshmallow fluff and chocolates in a large bowl.
3. Pour the boiled syrup over the chocolate mixture.
4. Beat until chocolate is all melted.
5. Grease a 15" ½ x 10 ½ " by 1 inch jelly-roll pan with Crisco or butter and pour fudge into pan.
6. Let harden at room temperature before cutting into 2-inch squares.

KITTY BISCUITS

(Best enjoyed on sunny summer porch afternoons)

Ingredients:

At least one kitty (better yet, two or three)
Kansas sun puddles
One porch facing southwest

Directions:

1. Rub kitty tummy.
2. Continue until kitty biscuits emerge.
3. Enjoy!

ACKNOWLEDGEMENTS

This book is a love letter to my mom for instilling in me a legacy of choosing happy. It is also a devotional to Kansas, my heart's landscape.

"Here are my favorite posts. You should write a book." A package with the note and a flashdrive from my childhood friend, Debra DeCordova, sent me on a journey. She had saved my facebook posts that became the seedlings for this book. Thank you, Debra. (and thank you for getting me through ninth grade algebra!)

Who could write a book without having read other books, particularly those we have read over and over again? Pens up to Harper Lee who wrote my all-time favorite book, To Kill A Mockingbird. Mom gave it to me for my tenth birthday, and I have read it every year since. Also, gratitude to Margery Williams for creating The Velveteen Rabbit, a story of friendship and belonging which stayed with me throughout my childhood. Then, as an early adolescent, I discovered a role model in Nancy Drew and saved my allowance every week to buy a new Nancy Drew book. I raise my magnifying glass to Carolyn Keene.

Who could write a book without others to read, re-read, word process, format, edit and encourage us?

In 2016, by Lake Michigan, I sorted thorough hundreds of posts and gave the 148,000 word document to Lisa Greenstreet who word processed it, approaching book format. I appreciate her attention span and ability to pull it all together. We certainly drank a lot of coffee.

After submitting the book for review and getting publisher feedback, I discovered the amazing Hazel Hart (HH). She became my go-to editor and polished the many posts into a beautifully written book. She looked at every word, space, and punctuation mark with only the goal of clarifying what I had written. She also pointed out how many times my "kitties made biscuits." I am honored to have her spirit in my book.

My heart editor is my dear friend and roommate from the University of Kansas, Leslie McClain, retired professor, University of

Wisconsin-Stevens Point. Leslie generously FaceTimed with me for six months as we read and edited our way through the book, page by page enriching every story. It was a celebration of our love and lifelong friendship.

It's not that hard to write a book. It's more of a challenge to find a publisher. Just by chance, I met Maureen Carroll (Micki) at the Lawrence writers' meeting in South Park. My heart and head clicked with her and she would become my publisher. Like the name of her publishing company, Anamcara Press LLC, she became my "soul" publisher. She is the flourish of my book and I have been enhanced by her creativity, knowledge and love of making the perfect book.

You have to get the world to find your book to read. For all of her marketing and promotion talents, I would like to give a round of applause to Linzi Garcia, my wicked wizard marketing guru. She created the magic to share my book with readers. She also held my hand when I felt overwhelmed with edits and revisions.

To Vann, my husband, who always knew there would be a "**book**." He has been a constant source of cheer for me in every aspect of my life.

Lastly, to my kitties, Jazzy, Queenie and Muffy, who sat on the computer, mouse and keyboard through every edit, purring and making biscuits.

Doing our best! Having fun!

ABOUT THE AUTHOR

Ann Vigola Anderson is a native Kansan and graduate of the University of Kansas. She is grounded in the sense of place and is committed to the preservation of mid-century Kansas memories.

Her work has appeared in Tennis Pro Magazine and Itty Bitty Writing Space. For six years her comic strip, "The Borregosons," appeared in the Borrego Springs, California, weekly newspaper, The Borrego Sun. Her writing was featured in the 2020 article by Sarah Smarsh (Heartland) "America's Postal service is a Rural Lifeline-and it's in jeopardy."

Ann is a featured writer on Kansas Foto Framed by Gwenna (Reich) with over 1,300 followers featuring Gwenna's photos and Ann's stories. Ann is also a contributor to Snapshot Kansas with over 19,000 on-line members. She is designated as a "virtual storyteller" with posting of her photos and descriptions of Kansas places.

She currently serves on the planning committee for The Museum on Main Street's Crossroads: Change in Rural American New Growth from Deep Roots in Wabaunsee County, a collaboration between the Smithsonian Institute and Humanities Kansas.

When she was six, Ann wrote her first story on a Big Chief tablet. Posts of A Mid-Century Kid: Doing my best. Having fun. is her first book.

Ann spends her days writing and teaching tennis at the Jayhawk Tennis Center, where she inspires baby jays and the "senior class" to explore their place at the net. She and her husband, Vann, live in Lawrence, Kansas with their three kitties, Jazzy, Queenie, and Muffy.

OTHER BOOKS YOU MIGHT ENJOY FROM ANAMCARA PRESS LLC

ISBN: 9781941237-33-5
$18.99

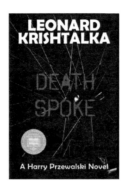

ISBN: 9781941237-30-4
$18.99

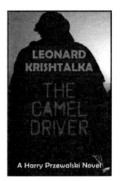

ISBN: 9781941237-32-8
$18.95

ISBN: 9781941237-13-7
$18.95

ISBN: 9781941237-18-2
$14.95

ISBN: 9781941237-08-3
$24.95

Available wherever books are sold and at:
anamcara-press.com

Thank you for being a reader! Anamcara Press publishes select works and brings writers & artists together in collaborations in order to serve community and the planet.
Your comments are always welcome!

Anamcara Press
anamcara-press.com